Frommer's®

Prague
day BY day

3rd Edition

FrommerMedia LLC

Contents

15 Favorite Moments 1
15 Favorite Moments 2

1 The Best Full-Day Tours 7
The Best in One Day 8
The Best in Two Days 16
The Best in Three Days 20

2 The Best Special-Interest Tours 25
Kafka's Prague 26
A Day at Prague Castle (Pražský hrad) 30
Communist Prague 38
Prague with Kids 44
Romantic Prague 48

3 The Best Neighborhood Walks 51
The Jewish Quarter (Josefov) 52
The Lesser Town (Malá Strana) 58
The Castle District (Hřadcany) 62
The Old Town (Staré Město) 64

4 The Best Shopping 69
Shopping Best Bets 70
Prague Shopping A to Z 74

5 The Best of the Outdoors 83
A Walk Across Petřín Hill 84
Lounging in Letná (Letenské sady) 88
The Hidden Gardens of Malá Strana 90

6 The Best Dining 93
Dining Best Bets 94
Prague Restaurants A to Z 98

7 The Best Nightlife 109
Nightlife Best Bets 114
Prague Nightlife A to Z 115

8 The Best Arts & Entertainment 121
Arts & Entertainment Best Bets 122
Prage A&E A to Z 126

9 The Best Lodging 133
Lodging Best Bets 134
Prague Lodging A to Z 138

10 The Best Day Trips & Excursions 149
Fairy-Tale Karlštejn 150
Charming Český Krumlov 152
Bone-Chilling Kutná Hora 156

The Savvy Traveler 159
Before You Go 160
Getting There 162
Getting Around 164
Prague's Architectural Mix 165
Recommended Films & Books 166
Fast Facts 169
Useful Phrases & Menu Terms 174

Index 179

Published by:

Frommer Media LLC

ISBN: 978-1-628-87028-2 (paper); ISBN 978-1-628-87058-9 (ebk)

Editorial Director: Pauline Frommer
Editor: Lorraine Festa
Production Editor: Erin Geile
Photo Editor: Seth Olenick
Cartographer: Elizabeth Puhl
Page Compositor: Heather Pope
Indexer: Kelly Henthorne
Front cover photos, left to right: Czech beer in Prague. ©Marci Dunn. Astronomical Clock detail in Old Town Square. ©SandyS. Týn Church. ©William Manning/Corbis.

For information on our other products and services, please go to Frommers.com.

Frommer's also publishes its books in a variety of electronic formats. Some content that appears in print may not be available in electronic formats.

Manufactured in China

5   4   3   2   1

About This Book

Organizing your time. That's what this guide is all about.

Other guides give you long lists of things to see and do and then expect you to fit the pieces together. The Day by Day guides are different. These guides tell you the best of everything, and then they show you how to see it in the smartest, most time-efficient way. Our authors have designed detailed itineraries organized by time, neighborhood, or special interest. And each tour comes with a bulleted map that takes you from stop to stop.

Hoping to follow in Kafka's footsteps or spend a day exploring Prague castle? Planning a walk through Prague's Old Town? Hoping to sample some Czech beers at a traditional pub? Whatever your interest or schedule, the Day by Days give you the smartest routes to follow. Not only do we take you to the top attractions, hotels, and restaurants, but we also help you access those special moments that locals get to experience—those "finds" that turn tourists into travelers.

The Day by Days are also your top choice if you're looking for one complete guide for all your travel needs. The best hotels and restaurants for every budget, the greatest shopping values, the wildest nightlife—it's all here.

Why should you trust our judgment? Because our authors personally visit each place they write about. They're an independent lot who say what they think and would never include places they wouldn't recommend to their best friends. They're also open to suggestions from readers. If you'd like to contact them, please send your comments our way at support@frommermedia.com, and we'll pass them on.

Enjoy your Day by Day guide—the most helpful travel companion you can buy. And have the trip of a lifetime.

About the Author

Mark Baker is a freelance journalist and travel writer based in Prague. He has authored more than a dozen guidebooks on Eastern and Central Europe. He has also written for *National Geographic Traveler* magazine, *BBC.com, LP.com, the Wall Street Journal, Wanderlust,* and many others. Before embarking on a freelance career, Mark worked as a correspondent for The Economist Group, Bloomberg News, and Radio Free Europe. You can see more of Mark's writing at http://centraleuropetraveler.com.

An Additional Note

Please be advised that travel information is subject to change at any time—and this is especially true of prices. We therefore suggest that you write or call ahead for confirmation when making your travel plans. The authors, editors, and publisher cannot be held responsible for the experiences of readers while traveling. Your safety is important to us, however, so we encourage you to stay alert and be aware of your surroundings.

Star Ratings, Icons & Abbreviations

Every hotel, restaurant, and attraction listing in this guide has been ranked for quality, value, service, amenities, and special features using a **star-rating system.** Hotels, restaurants, attractions, shopping, and nightlife are rated on a scale of zero stars (recommended) to three stars (exceptional). In addition to the star-rating system, we also use a **kids icon** to point out the best bets for families. Within each tour, we recommend cafes, bars, or restaurants where you can take a break. Each of these stops appears in a shaded box marked with a coffee-cup-shaped bullet ☕.

The following **abbreviations** are used for credit cards:

AE	American Express	DISC	Discover	V	Visa
DC	Diners Club	MC	MasterCard		

Travel Resources at Frommers.com

Frommer's travel resources don't end with this guide. Frommer's website, **www.frommers.com**, has travel information on more than 4,000 destinations. We update features regularly, giving you access to the most current trip-planning information and the best airfare, lodging, and car-rental bargains. You can also listen to podcasts, connect with other Frommers.com members through our active-reader forums, share your travel photos, read blogs from guidebook editors and fellow travelers, and much more.

A Note on Prices

In the "Take a Break" and "Best Bets" sections of this book, we have used a system of dollar signs to show a range of costs for 1 night in a hotel (the price of a double-occupancy room) or the cost of an entree at a restaurant. Use the following table to decipher the dollar signs:

Cost	Hotels	Restaurants
$	under $130	under $15
$$	$130–$200	$15–$30
$$$	$200–$300	$30–$40
$$$$	$300–$395	$40–$50
$$$$$	over $395	over $50

How to Contact Us

In researching this book, we discovered many wonderful places—hotels, restaurants, shops, and more. We're sure you'll find others. Please tell us about them, so we can share the information with your fellow travelers in upcoming editions. If you were disappointed with a recommendation, we'd love to know that, too. Please write to: Support@FrommerMedia.com

12 Favorite
Moments

12 Favorite Moments

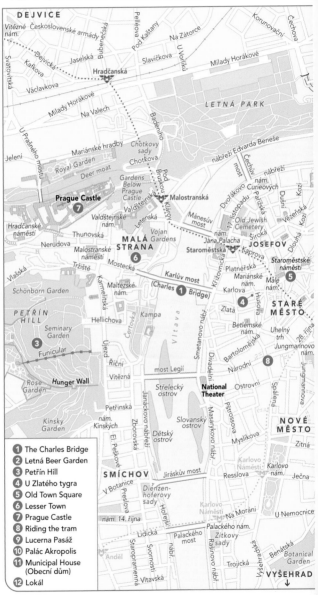

1 The Charles Bridge
2 Letná Beer Garden
3 Petřín Hill
4 U Zlatého tygra
5 Old Town Square
6 Lesser Town
7 Prague Castle
8 Riding the tram
9 Lucerna Pasáž
10 Palác Akropolis
11 Municipal House (Obecní dům)
12 Lokál

Previous page: The Charles Bridge at dawn.

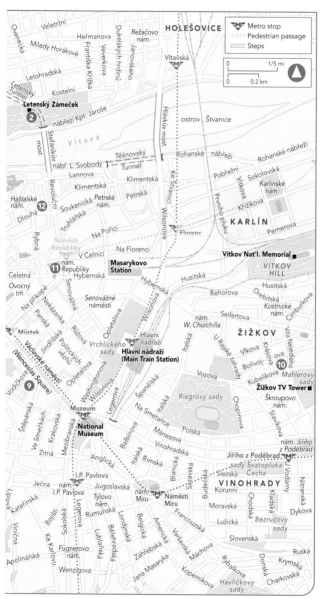

Legend

Metro stop
Pedestrian passage
Steps

0   1/5 mi
0   0.2 km

Ovenecká
Veletržní
Milady Horákové
Letohradská
Heřmanova
Veverkova
Dukelských hrdinů
Františka Křížka
Janovského
Kostelní
Řežačovo nám.
HOLEŠOVICE
Vltavská

Letenský Tunnel
Letenský Zámeček 2
Stefánikův most
nábřeží Kpt. Jaroše
V l t a v a
ostrov Štvanice
Hlávkův most

nábř. L. Svobody
Lannova
Klimentská
Revoluční
Soukenická
Klimentská
Dlouhá
Petrské nám.
Petrská
Těšnovský Tunnel
Rohanské nábřeží
Rohanské nábřeží
Pobřežní
Sokolovská
Vítkova
Karlínské nám.
Prvního pluku
Křižíkova
KARLÍN
Pernerova

Haštalské nám. 12
Rybná
Truhlářská
Na Poříčí
Náměstí Republiky
V Celnici
Na Florenci
Florenc
Ke Štvanici
Wilsonova

Celetná
Ovocný trh
nám. Republiky 11
Hybernská
Na příkopě
Nekázanka
Panská
Senovážná
Senovážné náměstí
Jindřišská
Politických vězňů
Opletalova
Hybernská
Na Florenci
Masarykovo Station
Husitská
Řehořova
Orebitská
Seifertova
Kostnické nám.
Cimburkova
VÍTKOV HILL
Husitská
Vítkov Nat'l. Memorial ■
VÍTKOV

Müstek
Václavské náměstí (Wenceslas Square)
Vodičkova
Štěpánská
Ve Smečkách
Krakovská
Žitná
National Museum
Muzeum
Vrchlického sady
Washingtonova
Wilsonova
Legerova
Opletalova
Růžová
Hlavní nádraží (Main Train Station)
nám. W. Churchilla
Italská
Španělská
Na Smetance
U Rajské zahrady
Vlkova
Bořivoj.
Kubelíkova
ŽIŽKOV
Krásová
Vita Nejedlého
Mahlerovy sady
Žižkov TV Tower ■
Škroupovo nám.
Slavíkova

Vodičkova 9
Kateřinská
I.P. Pavlova
nám. I.P. Pavlova
Ječná
Jugoslávská
Tylovo nám.
Rumunská
Lublaňská
Bělehradská
Sokolská
Legerova
Balbínova
Mánesova
Polská
Vinohradská
Italská
Římská
Blanická
Sázavská
Budečská
Slezská
Čecha
sady Svatopluka
KORUNNÍ
Korunní
Chodská
Moravská
Kladská
Nitranská
Dykova
Vozová
Riegrovy sady
Chopinova
Jiřího z Poděbrad
VINOHRADY
Bezručovy sady
Slovenská
Lužická

Lípová
Viničná
Apolinářská
Boiště
Fügnerovo nám.
Ke Karlovu
Wenzigova
nám. Míru
Náměstí Míru
Londýnská
Belgická
Americká
Francouzská
Záhřebská
Jana Masaryka
Koperníkova
Vašavská
Machova
Havlíčkovy sady
Rybalkova
Donská
Ruská
Krymská
Charkovská

Prague's breathtaking beauty has been discovered. The city now ranks among the most popular in Europe. That's great news for the economy and for people who live from the trade, but it means I need to plan my special moments carefully. I am a little reclusive by nature, and I love the feeling of having a place to myself. These are my tips for moving away from the masses. I hope you enjoy them too.

Relaxing at the Letná Beer Garden.

❶ An early-morning walk across the Charles Bridge. Charles Bridge is not exactly a hangout for recluses, particularly in mid-summer when the bridge is thronged. On the other hand, the crowds definitely thin out at key moments during the day. My favorite time to cross the bridge is early in the morning, approaching from the Old Town side, when the sun is behind your shoulder and Prague Castle is illuminated in the distance. Another good time is in the evening after sundown to enjoy the subtle play of light and shadow among the statues, the city spires, and the domes of Malá Strana in the distance. *See p 13.*

❷ A summer evening at the Letná Beer Garden, perched around a table of old friends. If you want to know where the whole city seems to go for that after-work beer in the summer, look no further than Letná.

Bankers, lawyers, students, mothers with kids, people with dogs— they're all here, sitting at picnic tables and drinking 35 Kč half-liters of beer out of big plastic cups. The spectacular views out over the Old Town lend a special feeling to the night. *See p 89.*

❸ Walking across Petřín Hill. It's the most inspiring view in the city, yet on a typical weekday it seems everyone else is too busy to notice. When I get the chance to slip away, I take the funicular up to Petřín and then make this trek across the top of the meadow toward Prague Castle. There's a little trail to follow and several benches to rest on. Occasionally, I run into another Prague resident (usually out walking his or her dog) who loves this place just as much as I do. *See p 85.*

❹ Drinking Pilsner Urquell at an authentic Czech pub like U Zlatého tygra or U Černého vola. The new watering holes in town are nice, but nothing beats the simplicity of a wooden table, a crowd of friends, and a half-liter of the beer that conquered the world. It's true that the stodgy food at these places could stand some improvement, but no one really comes for the food anyway. *See p 117 and 118.*

❺ **Hanging out on Old Town Square.** Yes, it's touristy, filled to overflowing most days with tour groups, dubious street musicians, festivals, and lots and lots of (admittedly average) restaurants. Still, somehow it works. No place in Prague feels more lively or connected to the outside world. Any time of day or night is fine, but evenings are my favorite. There's something about entering the square from the Malé náměstí side, rounding the Clock Tower, and catching those floodlit towers of the Týn Church and the dark Baroque facades below. Every night feels like a street party. *See p 65.*

❻ **Getting lost in the Lesser Town.** Malá Strana is special. It doesn't have the sheer number of traditional tourist sites that Old Town does, and it draws far fewer visitors. My favorite area is Kampa Island and the little bridges across the Čertovka that connect with the

The Old Castle Steps in Malá Strana.

A tram passing by the National Theater.

mainland. If I have lots of time and sunshine, I pack a lunch, book, and blanket and head for the grassy meadow of Kampa Park. From there, I like to walk back along the river off Na Kampě toward the Charles Bridge. The entire district feels timeless. *See p 59.*

❼ **Enjoying the splendor of Prague Castle,** especially strolling through St. Vitus Cathedral. If you've got the energy, climb the 287 steps of the South Tower for some inspiring views of the Castle complex below, and Malá Strana and Old Town out in the distance. When I come on my own, I rarely buy a ticket to go inside the Royal Palace. It's enough for me just to amble around the courtyards and soak in the atmosphere. *See p 31.*

❽ **Riding the tram.** It doesn't have to be in any particularly scenic area. The trams are to Prague what the subways are to New York—the lifelines of the city. Each car is a microcosm of society and wonderfully democratic, ferrying everyone from students to government ministers. When I have a few hours, I sometimes hop a tram heading in any direction just to see what's out there. You get 90 minutes of travel for 32 Kč. That's enough to cover a lot of ground. *See p 50.*

Lucerna Pasáž.

⑨ Poking around the Lucerna Pasáž. I am not much of a shopper, but I love coming here. It's not for the stores—most of the shops here seem to sell impractical, one-of-a-kind items like antique cameras. It's more the 1920s to '30s feel. Modern shopping malls promise a lifestyle experience, but this place actually delivers, with several great cafes, an old-fashioned movie theater, a big hall for balls and dances, and a great rock and jazz club in the basement. It's amazing that it's withstood the test of time. I fully expect in a few years it will be filled with lifeless chain stores, but for now, Lucerna is still something special. *See p 23.*

⑩ Catching a show at the Akropolis. Prague's changed a lot in the more than 20 years since the fall of Communism. Most of the changes have been for the better, but it sometimes feels like the city has lost its edge. This longtime nightclub and social staple in Žižkov still pulls in its share of great rock and folk acts from around the world. On quieter nights, it's good for just chilling out in the restaurant or cafe upstairs, or listening to the DJs spin tunes in the basement. This is the place to come when I want to feel that vibe that brought me to Prague in the first place. *See p 130.*

⑪ Getting tickets for a concert at the Municipal House. It's a rare treat to snag a good seat in the opulent Smetana Hall at the Obecní dům. Locals complain that concert programmers sometimes play it too safe, loading the card with crowd pleasers like Smetana, Janáček, and Dvořák. That's fine by me, and I'm sure by most visitors as well. Czech composers are too rarely played abroad, so come and hear them when you've got the chance. If you can't book something at the Smetana, the Rudolfinum will do just fine. *See p 9.*

⑫ Having a dinner out in "new Prague." Part of the thrill of watching a city recover from its Communist past and develop is witnessing the explosion of new businesses, places to go, and things to do. Nowhere is this dynamism more apparent than in the restaurant business. And you don't need to drop a lot of money to eat well. My favorite place at the moment is the pub Lokál (p 101), with great low-priced Czech food and beer to match. I also love Aromi (p 98), Kofein (p 100), and Čestr (p 98). They all revel in good food and know that to succeed in Prague, it's not enough to cater only to the tourists. ●

The Czech National Symphonic Orchestra performing at the Obecní dům.

The Best in One Day

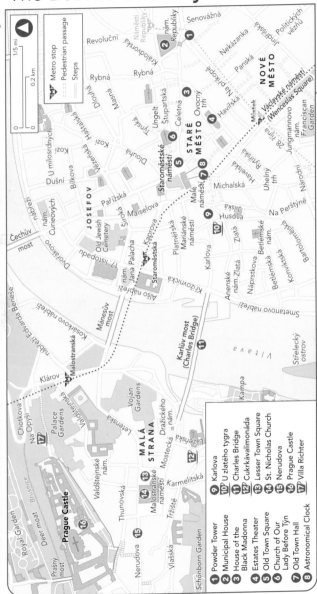

- **1** Powder Tower
- **2** Municipal House
- **3** House of the Black Madonna
- **4** Estates Theater
- **5** Old Town Square
- **6** Church of Our Lady Before Týn
- **7** Old Town Hall
- **8** Astronomical Clock
- **9** Karlova
- **10** U zlatého tygra
- **11** Charles Bridge
- **12** Cukrkávalimonáda
- **13** Lesser Town Square
- **14** St. Nicholas Church
- **15** Nerudova
- **16** Prague Castle
- **17** Villa Richter

Previous page: Old Town Square.

This 1-day tour follows the ancient coronation route of Bohemian kings. It's impossible to see all the major sights in a day, but this walk comes as close as humanly possible. You can do it in 3 or 4 hours without stops. If you decide to poke your nose in here or there, it can stretch into a whole day. *Be forewarned:* There's a lot of ground to cover from the Powder Tower to Prague Castle, so get an early start and wear comfortable shoes. START: **Náměstí Republiky.**

❶ ★ **Powder Tower (or Powder Gate) (Prašná brána).** The late-Gothic Powder Tower is one of the last standing remnants of the Old Town's original fortification system and marks the start of the royal coronation route. The name derives from the tower's early purpose: to hold gunpowder for defending the city. The tower dates from the 15th century, but the trademark golden spires were a relatively late addition in the 19th century. You can clamber up to the top for a view out over the Old Town, but better to save your strength for one of the many other towers that lie on the road ahead. ⏱ *20 min. Náměstí Republiky 5. 75 Kč. Apr–Sept daily 10am–10pm, Mar, Oct daily 10am–8pm, Nov–Feb daily 10am–6pm. Metro: Náměstí Republiky.*

❷ ★★ **Municipal House (Obecní dům).** Before proceeding down Celetná and starting the Royal Route, take a peek inside this ornate Art Nouveau building from the early days of the 20th century. The Municipal House was built as an expression of Czech nationalism (at a time when Czechs and Germans were rivals for cultural supremacy). The architects consciously mimicked the elaborate Parisian variant of Art Nouveau over the more subdued "Secession" style favored in Vienna. Today, it's home to one of the leading orchestras, the Prague Symphony Orchestra (see chapter 8), as well as a cafe, French restaurant, traditional pub,

Powder Tower.

and cocktail bar. Fans of Art Nouveau should take one of the guided tours of the interior (see the website for details; tours normally leave at 11am, 1pm, and 3pm). ⏱ *15 min., 1½ hr. with tour. Náměstí Republiky 5. ☎ 222-002-101 (ticket office). www.obecni-dum.cz. 290 Kč adult, 500 Kč family. Metro: Náměstí Republiky.*

❸ ★ **House of the Black Madonna (Dům U černé Matky Boží).** This former department store—with a beautiful 1920s-era cafe on the first floor—is one of the best examples of Cubist architecture from the first decades of the 20th century. Cubism is a style

Detail of the House of the Black Madonna.

that most people associate with painting, but Prague architects saw in the style a modern alternative to the boring historicist trends of the 19th century. Cubist buildings, like the paintings, are noted for their creative use of geometric shapes and designs. ⏱ *15 min. Celetná 34.*

④ ★ **Estates Theater (Stavovské divadlo).** A short detour along the Ovocný trh (the pedestrian zone leading off to the left) brings you to this historic theater, which in 1787 saw the world premiere of Mozart's opera *Don Giovanni*, conducted by Mozart himself. The building is not normally open to the public. Tickets for evening performances are sold at the National Theater box office at Národní 4. ⏱ *15 min.*

⑤ ★★★ **Old Town Square (Staroměstské nám.).** Returning to Celetná and continuing the walk soon takes you into the heart of Old Town: "Staromák," as Czechs affectionately refer to Old Town Square. The square has been at the center of the city's economic life for nearly 1,000 years and is one of the most beautifully preserved Gothic and Baroque spaces in Europe. To get your bearings, stand with the twin-spire Church of Our Lady Before Týn (or simply "Týn

Church") to your immediate right; a statue of Czech religious reformer Jan Hus stands in the middle. Diagonally across is the white St. Nicholas Church (not to be confused with the church of the same name in Malá Strana). Straight ahead is the Old Town Hall (Staroměstská radnice), with a clock tower on top and fascinating medieval astronomical clock on the side. ⏱ *20 min.*

⑥ ★★ **Church of Our Lady Before Týn (kostel Matky Boží před Týnem).** There's something undeniably bewitching about this Gothic church's spires rising up over a row of Baroque facades below. At night, brilliant floodlights illuminate the towers, making the effect even more powerful. The church dates from the 14th century and was once Prague's leading Hussite (Protestant) church. In fact, its spires once held a giant golden chalice (the sign of the Hussites) between them, which the Catholics promptly melted into a golden Madonna (still visible on the front of the church). The interior is largely Baroque. To the right of the main

The National Theater performs an experimental version of Don Giovanni *at Estates Theater every year.*

Brightly painted facades in Old Town Square.

altar you'll find the tomb of famed Danish astronomer Tycho Brahe of the court of Rudolf II. Enter through the arcades under the red address marker 604. ○ *30 min. Staroměstské nám. 14. Free admission. Tues–Sun 10am–1pm, 3–5pm.*

⑦ ★★ Old Town Hall (Staroměstská radnice).

If you have legs for only one tower climb, make it this one. The view to the square below is beloved by photographers everywhere—it's one of the signature views of Prague. There's an elevator if you're not up for the narrow steps. You can also take a guided tour to see the historic rooms. The Old Town Hall occasionally hosts art and photo exhibitions. It's also home to a branch of the tourist office. Before leaving, walk over to where the Town Hall fronts the square. On the ground you'll find 27 X's marking the spot where in 1621 the Habsburgs beheaded 27 Bohemian noblemen in hopes of frightening the local populace into accepting Austrian rule. It apparently worked. Austria remained in control for 300 years until the end of World War I. ○ *30 min. Staroměstské nám. 1/3.* ☎ *775-443-438. www.prague welcome.cz. 100 Kč (tower), 100 Kč*

(tour with guide). Tower open Mon 11am–10pm, Tues–Sun 9am–10pm. Guided tours Mon 11am–6pm, Tues–Sun 9am–6pm.

⑧ ★★★ Astronomical Clock (Orloj).

If it's close to the top of the hour, race over to the city's number-one crowd pleaser: the medieval astronomical clock. The clock was not used to tell time; instead it was meant to mark the phases of the moon, the astrological signs, the seasons, and the

Týn Church.

One of Old Town Hall's intricate windows.

Christian holidays. At the top of the hour, a brief, eerie, medieval morality play unfolds. Two doors slide open and the 12 apostles glide past, while the 15th-century symbols of

Huge crowds gather in front of the astronomical clock every hour.

evil—death, vanity, corruption, and greed—shake and dance below. Legend has it that Master Hanuš, one of the clock's designers, was blinded by the Municipal Council after he finished repairing the masterpiece so that he couldn't build an even more spectacular clock somewhere else. ⏱ *15 min.*

❾ ★ **Karlová.** From the astronomical clock, walk toward the adjoining Small Square (Malé nám.), passing the ornate Renaissance sgraffito of the "House at the Minute" (Dům u minuty). Franz Kafka lived here as a kid. Karlová street begins at the corner of the Small Square and wends its way eventually to the Charles Bridge (Karlův most). Not long ago this street was filled with student cafes and pubs. Now, with the massive influx of tourists, it's mostly T-shirt and glass shops, but still fun to meander. Astronomy buffs will be interested in the house at no. 4, once the residence of Johannes Kepler. It was Kepler who finally figured out the elliptical orbits of the planets, settling once and for all the debate over whether the earth or the sun lies at the center of the solar system. ⏱ *20 min.*

10 **U zlatého tygra.** If it's after 3pm, stop at the intersection of Karlová and Husová for a quick beer or a light meal at one of the few remaining authentic Czech pubs in the center of the city. The Pilsner Urquell beer here is rumored to be the freshest in the city. It's still considered an "old man's pub," so you'll need to show respect for the regulars. This pub's place in Prague lore looms so large that the late Václav Havel even invited U.S. president Bill Clinton to have a beer with him here in 1994. *Husová 17.* ☎ *222-221-111. $.*

11 ★★★ **Charles Bridge (Karlův most).** Karlová eventually deposits you at the start of what is arguably Prague's most stunning architectural attraction. When this bridge was first built in the 14th and 15th centuries, it was considered one of the wonders of the known world. It was commissioned by Charles IV and laid out by Peter Parléř, one of the original architects of St. Vitus Cathedral. The Baroque statues that lend the bridge its unique character date from the 17th century. The stark religious imagery was the work of the conquering Habsburgs and represents their attempt to re-Catholicize the stubbornly Protestant Czechs. Before crossing the bridge, stop first to admire the **Old Town Bridge Tower** (Staroměstská mostecká věž). The eastern side of the tower, facing the Old Town, shows the original facade of the coats of arms of the Bohemian kings and the Holy Roman Empire. The western side was damaged in battle by Swedish troops at the end of the Thirty Years' War. If you're up for a climb, there's a picture-perfect view of the bridge waiting for you at the top. Most of the 30 or so statues that line the bridge are reproductions. Not all are considered artistic masterpieces, but each has a story to tell. The statue of the Bronze Crucifix (third on the right) is the oldest on the bridge and stands on a spot once occupied by a wooden crucifix. Legend has it the Hebrew inscription that reads HOLY, HOLY, HOLY GOD was forcibly paid for by an unknown Jew who had mocked the crucifix. The statue of St. John of Nepomuk (eighth on the right) is the most

Karlová street.

Charles Bridge.

popular. He was allegedly tossed from this bridge and drowned; touching his relief on the statue (now shiny gold) is said to bring good luck. Art critics judge the statue of St. Luitgarde kissing Christ's wounds (12th on the left), done by Baroque master Matthias Braun, as the most valuable. ○ *45 min. 75 Kč (to climb the Old Town Bridge Tower).*

12 **kids** **Cukrkávalimonáda.** You'll find several dining options within easy reach of this side of Charles Bridge for a full course meal with all the trimmings (see chapter 6), but if you're just looking for a quick sandwich or bowl of soup, try this welcoming and beautifully designed cafe and sandwich shop. If it's close to a meal time, you may have to fight for a table, but it's worth the effort for freshly made soups and healthy salads. *Lázenská 7.* ☎ *257-225-396. www. cukrkavalimonada.com. $$.*

13 **Lesser Town Square (Malostranské nám.).** Walk below the Lesser Town Towers (Malostranské mostecké věže), noting the smaller tower on the left. It

was built in the 12th century and actually predates the bridge itself. Mostecká is the picturesque street that leads you to the focal point of the Lesser Town, Malostranské náměstí. There's not much to see here, but the square continues to function as an important transportation junction. ○ *10 min.*

St. Nicholas Church in Malá Strana (not to be confused with the church of the same name in Old Town Square).

⑭ ★★ St. Nicholas Church (Kostel sv. Mikuláše).

This 18th-century church, the work of Killian Dienzenhofer and his son, is considered a masterpiece of high Baroque. In general, Czechs tend to favor Gothic over Baroque, associating the latter with the Austrian Habsburg occupation, but nearly everyone loves this church. The voluptuous marble columns, the statues, and the frescoes are over-the-top in almost every way, but the exuberant interior somehow works. The exterior dome is especially lovely when viewed from the Charles Bridge. The church also has a tower that you can climb, but for our money, better views can be had from the Old Town Hall Tower and the Old Town Bridge Tower (both described above). The church is one of the better venues for concerts. ⏱ 20 min. Malostranské nám. 1. ☎ 257-534-215. www.stnicholas.cz. 75 Kč (tower). Daily 9am–8pm.

Fighting giant statues atop Prague Castle's main entrance gate.

⑮ ★ Nerudova.

From St. Nicholas Church, follow this street uphill for the trek to Prague Castle. The street takes its name from Czech author Jan Neruda, who was born here in the 19th century. The Nobel prize–winning Chilean poet Pablo Neruda so admired Jan Neruda's writings that he adopted "Neruda" as a pen name. The street is lined with stunning Baroque palaces. Many have been given cute descriptive names. The house at no. 12, for example, is "The House of the Three Violins" (U tří housliček). My favorite is no. 11: "The House of the Red Lamb" (U červeného beránka). ⏱ 20 min.

⑯ ★★★ Prague Castle (Pražský hrad).

At the top of Nerudova are steps leading to Prague Castle. The castle complex, including the Royal Palace and St. Vitus Cathedral, has been the seat of political and religious authority in the Czech lands for nearly as long as there have been Czech lands. Unless you've jogged the entire Royal Route, it's unlikely that you'll have the time to make a full tour. Instead, save a more in-depth exploration of the castle for Day 2 (see the tour starting on p 17), and just take a peek at the grounds inside the gate to get your bearings. If this is your only chance to see the castle area, be sure to check out St. Vitus. ⏱ 30 min.

⑰ ★★ Villa Richter.

This hilltop vineyard just as you exit the Prague Castle complex on the eastern end has something for everyone. There's a relatively inexpensive wine bar where you can get tastings for 45 Kč a glass, as well as small items to eat like sandwiches and snacks. Also onsite is Piano Nobile, a gourmet restaurant offering very good Czech and international cooking and a wine vault with some 2,000 bottles. A three-course tasting menu goes for 990 Kč. Staré zámecké schody 6. ☎ 257-219-079. www.villarichter.cz. $$–$$$$.

The Best in Two Days

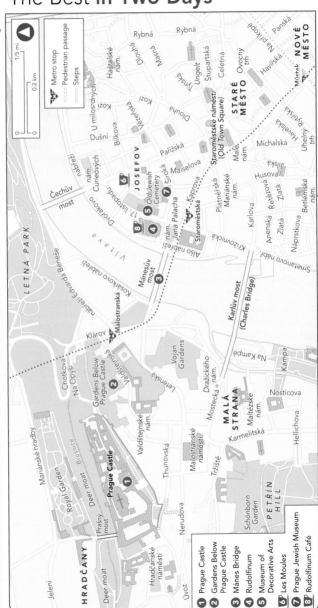

Legend:
- **M** Metro stop
- ::::: Pedestrian passage
- ••••• Steps

Scale: 1/5 mi, 0.2 km

1. Prague Castle
2. Gardens Below Prague Castle
3. Mánes Bridge
4. Rudolfinum
5. Museum of Decorative Arts
6. Les Moules
7. Prague Jewish Museum
8. Rudolfinum Café

The 1-day tour of Prague was all about covering ground. This second-day tour is more about drilling down and focusing on the city's two world-class attractions: Prague Castle (Pražský hrad) and the Prague Jewish Museum (Židovské muzeum v Praze). Both tend to attract hordes of visitors, but they are well worth any minor inconvenience. The tour is set up to begin at the castle and move across the river to the Jewish Museum, but it can easily be done in reverse. The important thing is to get an early start and don't try to push too hard. Budget a half-day for each and reward yourself with a nice lunch in between. This walk can easily be combined with the neighborhood tours of the Castle District (Hradčany) and the former Jewish Quarter (Josefov) described in chapter 3 and the Prague Castle special interest tour in chapter 2, but bear in mind that the more you tack on, the more time you'll need to finish.

START: Hradčanské nám. in front of the main castle entrance.

❶ ★★★ Prague Castle (Pražský hrad).

The Prague Castle complex includes both the Royal Palace (Královský pálac), the residence of the early kings, and St. Vitus Cathedral (Chrám sv. Víta), the country's spiritual center. You can wander the castle grounds for free, but to fully explore the major attractions, including entering St. Vitus, you need to buy a combined-entry ticket. Two types of tickets—full-price and reduced admission—are available; which to choose depends on the amount of time you have and your level of interest. Both tickets are valid for the major attractions, including the Royal Palace, St. Vitus Cathedral, St. George's Basilica (Kostel sv. Jiří), and Golden Lane (Zlatá ulička). A full-price ticket also includes the Prague Castle Picture Gallery (Obrazárna Pražského hradu) and a special permanent exhibition in the Royal Palace titled "The Story of Prague Castle." If you're not well versed in the ups and downs of Czech history, consider renting a portable headset audioguide. The English-language commentary runs long but provides badly needed context. For help navigating the castle, see the Prague Castle tour in chapter 2 on p 30. ⏱ 3 hr. Hradčanské nám. ☎ 224-373-368. www.hrad.cz. Full admission 350 Kč adults, 175 Kč children, 700 Kč family; reduced admission 250 Kč adults, 125 Kč children, 500 Kč family.

Stained-glass window in St. Vitus Cathedral, in the Prague Castle complex.

Audioguide 350 Kč (1 hr.). Daily Apr–Oct 9am–5pm; Nov–Mar 9am–4pm. Metro: Malostranská plus tram 22, two stops.

② ★★ Gardens Below Prague Castle (Zahrady pod Pražským hradem).

Exit the castle complex on the lower end and turn immediately right to see the gardens that run along the castle's southern side. Walk down a few steps to find the entrance to these five interconnected Baroque gardens that run downhill toward Malá Strana. One admission price gives you entry into all five gardens. The gardens are more fully described in the Hidden Gardens of Malá Strana tour on p 90. Make your way downhill and exit on Valdštejnská. **Note:** If you've already seen the gardens or don't want to pay the 80 Kč entrance fee, continue walking straight as you exit the castle complex, following the steps downhill until you come to the Malostranská metro station. ⏱ 40 min. ☎ 257-214-817. www.palacove-zahrady.cz. 80 Kč. Apr–Oct daily 10am–7pm.

③ Mánes Bridge (Mánesův most).

From Valdštejnská, walk past the Malostranská metro station and cross the Vltava River via this modern bridge. The Mánes Bridge has nothing on the Charles Bridge in terms of beauty, but it provides a nice perspective on the impressive length of the Charles Bridge, which is quite a structure given the engineering limitations of the 14th century. ⏱ 10 min.

④ Rudolfinum.

Standing on your left as you leave the Mánes Bridge on the Old Town side, the 19th-century neo-Renaissance Rudolfinum is the leading concert house in the Czech Republic and home to the Czech Philharmonic Orchestra (p 128). It's not normally open to the public for a look inside, but it's well worth trying to snag tickets to a performance. ⏱ 10 min. Alšovo nábřeží 12. ☎ 227-059-227 (ticket information). www.ceskafilharmonie.cz.

⑤ ★★ Prague Museum of Decorative Arts (Uměleckoprůmyslové muzeum v Praze).

If you have time before lunch and want a quick diversion, this often-overlooked museum across the street from the Rudolfinum is worth a detour. The collection covers applied arts from the 16th to the 20th century, but the strong suit is the collection of early-20th-century Cubist, Art Nouveau, and Art Deco jewels, glass, textiles, and posters. Also be sure to head upstairs to the Votive Hall (Votivní sál) to see a set of 14th-century silver ornaments that

The Rudolfinum.

The Old Jewish Cemetery.

were discovered hidden in the walls of Karlštejn Castle. The museum has a great (if small) gift shop and a popular on-site cafe that's a lifesaver when you're starting to wear down. ⏲ *45 min. 17. listopadu 2.* ☎ *251-093-111. www.upm.cz. 120 Kč. Tues–Sun 10am–6pm.*

---

⑥ **Les Moules.** Before tackling the Jewish Museum, have lunch at this Belgian-style bistro just around the corner from the museum's entrance. The specialty is mussels, but there are plenty of decent meat entrees. Good Belgian beer on tap (and, naturally, excellent Czech beer as well). *Pařížská 19.* ☎ *222-315-022. www.lesmoules.cz. $$.*

---

⑦ ★★★ **Prague Jewish Museum (Židovské muzeum v Praze).** After Prague Castle, this is arguably the second most important tourist attraction in town. The Jewish Museum is a collection of surviving synagogues and the Old Jewish Cemetery (Starý židovský hřbitov) that date from the 15th to the 19th century, when Jews were forced to live in this tiny parcel just north of Old Town Square. The city of Prague cleared the Jewish Quarter and razed most of the buildings at the end of the 19th century after it had become a slum. Each of the four synagogues (Maisel, Pinkas, Klaus, and Spanish) has a separate exhibition on Jewish life, but the real highlight is the

somber but spiritual Old Jewish Cemetery, crammed with some 12,000 tombstones. A combined-entry ticket gets you into the museum's four synagogues, plus the cemetery and the adjoining Ceremonial Hall. A separate ticket is required to visit the Old New Synagogue, the oldest still-functioning Jewish place of worship in Europe. For help navigating the Jewish Museum, see the Jewish Quarter neighborhood tour on p 52. ⏲ *3 hr. U Starého hř bitova 3a.* ☎ *222-317-191. www.jewish museum.cz. Jewish Museum 300 Kč adults, 200 Kč children; Old New Synagogue 200 Kč adults, 140 Kč children; combination ticket 480 Kč adults, 320 Kč children. Apr–Oct Sun–Fri 9am–6pm; Nov–Mar Sun–Fri 9am–4:30pm. Closed on Jewish holidays.*

---

⑧ **Rudolfinum Café.** Not many people know it, but the Rudolfinum (④ above) houses a beautiful cafe that makes for the perfect, peaceful place to repair to and rejuvenate after the throngs of the former Jewish quarter. In addition to tea and coffee drinks, there's a small selection of light food items, like soups, salads, quiches, and cakes. The entrance to the cafe is on the side of the building that fronts the river. Simply tell the guard at the door you want to go to the cafe, and he or she will point you in the right direction. *Alšovo nábřeží 12.* ☎ *774-128-496 www.caferudolfinum.cz. $.*

The Best **in Three Days**

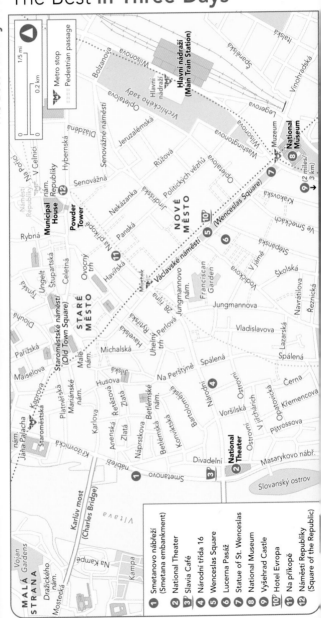

1. Smetanovo nábřeží (Smetana embankment)
2. National Theater
3. Slavia Café
4. Národní třída 16
5. Wenceslas Square
6. Lucerna Pasáž
7. Statue of St. Wenceslas
8. National Museum
9. Vyšehrad Castle
10. Hotel Evropa
11. Na příkopě
12. Náměstí Republiky (Square of the Republic)

You can congratulate yourself at this point. If you've followed the previous days' tours, you've definitely hit the major sights, but what's missing is a feel for the modern city—that part of Prague life that takes place outside the tourist strongholds of the Old Town Square and Prague Castle. This tour is a grab bag—a little relaxing, a little shopping, and a little taste of the big city. START: Staroměstská metro station.

View from Smetanovo náb.

1 ★ **Smetanovo nábřeží (Smetana Embankment).** From the metro station, find the tram stop on Křižovnická ul. and follow the street in the direction of the Charles Bridge. Pass the bridge and continue walking south, finding the sidewalk that takes you along the river. This is Smetana Embankment, named for Czech composer Bedřich Smetana, author of probably the best-known piece of Czech music outside the country: "The Moldau" (*Vltava*). This also happens to be the place for that killer photograph, the one with the Charles

Bridge to the right and the castle above and behind. The best time to catch the view is mid-morning, with the sun over your shoulder as you look out over the water. ⏱ *20 min.*

2 ★ **National Theater (Národní divadlo).** Continue walking until you reach the main cross street, Národní. You can't miss this neo-Renaissance masterpiece of a theater, a symbol of Czech nationalism, dating from the late 19th century. The theater took decades to build, but when it finally opened in 1881, it was destroyed by fire after only 12 performances. It was

The National Theater.

Wenceslas Square.

quickly rebuilt and opened again in 1883. Smetana composed the opera *Libuše* for the occasion. It's still the leading theater in the country and maintains a rotating program of theater, opera, and dance. It's rarely open to the public, but occasionally the city tourist office, Prague Welcome (www.praguewelcome.cz), offers guided tours. Try to get tickets to see something here (p 131). ⏱ *10 min. Národní třída 2.* ☎ *224-901-448 (ticket information). www.narodni-divadlo.cz.*

3 **Slavia Café.** Stop for coffee at this legendary dissident cafe that has the added advantage of a perfect view over the river toward Prague Castle. The Slavia was once a meeting point for the late president and playwright Václav Havel and other dissident intellectuals from the theater and film worlds. At one point in the 1980s, half of the cafe would be filled with dissidents and the other half with secret police. Now it's mostly for tourists, but serves good coffee and light meals. *Smetanovo náb. 2.* ☎ *224-218-493. www.cafeslavia.cz. $$.*

4 **Národní třída 16.** Stop here under an arcade to see a small plaque honoring the students who started the Velvet Revolution in 1989 that overthrew the Communist government. The Communist Prague tour on p 38 goes into more detail, but it was at this point where the police stopped a group of student demonstrators on that fateful night of November 17, 1989. That event marked the beginning of the end for the authorities, as the demonstrations each night grew bigger and bigger. Ultimately there were hundreds of thousands of protesters. ⏱ *10 min. Národní třída 16.*

5 ★★ **Wenceslas Square (Václavské náměstí).** Follow Národní to the end and then along a pedestrian walk to the base of Wenceslas Square. After Old Town Square, this upwardly sloping boulevard is the most famous "square" in the city. It began life in the 14th century as Prague's horse market but has since evolved into the commercial heart of the city and also the symbolic center of the nation's conscience. Crowds have gravitated here to celebrate every milestone, or protest every defeat, for the past 200 years—independence from Austria-Hungary in 1918, the Nazi occupation in 1939, the Soviet-led invasion in 1968, the funeral for student martyr Jan Palach in 1969, the Velvet Revolution in 1989, and even the ice hockey gold medal at the 1998 Olympic Games in Nagano, Japan. The square was built up in the 19th and 20th centuries and lacks the harmony of the Old Town Square. Nearly all of the architectural fashions in vogue during this time can be seen here, from the neo-Renaissance National Museum at the top of the square to the turn-of-the-century Art Nouveau style of the Hotel Evropa (no. 25) and the functionalist style of the 1920s and 1930s (Bata shoe store, no 6). ⏱ *30 min. Václavské nám.*

⑥ ★★ Lucerna Pasáž. Walk up the square on the right-hand side. Fans of the 1920s and 1930s will love the retro styling of the Lucerna Pasáž shopping center, the most attractive of the many shopping arcades on both sides of the square. There's not much to buy here, but there are a number of interesting cafes, a 1920s-era cinema, and even a statue of St. Wenceslas riding on an upside-down horse hanging from the ceiling, courtesy of Czech artist David Černý. You can enter the Lucerna Pasáž from either Vodičková or Štěpánská streets. ⏱ *15 min. Štěpánská 61.* ☎ *224-224-537. www.lucerna.cz.*

⑦ Statue of St. Wenceslas. At the top of the square stands the very equestrian statue that Černý was poking fun at. St. Wenceslas, a former Bohemian prince, is one of the patron saints of the Czech lands, and it was from the base of this statue that the proclamation of Czechoslovak statehood was first read out in 1918. Love it or loathe it, the statue plays a practical role as the most popular meeting spot in the city—if a Prague resident suggests that you meet "at the horse," this is where you should go. ⏱ *10 min.*

⑧ Národní Muzeum (National Museum). Like the National Theater and the Rudolfinum, the construction of the National Museum was closely tied up in the Czech national revival movement of the 19th century. The stern neo-Renaissance facade was badly damaged in the 1968 Warsaw Pact invasion when it was fired on by Russian troops. Normally the museum houses enormous collections of

Statue of St. Wenceslas, with the National Museum in the background.

minerals, remnants from archaeological digs, folk costumes, pottery, coins, textiles and sheet music, among other things, but the museum is currently closed until 2015 to allow for a thorough renovation inside and out. ⏱ *15 min to view façade. Václavské nám. 68. Closed until 2015 for renovations.*

⑨ ★★ Vyšehrad. If it's a beautiful day and you feel like getting out of the city, skip the rest of the tour and instead hop the metro (C line) two stops south to the ruins of the former Vyšehrad Castle. Vyšehrad was the seat of the first Czech kings in the Přemyslid dynasty going back to before the turn of the first millennium. Legend has it that well over a thousand years ago, Princess Libuše (of Smetana opera fame) looked out over the Vltava river valley from this spot and predicted the founding of a great city. Today, the main fortifications remain on rocky cliffs, blocking out the noise below. The grassy bluffs are perfect for a picnic. There are a couple of galleries up here as well as the castle wall's old casemates. You can also peek inside the impressive neo-Gothic Sts. Peter and Paul Cathedral. The Vyšehrad Cemetery (Vyšehradský hřbitov) is one of the most important in the country. It's

Vyšehrad Castle at night.

the final resting place of composers Antonín Dvořák and Bedřich Smetana and Art Nouveau painter Alfons Mucha, among others. *Soběslavová 1.* ☎ *241-410-348. www.praha-vysehrad.cz. Free to enter the grounds and visit the cemetery, separate admission charges for various attractions, galleries, and to enter the cathedral. Metro: Vyšehrad (plus a 15-minute walk).*

10 **Hotel Evropa.** If you decide not to head out to Vyšehrad Castle, continue the tour here. From the top of Wenceslas Square, turn back toward the lower end, walking along the opposite side of the square. The cafe of this glorious Art Nouveau hotel is the perfect perch to take a break. In the summer, sit on the terrace; in winter, relax amid the turn-of-the-century splendors. It's the most ornate interior on the square, bar none. *Václavské nám. 68.* ☎ *224-215-387. www.evropahotel.cz. $.*

11 **Na příkopě.** Turn right at the bottom of Wenceslas Square onto the broad pedestrian street Na příkopě. The name of the street means "at the moat," referring to a time when this street was a moat separating the Old Town (Staré Město) to the left from the New Town (Nové Město) to the right. Despite its historic name, today it commands some of the highest office-rental prices in Europe, and is home to some of the city's best shopping. ○ *20 min.*

12 **Náměstí Republiky (Square of the Republic).** Na příkopě leads to Náměstí Republiky and numerous tram and metro connections. Although Náměstí Republiky itself holds two of Prague's finest buildings (the Powder Tower and the Municipal House), it's an architectural potpourri that's never really worked as a public square. On the plus side, there's a huge shopping mall, the Palladium, at the far end of the square (note the big pink building), and plenty of bars and cafes to relax in after the tour. ○ *10 min.* ●

Hotel Evropa.

Kafka's Prague

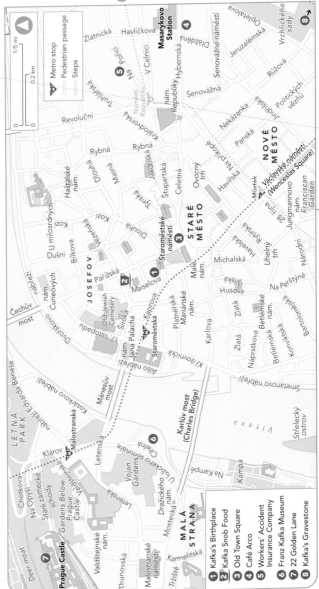

Metro stop
Pedestrian passage
Steps

0 1/5 mi
0 0.2 km

Masarykovo Station ❹

Zlatnická
Havlíčkova
V Celnici
Na poříčí ❺
Truhlářská
Náměstí Republiky
nám. Republiky
Hybernská
Senovážné náměstí
Opletalova
Diažděna
Jeruzalémská
Vrchlického sady ❽
Revoluční
Zlatnická
Havlíčkova

Rybná
Rybná
Jakubská
Dlouhá
Masná
Ovocný trh
Celetná
Štupartská
Havířská
Na příkopě
Panská
Nekázanka
Jindřišská
Ružová
Politických vězňů

NOVÉ MĚSTO
Václavské náměstí (Wenceslas Square)

Hašталská nám.
Kozí
Kozí
Vězeňská
Dušní
Bílkova
Týnská
Dlouhá
Pařížská
STARÉ MĚSTO
Staroměstské náměstí ❶
Malé nám.
Michalská
Havelská
Uhelný trh
Jungmannovo nám.
28. října
Františcán Garden

JOSEFOV
Old Jewish Cemetery
Maiselova
Široka
17. listopadu
Kaprova
Staroměstská
Platnéřská
Mariánské nám.
Husova
Na Perštýně
Bartolomějská

❷
Maiselova

Dvořákovo nábřeží
nám. Curieových
náb řeží
U milosrdných

Čechův most

Jana Palacha
Staroměstská
Karlova
Zlatá
Zlatá
Betlémské nám.
Konviktská
Náprstkova
Betlémské nám.

Alšovo nábřeží
Křižovnická
Smetanovo nábřeží
Národní

Mánesův most

LETNÁ PARK
nábřeží Edvarda Beneše
Kosárkovo nábřeží
Klárov
Malostranská ❻
Letenská
Valdštejnská

Karlův most (Charles Bridge)

Vltava

Strelecký ostrov

U lužického semináře
Vojan Gardens
Dražického nám.
Na Kampě
Kampa

Chotkova
Na Opyši
Staré zámecké schody
Gardens Below Prague Castle

Prague Castle ❼
Deer moat

Valdštejnské nám.
MALÁ STRANA
Malostranské náměstí
Mostecká
Kamelitská
Tržiště
Thunovská
Valdštejnská
Letenská

❶ Kafka's Birthplace
❷ Kafka Snob Food
❸ Old Town Square
❹ Café Arco
❺ Workers' Accident Insurance Company
❻ Franz Kafka Museum
❼ 22 Golden Lane
❽ Kafka's Gravestone

Previous page: Detail of Vyšehrad Castle door.

The former Communist government was never entirely comfortable with Franz Kafka, the German-Jewish writer who was born in Prague in 1883. Kafka's themes of bureaucracy and alienation were too close to the grim reality of day-to-day life of pre-1989 Prague, and Kafka was all but ignored by the Communist government. All of that changed after the Velvet Revolution in 1989, and a caricature of Kafka's familiar face—complete with his overly elongated ears—can be found on posters, T-shirts, and coffee mugs in every souvenir shop in town. Perhaps it's ironic that a somber German-Jewish intellectual—the father of the modern novel—should somehow be adopted by the flashy local tourist industry as one of the faces of new Prague. On the other hand, given the city's turbulent history of Nazi occupation followed by Communist dictatorship, perhaps it's more than fitting. Although Kafka died 15 years before the start of World War II and 24 years before the Communist coup d'etat in 1948, his novels now seem eerily prophetic of what was to come. START: **Old Town Square (Staroměstské nám.).**

❶ ★ Kafka's Birthplace. Just beside the St. Nicholas Church (Chrám sv. Mikuláše) stands the house where Kafka was born. At the time, the neighborhood was still pretty seedy, just on the edge of the then-Jewish ghetto. The actual house was destroyed by fire and the only element remaining is the impressive doorway. The plaque on the side of the house reads in Czech FRANZ KAFKA WAS BORN HERE ON JULY 3, 1883. There's not much to see here, but in summer, there's a small cafe on the street level called—what else? —Kafka Café. ⏱ 10 min. U radnice 5. Not open to the public. Metro: Staroměstská.

❷ Kafka Snob Food. Despite the ridiculous name (how could shy Kafka ever be construed as a snob?), this restaurant and cafe around the corner from Kafka's birthplace is a better choice than Kafka Café for very good cakes and coffee drinks or a light meal. Most of the food entrees have an Italian influence. *Široká 12.* ☎ 725-915-505. $$.

❸ ★★★ Old Town Square (Staroměstské nám.). Kafka spent many of his formative years on Old Town Square and the surrounding streets. Kafka's father, a haberdasher, married well, and

This plaque marks Kafka's birthplace.

Einstein plaque at Staroměstské nám. 17.

the family was moving up the social ladder. One of their nicer apartments was at Staroměstské nám. 2 (the Renaissance house "U Minuty") just beside the Astronomical Clock. As a boy, Kafka attended the German grammar school across the square at the bright-pink Kinský Palace (Staroměstské nám. 12). His father ran a haberdashery in the same building (commemorated by a plaque on the courtyard wall). Later in his life, ill with tuberculosis, Kafka lived again with his family at Staroměstské nám. 5. Here he worked on probably his most famous book, *The Castle*, and several short stories. My favorite Kafka memorial is found at Staroměstské nám. 17, the former home of socialite Berta Fanta, who ran a weekly salon in her drawing room. A plaque on the house reads: HERE IN THIS SALON OF MRS. BERTA FANTA, ALBERT EINSTEIN, PROFESSOR AT PRAGUE UNIVERSITY IN 1911 TO 1912, FOUNDER OF THE THEORY OF RELATIVITY, NOBEL PRIZE WINNER, PLAYED THE VIOLIN AND MET HIS FRIENDS, FAMOUS WRITERS, MAX BROD AND FRANZ KAFKA. Wow. ⏱ *20 min. Metro: Staroměstská.*

❹ **Café Arco.** Leave the square walking down Celetná, passing another of the Kafka family residences at no. 2. Continue straight beyond the Powder Tower, following the street Hybernská to find the Café Arco. Unfortunately, little remains of this once-illustrious cafe, one of the centers of German-Jewish intellectual life in the early years of the 20th century. The Arco now houses a depressing

cafeteria for police officers and some other random offices. It was also a favorite of Max Brod, Kafka's faithful friend and the man arguably most responsible for Kafka's posthumous fame. On his death, Franz Kafka asked that his writings be destroyed. Brod instead cobbled them together, edited them, and sought out a publisher. The rest is literary history. The Arco was not the only cafe Kafka frequented. He occasionally favored the Café Louvre at Národní třída 22 and the now-defunct Café Continental at Na příkopě 17. ⏱ *10 min. Hybernská 16.* ☎ *974-863-542. Metro: Náměstí Republiky.*

❺ ★ **The former Workers' Accident Insurance Company.** Franz Kafka lived a double life. By night he was the consummate haunted intellectual, scribbling about alienation and the modern condition. By day, he was a mild-mannered claims adjuster for the insurance company that once stood at Na poříčí 7. The original building still exists, but today houses the Mercure Hotel (called: "Hotel Century Old Town"). Kafka's office was located where room 214 now stands, and the receptionist will happily show you the room if it's empty. Real fans can book the room for the night, but it's not much different from any other room. ⏱ *15 min. Hotel Mercure. Na poříčí 7.* ☎ *221-800-800. www.accorhotels.com. Metro: Náměstí Republiky.*

Photograph of Franz Kafka.

Kafka once lived in this blue house at 22 Golden Lane.

❻ ★ Franz Kafka Museum.

The tour picks up across the river in Malá Strana. The easiest way to get here from the previous stop on the tour is to catch the metro at Náměstí Republiky (Line B), changing lines at Mustek (Line A) and continuing to Malostranská. From Malostranská station, the Kafka Museum is about a 10-minute walk. This museum is a serious treatment of Kafka's life and work and as such may be more suited to true fans than those with only a passing interest. The museum has two sections, one focusing on the influence of Prague on Kafka's work and the other a video display of Kafka's Prague. ◷ *1 hr. Hergetova Cihelná. Cihelná 2b.* ☎ *257-535-373. www. kafkamuseum.cz. 180 Kč. Daily 10am–6pm. Metro: Malostranská.*

❼ ★★ 22 Golden Lane (Zlatá ulička 22).

The next stop is within the Prague Castle complex on a tiny street that once housed castle artisans. From the Kafka museum, you can return to the Malostranská metro station and then hike up the steps that lead up to the castle from the right of the station—though it's best to combine your visit here with a full castle tour (see "A Day at Prague Castle," below), because the admission price to Golden Lane is included in the ticket. Kafka's sister rented this tiny room from 1916 to 1917 and allowed her brother to live and work here for a time. During the early years of the 20th century, Golden Lane was a kind of eclectic Bohemian ghetto filled with eccentrics and creative types. Now it's mostly T-shirt and glass shops. There's a small gift shop here and a tiny marker on the house that states in Czech: FRANZ KAFKA LIVED HERE. ◷ *30 min. Zlatá ulička 22. Hradčany. Metro: Malostranská (plus tram 22 two stops).*

❽ ★★ Kafka's Gravestone.

Kafka died in 1924 of tuberculosis at a sanitarium near Vienna. He was only 41 years old. He's buried in the New Jewish Cemetery in the Prague suburb of Strašnice. To reach the cemetery from the center, take metro line A to Želivského. From here it's just a short walk to the cemetery and signs will point you along the way to sector 21, where Kafka's grave

marker stands. "Dr. Franz Kafka" is buried under a simple white stone along with his parents, Hermann and Julie Kafka. A small plaque below is dedicated to Kafka's three sisters, all of whom died in Nazi concentration camps during World War II. ◷ *30 min. New Jewish Cemetery (Nový židovský hřbitov). Metro: Želivského.*

Kafka's gravestone, in the New Jewish Cemetery.

A Day at Prague Castle (Pražský hrad)

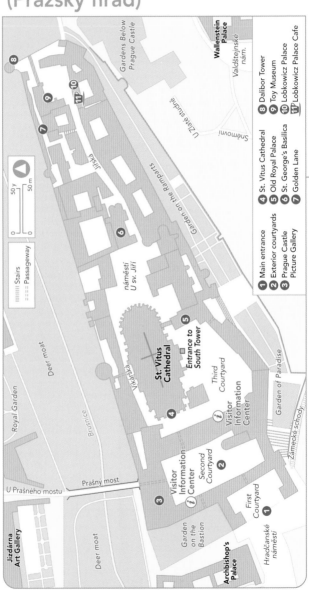

1 Main entrance
2 Exterior courtyards
3 Prague Castle Picture Gallery
4 St. Vitus Cathedral
5 Old Royal Palace
6 St. George's Basilica
7 Golden Lane
8 Dalibor Tower
9 Toy Museum
10 Lobkowicz Palace
11 Lobkowicz Palace Cafe

Touring Prague Castle can be a bewildering proposition. First there's the sheer size. It's the largest castle complex in the world. Then there's the fact that the historical events and personalities behind the buildings are not well known to most visitors. You may have some dim recollection of Charles IV or Rudolf II from a past European history class, but what about Adalbert or Sigismund or the Přemyslid dynasty? Still, the castle complex—which includes St. Vitus Cathedral, the Old Royal Palace, St. George's Basilica, Golden Lane, and other major sights—is such a treasure-trove of art, architecture, jewels, tombs, and jaw-dropping views that it's well worth the effort. Be sure to leave yourself at least a good half a day to cope with crowds and to do it justice, and try to take in some of the sumptuous gardens that surround the complex. See the box "Prague Castle: Practical Matters," later in this chapter, for ticket information. START: **Hradčanské nám.**

❶ ★ **Main entrance.** The main entry to the castle complex, fronting Hradčanské nám., was built to impress. Note the oversized gates and imposing statues of the Battling Titans above. Two guards stand watch and every hour on the hour there's a ritual changing of the guard; at noon there's a more elaborate ceremonial changing of the guard that goes on for about 20 minutes. Feel free to stand alongside for a photo—the guards are trained not to pay attention but sometimes their eyes do stray.
🕐 *15 min.*

Prague Castle's Main Gates.

❷ **Exterior courtyards.** Proceed through the main gate (entry is free) and walk into the First Castle Courtyard (První hradní nádvoří), passing through another impressive entryway—the Matthias Gate (Matyášova brána)—into the Second Castle Courtyard (Druhé hradní nádvoří). As you go through the Matthias Gate, look to the right to see the offices of the Czech presidency (closed to the public). Both the first and second courtyards, which reflect the formal tastes of the 18th-century Austrian aristocracy, are admittedly on the bland side. 🕐 *10 min.*

❸ ★ **Prague Castle Picture Gallery (Obrazárna Pražského hradu).** The entrance to the gallery lies to the left as you enter the second courtyard. We can only imagine the treasures it once held as the court gallery for Rudolf II. Unfortunately, the holdings were plundered in the Thirty Years' War, and those scattered pictures that survived, more often than not, were carted off to galleries in Vienna. A few masterpieces remain, including works by court favorites Hans von Aachen and Bartholomeus Spranger. 🕐 *30 min.* ☎ *224-373-531. Entry is included in the full-price* *ticket to the castle complex. Separate admission is 150 Kč. Daily Apr–Oct 9am–6pm; Nov–Mar 9am–4pm.*

❹ ★★★ St. Vitus Cathedral (Chrám sv. Víta).

Follow the small entryway that leads to the Third Castle Courtyard (Třetí hradní nádvoří) and prepare for a shock—an enormous Gothic cathedral squeezed in among the castle walls. It's hard to exaggerate the importance of St. Vitus Cathedral to the national identity, even if the Czechs are not considered overly religious. Construction began in 1344 on order of Charles IV, but the cathedral was not finished until 1929. In addition to serving as the center of the Catholic Church, the cathedral's crypts hold the remains of the land's most famous rulers, including Charles IV and his four wives, as well as Rudolf II, Wenceslas IV, and King George of Poděbrady. Each of the chapels that line the sides of the church seems to hold yet another legend dear to the hearts of Czechs. Leave at least an hour to tour the cathedral.

St. Vitus Cathedral.

The entrance to the cathedral is through the left-hand door at the front and foot traffic moves clockwise once inside. The left side of the front half of the church is lined with small chapels—the most interesting one being the third, with its stained-glass windows painted by the Czech Art Nouveau master Alfons Mucha. Farther along on the left-hand side are the confessionals and, above, a loft with an amazing 18th-century organ. As you move deeper into the church, you enter the older section. Here the chapels hold the remains of some of the earliest rulers of the Czech lands, going back nearly 1,000 years. As you proceed around the back, you come to the gaudy, silver sarcophagus of St. John of Nepomuk, a jarring Baroque contrast to the more subdued Gothic of much of the rest of the church. A little farther on, you come to the most beautiful of the 22 side chapels: the Chapel of St. Wenceslas (Svatováclavská kaple). Wenceslas—immortalized as a "king" in Christmas carols—was in fact an early Christian prince who was killed by his power-hungry brother Boleslav in A.D. 935. He was canonized soon thereafter. The chapel is considered the spiritual heart of the cathedral and was built over Wenceslas's tomb. Access to the chapel is restricted, but notice the inlaid jewels that cover the walls and altar. A doorway at the back leads to the Crown Chamber and the repository of the Bohemian crown jewels (not open to the public). Once outside of the cathedral, turn left and circle around the south side of the cathedral to find the entrance to the South Tower lookout gallery (entry requires a separate ticket). The view from the top is picture perfect, but keep in mind it's 287 steps to climb up, and the steps get more and more crowded

The Riding Hall at Royal Palace.

the higher you go. ⏱ *60 min., not including tower climb. Entry to St Vitus Cathedral is included in both the full- & reduced-price Castle admissions. To climb the South Tower costs 150 Kč (no discounts for children).*

❺ ★★★ Old Royal Palace (Starý Královský pálac). The entrance to the Old Royal Palace lies to the right of the cathedral (if you are standing in front of the cathedral facing the church's main entrance). Until the 16th century the Old Royal Palace was the main residence of the castle complex. The chief sight here is the enormous Vladislav Hall (Vladislavský sál), noted for its size and its rib-vaulted ceilings—the work of celebrated late-Gothic architect Benedikt Ried. At the time it was a tremendous technical feat to have an enclosed room of this size without supporting pillars. Over the centuries, the room has hosted jousting matches, coronations, feasts of all kinds, and in modern times the inaugurations of Czech presidents. At the end of

the Vladislav Hall a door leads to the Ludwig Wing, the site of the infamous 1618 defenestration of two Catholic governors and their secretary that led to the carnage of the Thirty Years' War. Also here is the Old Diet (Stará Sněmovná), the former court where the king would meet with the high representatives of the church on one side and the nobility on the other. ⏱ *45 min. Entry to the Old Royal Palace is included in both the full- & reduced-price Castle admissions.*

❻ ★★ St. George's Basilica (Kostel sv. Jiří). Just down from the Royal Palace, you can't miss the simplicity of St. George's Basilica, Prague's oldest surviving Romanesque building dating from the 10th century. After the opulence of St. Vitus Cathedral, St. George's appears positively quaint and welcoming. The main sights here are the building itself and the tomb of St. Ludmila, the grandmother of St. Wenceslas. Next to the basilica is the St. George Convent, the oldest

St. George's Basilica.

convent in the country (not open to the public at the time of research). ⏱ *30 min. Entry to St. George's Basilica is included in both the full- & reduced-price Castle admissions.*

7 ★★ Golden Lane (Zlatá ulička). The ramshackle houses here on this street are impossibly tiny—usually simple one- or two-room abodes, without anything like a kitchen or a bathroom to make them livable. Nonetheless, they housed the castle guards in the 16th century and continued to function as more or less normal dwellings up until the 20th century. Franz Kafka was perhaps the most famous resident, living for a short time at no. 22. ⏱ *20 min. Entry to Golden Lane is included in both the full- & reduced-price Castle admissions. Separate admission is 70 Kč.*

8 Dalibor Tower (Daliborka). Continuing on down toward the end of the complex brings you to a tower that once held the castle's prison. Dalibor, one of the first prisoners here, was a nobleman accused of leading a popular revolt in the 15th century. He apparently learned to play the violin while imprisoned here, and according to legend, the citizens of Prague would gather round to listen to him play. The music stopped in 1498 with his execution. ⏱ *10 min.*

9 Toy Museum (Muzeum hraček). Walking through a series of doorways and exit signs takes you to a small courtyard that houses a cafe and this toy museum, housed in what was once the Supreme Burgrave, the seat of the castle administration. Younger children will enjoy this collection of traditional toys, including classic dolls, wooden figures, and trains. The most valuable item is a 2,000-year-old doll from ancient Greece. Note that this is one of the few attractions within the castle complex not included within the general admission price. Nice to know before you've hiked the three flights of

stairs to the ticket office. ⏱ *30 min.
Jiřská 6.* ☎ *224-372-294. 70 Kč.
Daily 9:30am–5pm.*

⑩ ★★ **Lobkowicz Palace.** Just
outside the courtyard, this former
16th-century residence of the noble
Lobkowicz family now houses a private exhibition called "The Princely
Collections," highlighting the family's fascinating holdings of paintings, sheet music, rare books, and
arms. The paintings include works
by Brueghel the Elder and
Velázquez, among others. Entry is
not included in the castle admission
price. ⏱ *60 min. Jiřská 3.* ☎ *233-
312-925. www.lobkowicz.cz. 275 Kč,
200 Kč children 7–15. Daily
10:30am–6pm.*

Lobkowicz Palace and Dalibor Tower.

History 101: Prague Castle

Prague Castle has been at the center of political and religious
authority throughout the history of the Czech lands. Archaeologi-
cal finds indicate there's been a castle on this site since the 9th
century, and the complex of royal residences, monasteries, and
churches was built up and added to piecemeal over the years. The
high point came in the 14th century during the reign of Holy
Roman Emperor Charles IV, who made the castle his Imperial residence. He rebuilt the Royal Palace and began work on St. Vitus
Cathedral, emulating the best of French Gothic cathedrals of the
day. The castle's fortunes waxed and waned with the fate of the
Czech lands, falling into ruin during the Hussite wars of the 15th
century, then returning to glory during the reign of Holy Roman
Emperor Rudolf II at the turn of the 17th century. The defenestration at Prague Castle in 1618—when a group of Protestant noblemen pushed two Catholic governors from a high window and onto
a dung heap below—sparked a religious conflagration that spread
throughout Europe: the Thirty Years' War. The castle complex
languished during the 300 years of Habsburg occupation until
1918, but once again became the seat of power with the founding
of independent Czechoslovakia at the end of World War I. During
World War II, the Nazi ruler of Bohemia and Moravia, Reinhard
Heydrich, took up residency here. Today the castle serves as the
official residency of the Czech president.

German troops marching through the Prague Castle gates in 1939, during their invasion of Czechoslovakia.

11 Lobkowicz Palace Cafe. By this time, you'll be long overdue for coffee or a snack. Even if you don't visit the palace, stop by the courtyard cafe just to the right of the palace entrance. The castle area is not generally known for good or reasonably priced refreshments. Here, the prices are just as high as elsewhere, but the soups, sandwiches, and wraps are freshly made, and you may even be serenaded by palace musicians. *Jiřská 3.* ☎ *233-356-978. www.lobkowicz.cz. Daily 10am–6pm. $$.*

Finish the tour by hiking downhill in the direction of Malá Strana. Steps here can take you down to the Malostranská metro station. If you're ready for a serious meal or at least a good glass of wine, you'll find the archway leading to the Villa Richter restaurant and vineyard complex (see p 105) just to the left before you begin your descent. If you've got some daylight left and want to spend more time around the castle, check out the amazing gardens that surround the complex on the castle's south side (walk to the right as you are leaving the castle complex). Note that you can also find the upper entrance to the Gardens Below Prague Castle (Zahrady pod Pražským hradem; p 91) to the right as you exit the castle compounds and follow the signs.

Prague Castle: Practical Matters

Entry into the castle grounds is free, but to tour St. Vitus Cathedral, the Old Royal Palace and other major sights requires a ticket. Buy tickets at one of two Prague Castle Information Centers (located in the second and third courtyards after you pass through the main gates). Two types of tickets are available. Full-price admission (350 Kč adults, 175 Kč children, 700 Kč family) gets you into St Vitus Cathedral, the Old Royal Palace, St. George's Basilica, Golden Lane, the Dalibor Tower, the Prague Castle Picture Gallery, and a special permanent exhibition in the Old Royal Palace titled "The Story of Prague Castle." A reduced admission (250 Kč adults, 125 Kč children, 500 Kč family) includes only the Old Royal Palace, St. Vitus Cathedral, St. George's Basilica, and Golden Lane. Most visitors will be more than satisfied with a reduced price ticket. Both tickets are valid for two days. If you're intent on getting the most out of the experience, rent a small "audioguide," a hand-held recording that takes you to about 50 sights in the cathedral and the castle. The commentary, available in several languages, is a little on the long side (you can fast-forward through the slow parts), but adds much-needed context. Audioguides cost 350 Kč for 2 hours, and 500 Kč all day. One or two audioguides are sufficient to share among a small group. Hradčanské náměstí. ☎ 224-372-423; www.hrad.cz. Open daily April to October from 9am to 6pm, November to March from 9am to 4pm. Metro: Malostranská plus tram 22 two stops.

Communist Prague

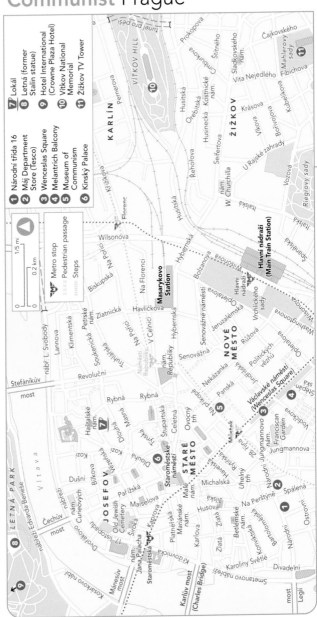

1. Národní třída 16
2. Máj Department Store (Tesco)
3. Wenceslas Square
4. Melantrich Balcony
5. Museum of Communism
6. Kinský Palace
7. Lokál
8. Letná (former Stalin statue)
9. Hotel International (Crowne Plaza Hotel)
10. Vitkov National Memorial
11. Žižkov TV Tower

alking around this colorful and lively city today, it's hard to believe that a little more than 2 decades ago the Czech Republic was part of the Eastern Bloc and the Warsaw Pact—as grey and "Soviet" as Leonid Brezhnev's ashen face. Happily, those days are long gone, but a few interesting relics remain scattered around the city as a reminder of those bad old days. This tour begins by following the trail of the moving 1989 student protest known as the Velvet Revolution that peacefully ended 40 years of Communist rule. The start of the tour is easy to walk, and each sight follows closely from the previous one. The last three stops on the tour, though, are more spread out. You may want to choose one or two of the destinations and leave the others for another day. START: **Národní 16, Metro to Mustek (Line A or B).**

❶ ★★ **Národní třída 16.** This address on one of the city's major arteries, Národní třída (National Ave.), near the intersection with Mikulandská ul., marks the spot where the Velvet Revolution began and Czechoslovak Communism finally defeated. On the night of November 17, 1989, a group of students and activists—encouraged by anti-Communist revolutions elsewhere in Eastern Europe and tired of 40 years of repressive rule here—assembled near the Vltava river and began marching up Národní on their way to Wenceslas Square. The group got as far as this building at no. 16—now memorialized by a simple plaque—before police confronted them and tried to drive them back. It's not clear what really happened that night (there was even a rumor—later disproved—that one of the students, Martin Šmíd, had been killed), but word of the confrontation quickly spread across the country, sparking weeks of huge demonstrations. By the end of the year, the

Communists had capitulated and the revolution's spiritual hero, the dissident playwright Václav Havel, was president. ⏱ *15 min. Národní třída 16, Prague 1. Metro: Mustek.*

❷ **Máj Department Store (My Tesco).** Walk down Národní třída a couple of blocks toward Wenceslas Square to the intersection with Spalená ul. When this department store was built in the mid-1970s, the building's "love it or loathe it" Brutalist architecture was hailed as a high point of Communist-era design. Brutalism was a popular international style that emphasized exposing a building's inner workings (like pipes and ducts) on the outside. The architects modeled the building loosely on Paris's Centre Georges Pompidou, but there's little resemblance. Critics later derided Brutalism as hideously ugly (the world's most vocal critic was probably Britain's Prince Charles, who famously labeled Brutalist buildings "carbuncles"). Some years ago, the current

Velvet Revolution marker.

Soviet troops invading Prague in August 1968 to crush the "Prague Spring" reform.

owner, the British retailer Tesco, announced plans to knock the building down and start over. Fans of Communist architecture then complained, and now the building—much like the Charles Bridge and the Old Town's Astronomical Clock—is an officially protected cultural landmark. ⏱ *10 min. Národní třída 26, Prague 1. Metro: Mustek.*

❸ ★★ **Wenceslas Square (Václavské nám.).** Continue walking along Národní třída to one of the biggest and best-known squares in Prague. Wenceslas Square has always found itself at the heart of turbulent times. At the end of World War I, thousands gathered here to demand independence from Austria-Hungary; in the run-up to World War II, thousands more came here to protest the Nazi occupation. The tradition continued during the Velvet Revolution. Night after night in those heady days of November 1989, hundreds of thousands of Czechs (and Slovaks) came here to voice their opposition to the Communist regime and to jangle their keys (a way of telling their geriatric overlords it was time to leave). About three-quarters of the way up the square, just below the

statue of the horseman, you'll find a small monument (often strewn with flowers) to the "Victims of Communism." You'll also see plaques marking the memory of two Czech students, Jan Palach and Jan Zajíc, who immolated themselves at separate times in 1969 to protest the Soviet-led invasion of the country a year earlier. That invasion, in August 1968, devastated Czechoslovakia and put a bitter end to a period of hope and political reform known as the "Prague Spring." It ushered in 20 more years of dreary, Soviet-style Communism. ⏱ *45 min. Václavské nám., Prague 1. Metro: Mustek or Muzeum.*

❹ ★ **Melantrich Balcony.** Not far from the memorial to the Victims of Communism, at no. 36 Wenceslas Square (now a branch of the British Marks & Spencer store), you will see a balcony jutting from the Melantrich publishing house. This is where, in late November 1989, the dissident playwright (and soon-to-be president) Václav Havel made his first historic appearances in front of the hundreds of thousands of people who were clamoring for his leadership. His mumbling yet defiant speeches solidified his position as the popular choice to guide Czechoslovakia out of those dark days. On at least one famous occasion, Alexander Dubček—the popular, ousted leader of the "Prague Spring" reforms—joined Havel on the balcony. By then, Dubček was an old man and had been out of the spotlight for 20 years, but the crowds cheered him on anyway. ⏱ *10 min. Václavské nám. 36, Prague 1. Metro: Mustek.*

5 ★★★ Museum of Communism. Walk back to the bottom of Wenceslas Square and follow the pedestrian street Na příkopě that leads off to the right. You'll find the "Museum of Communism" a couple of blocks down in a small passageway next to a McDonald's restaurant. Leave it to an American to find a way of making money from Communism. For years after 1989 there was no museum or central focal point to remember the 40 years of Soviet domination here, and in 2001 American entrepreneur Glenn Spicker and his partners decided to fill the gap. The museum is stuffed with kitschy displays of Communist-era apartments and grocery stores, but the entry hall has an excellent series of wall posters explaining the major events of the Communist period, from the 1948 Communist coup, to the

stagnation of the 1950s, the 1968 Warsaw Pact invasion, and finally the 1989 Velvet Revolution. It's a great primer for recent history. The best part is a moving 15-minute film loop (with English subtitles) mixing images of the Velvet Revolution with Czech folk songs. ⏱ *1 hr. Na příkopě 10. ☎ 224-212-966. www.muzeumkomunismu.cz. Admission 190 Kč. Daily 9am–9pm. Metro: Mustek.*

6 ★ Kinský Palace. Follow the little street, Havířská, that leads off Na příkopě and continue walking to Old Town Square. This lively Baroque palace, at no. 12 on Old Town Square, is normally highlighted in guidebooks as the biggest and pinkest of the square's many palaces (and the site of Franz Kafka's grammar school), but it has another distinction related to the country's Communist past. It was from this balcony in February 1948 that the country's first Communist leader, Klement Gottwald, proclaimed an effective coup d'état by Communist forces. The announcement was greeted with euphoria by the thousands amassed that day on the Old Town Square. Memories of the horrors of World War II were still fresh, and many hoped (naively, in retrospect) that Communism would bring long-desired peace

Kinský Palace balcony.

and prosperity. For fans of Czech-born author Milan Kundera, Gottwald's address from this balcony is humorously and ironically recounted in the first chapter of the novel *The Book of Laughter and Forgetting*. 🕐 *15 min. Staroměstské nám. 12, Prague 1. Metro: Staroměstská.*

7 **Lokál.** Lokál is a modern pub that plays on the country's Communist past to good effect. The decor is done up to look like a Communist-era pub from the 1970s, complete with period advertisements on the restroom walls. Fortunately, the food and the beer are much better than you would have gotten back then. To find it, exit the Old Town Square to the right just beyond the Kinský Palace, following Dlouhá for about 5 minutes. *Dlouhá 33.* ☎ *222-316-265. www.ambi.cz. $.*

8 ★★ **Letná (former Stalin statue).** From the Old Town Square, follow the fashionable street Pařížská to the Vltava river, then cross the bridge and ascend one of the walkways leading up to Letná park. It was here, at the top of the stairs, where a metronome now sways, that the world's largest

The world's largest statue of Stalin once stood where this metronome now sways.

Stalin statue—a full 50m (164 ft.) tall—once stood. The statue was commissioned in the early '50s at the height of the former Soviet dictator's cult of personality and was finished in 1955. Unfortunately for Czechoslovakia's Communist leaders, by the time the statue was done, Stalin was falling out of favor in the Soviet Union. The statue hovered uneasily over the city for several years, but by the 1960s it was clear it had to go. In 1962, the city dynamited it out of existence with nearly 2,000 pounds of explosives that knocked out windows all around the city. The statue's creator, Otakar Švec, didn't live to see his work demolished—he had committed suicide several years earlier. The Museum of Communism (see above) has several good photographs of the statue and even one of its demolition. The statue's design, depicting Stalin standing at the head of a line of workers, soldiers, and citizens, was dubbed by local wags at the time as "the world's largest bread line"—a reference to the notorious shortages of food staples. City officials are not quite sure what to do with this area, and for now most of it stands empty, with only the metronome forlornly marking time. 🕐 *15 min. Letná, Prague 1. Metro: Staroměstská.*

9 ★ **Hotel International (Crowne Plaza Hotel).** This hotel, about 3km (2 miles) northwest of Letná, in the suburb of Dejvice, is the city's best example of 1950s Socialist-Realist architecture. If you've been to Moscow or seen Warsaw's Palace of Science and Culture, you'll recognize this Stalinist skyscraper's signature wedding-cake style. In the years following World War II, Stalin marked his turf in the newly acquired Eastern bloc by offering these skyscrapers as "gifts" (that could not be refused).

For years, the building operated as a mid-range hotel for party functionaries until it was taken over by the Holiday Inn group in the 1990s and retrofitted into a modern luxury hotel. Today, the building is noteworthy for its overall design and exterior mosaics. Take a look, too, at the lobby, which retains much of its overall 1950s appearance. ⏱ *20 min. Koulová 15, Prague 6. ☎ 296-537-111. Metro: Dejvická (plus tram 8 to Zelena).*

⑩ ★★ Vítkov National Memorial. For more Socialist Realist style and out-and-out Communist kitsch, make a special trip across town to the suburb of Žižkov to a monument that once held the mummified remains of Czechoslovakia's first Communist leader, Klement Gottwald (in much the same way Lenin's remains were preserved at Moscow's Red Square). The complex, which includes the world's largest statue of a horse, was originally designed in the 1920s to honor the founding of the Czechoslovak state after World War I, but Gottwald co-opted the site in the '50s to function as a kind of Socialist sanctuary for Communist anniversaries and Labor Day celebrations. When Gottwald died in 1953—in keeping with the Communist fashion of the day—his remains were preserved here and put on public display. Unfortunately, the Czech embalmers were not as skilled as their Soviet comrades and it wasn't long before Gottwald's body began to deteriorate. The body had to be re-embalmed every 18 months and was permanently withdrawn from public view in 1961. After 1989, this monument was forgotten until 2010, when the National Museum opened a highly worthwhile permanent exhibition to modern Czech history. Gottwald's original embalming and preservation equipment is still on display in an eerie room downstairs. ⏱ *1 hr. U památníku 1900, Prague 3. ☎ 222-781-676. www.nm.cz. 110 Kč adults. Tues–Sun 10am–6pm. Metro: Florenc plus bus 175, 133, or 207.*

⑪ ★★ Žižkov TV Tower. Easily visible from the Vítkov National Memorial, Prague's multistory TV tower is arguably the ugliest building ever built in the Golden City. At the same time, there's something undeniably alluring about its ultra-smooth shape and sheer scale—it dwarfs everything around it. The tower dates from the late 1980s and was built to broadcast TV and radio signals, but there's always been an undercurrent of suspicion that the real purpose was to jam signals coming in from the BBC and Radio Free Europe. The sculptures of babies crawling up and down—by local jokester-artist David Černý—lend a surreal effect. Take the high-speed elevators up to the observation deck for impressive views of the city. ⏱ *30 min. Mahlerovy Sady 1, Vinohrady. ☎ 210-320-081. www.towerpark.cz. 150 Kč adults, 80 Kč children. Daily 8am–11pm. Metro: Jiřího z Poděbrad.*

Žižkov TV tower.

Prague with Kids

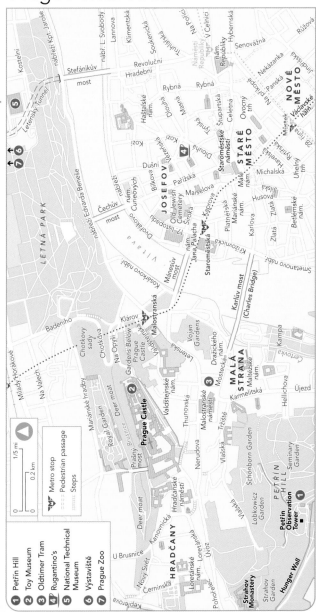

1 Petřín Hill
2 Toy Museum
3 Oldtimer Tram
4 Rugantino's
5 National Technical Museum
6 Výstaviště
7 Prague Zoo

Metro stop
Pedestrian passage
Steps

1/5 mi
0.2 km

Prague is not an easy city for kids. Younger children will like the castles, bridges, puppets, and trams, but shuffling the kids around from place to place (over lots of cobblestones) will be a constant challenge. Older kids will probably show only a passing interest in the city's history and architecture and could very well buckle (as anyone would) after an overly long day at Prague Castle. The tourist authorities have been slow to add attractions aimed at younger visitors but fortunately there are a few standbys that have nothing to do with Gothic or Baroque architecture. This is a lot to pack into 1 day; you may have to choose just one of the last two stops depending on your interest. START: **Žluté lázně** (Yellow Beach) or **Podolí.**

① ★★ **Petřín Hill.** The Petřín Hill that rises above Malá Strana is filled with great things for kids. You can follow the Petřín tour on p 85, or take the funicular train (lanová dráha) to the top and just wander around from there. In addition to a mock Eiffel Tower (built to a quarter of the size of the original) that you can climb to the top, you'll find an old-fashioned mirror maze ("Bludiště") as well as the Štefánik Observatory, open for stargazing on clear nights. ⏱ 60 min. *Petřín. Petřín Tower (Petřínská rozhledna).* ☎ 224-816-772. www.petrinska-rozhledna.cz. 105 Kč, 55 Kč for children. May–Sept 10am–10pm; Oct–Apr 10am–6pm. *Bludiště :* 75 Kč, 55 Kč for children. May–Aug 10am–10pm; Sept–Apr 10am–6pm. *Štefánik Observatory:* 65 Kč. Mon–Fri 2–7pm, 9–11pm; Sat–Sun 10am–noon, 2–7pm, 9–11pm. Metro: Malostranská plus tram 12, 20 or 22 south three stops to Újezd).

② ★ **Toy Museum (Muzeum hraček).** When you're 6 or 7 years old, Gothic cathedrals are not very riveting. Fortunately, the Prague Castle complex has something for young kids as well. This multi-level toy museum

Inside the maze of mirrors on Petřín Hill.

features loads of traditional wooden toys, dolls, construction sets, train sets, and lots of other amusements. It's housed in the offices of the former Supreme Burgrave, the seat of the castle administration (see the tour "A Day at Prague Castle," above). Entry to the museum is not included in the general castle admission. ⏱ 30 min. *Jiřská 6, Hradčany.* ☎ 224-372-294. 70 Kč adults, 30 Kč children. Daily 9:30am–5pm. Metro: Malostranská plus tram 22 to Pražský hrad.

③ ★ **Oldtimer Tram.** On weekends from March until November, an old-fashioned tram, no. 91,

TOY ◄ MUSEUM HRAČEK

This sign marks the entrance to the Toy Museum at Prague Castle.

Splish, Splash

As any seasoned parent knows, one of the best ways to keep kids occupied and happy is to let them splash around in some water. Fortunately, Prague has a couple of good options.

In good weather, head to **"Yellow Beach"** (Žluté lázně) for some outdoor fun (Podolské nábřeží, Podolí; ☎ 244-463-777; www.zlutelazne.cz). This popular grassy riverside beach is located south of town on the Old Town side of the Vltava. It has a nice outdoor swimming area and lots of activities for both big and little kids. A decent on-site restaurant means you can make a day of it. Admission is 80 Kč. It's open June to September from 9am to 8pm.

If it's too cold for Žluté lázně, come to the **Podolí indoor pool** and recreation center situated just across the street (Podolská 74. Podolí; ☎ 241-433-952; www.pspodoli.cz). There are actually two big outdoor pools here too, making it a good choice in winter or summer. A mock beach, solarium, and sauna are also on premises. Open daily from 6am to 9:45pm. Admission is 160 Kč, 90 Kč for children to age 12. To get to either spot, take the Metro to Karlovo náměstí, then tram 3, 16, 17, or 21 to the Dvorce stop.

clanks along a special circuit around town that takes it through major stops at Malostranské nám., Národní třída, Václavské nám., and others. You are free to jump aboard and exit the tram at any stop you choose. Buy a special ticket from the on-board conductor. ⏱ *45 min. Major tram stops around the city. No phone. www.dpp.cz. 35 Kč, 20 Kč children. Daily 10am–6pm.*

The whole family can blow off some steam at the Podolí pools.

4 ★★ **Rugantino's.** Just near Old Town Square and down a small side street, you'll find the most family-friendly restaurant in the city. Czechs don't often take their children out to restaurants, but here the owners and waitstaff welcome kids with open arms. While you're wading through a menu of some of the best pizzas in the city, the staff will be handing out colored pencils and doodling paper to the little guys and girls. Popular venue for children's parties. Dušní 4. ☎ 222-318-172. www.rugantino.cz. Metro: Staroměstská. $$.

5 ★★ **National Technical Museum (Národní technické museum).** Head north from the city square, across the river, to this fascinating museum stuffed with classic automobiles, historic airplanes, full-sized trains, old bikes, and just about every other mode of

The building facade at Výstaviště.

transport ever invented. It was recently remodeled, bringing in loads of interactive exhibitions and making it even more kid-friendly. ⓧ *2 hr. Kostelní 42, Letná.* ☎ *220-399-111. www.ntm.cz. 170 Kč, 90 Kč children 6–15. Tues–Fri 9am–5:30pm, Sat–Sun 10am–6pm. Metro: Vltavská plus trams 1, 25, 26 to Kamenická.*

❻ ★★ **Výstaviště.** Beyond the technical museum in the outlying district of Holešovice is another kids' mecca: the Výstaviště fairgrounds complex. The fairgrounds were built around the turn of the 20th century in Art Nouveau architecture, and although the complex is slightly run-down, it's got a small amusement park (with a merry-go-round and a few "Tilt-O-Whirl"-type rides), a singing fountain (with water and lighting timed to classical and popular music after sundown), and a small Sea World–style aquarium called "Mořský svět." Entry to the amusement park is free, but separate admissions are charged for the fountain and Mořský svět. ⓧ *2 hr. Křižík's Fountain (Křižíkova fontána):* ☎ *723-665-694. www.krizikovafontana.cz. 220 Kč. Apr–Oct 7–11pm. Seaworld (Mořský svět):* ☎ *220-103-275. www.morsky-svet.cz. 280 Kč, 180 Kč children 4–15. Daily*

10am–7pm. Metro: Nádraží Holešovice or tram 12, 14, 17 to Výstaviště.

❼ ★★ **Prague Zoo.** Moving farther north from Výstaviště, Prague's zoo has improved dramatically in recent years. It was nearly totally inundated in floods that struck the city in 2002 and 2013, and the authorities have had to invest heavily in new facilities. The collection of giraffes is one of the finest in Central Europe. ⓧ *2 hr. Best on weekdays, when it's less crowded. U Trojského zámku 120.* ☎ *296-112-111. www.zoopraha.cz. 200 Kč, 150 Kč children, 600 Kč families. Apr–Oct 9am–6pm; Nov–Mar 9am–4pm. Metro: Nádraží Holešovice then bus 112.*

Tiger at the Prague Zoo.

The Best Special-Interest Tours

Romantic Prague

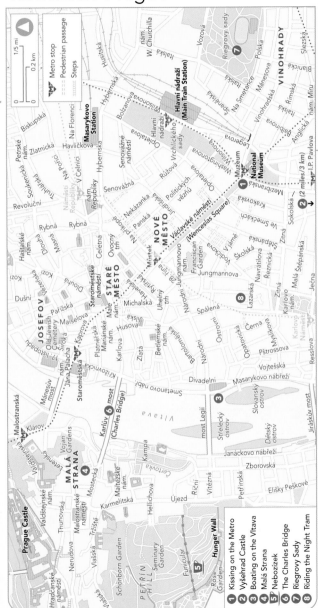

Legend:
- W Metro stop
- ▪▪▪ Pedestrian passage
- ⋯⋯ Steps

0 1/5 mi
0 0.2 km

1. Kissing on the Metro
2. Vyšehrad Castle
3. Boating on the Vltava
4. Malá Strana
5. Nebozízek
6. The Charles Bridge
7. Riegrovy Sady
8. Riding the Night Tram

If you've ever read any books by Czech authors Milan Kundera or Ivan Klima, you know that a deep, abiding affection—bordering on obsession—for the opposite sex lies just below the surface here. Prague romance is not the "candlelight and flowers" variety. Czechs, in general, are far too pragmatic. There's no need to waste time on a box of chocolates. Under Communism, flirting and drinking beer were practically the only two pleasures left in life, and Czechs made good use of both. Attitudes remain refreshingly relaxed, and you'll see couples holding hands and kissing on park benches, on trams, and in the pubs. It's infectious and there's no point in resisting. So take a walk, hold hands, and do what comes naturally. No one's paying any attention. START: **Metro to Muzeum.**

1 Kissing on the Metro. Kissing on the metro has a long and honored history in Prague, going back to the days under Communism when whole families would live in tiny two- or three-room apartments. Young couples were often at a loss for privacy and had to make do with any space available. Any metro line works, but the C line (Red) between Muzeum and Háje might be the best for this purpose. The gaps between stations seem to stretch on for miles.

2 ★★ Vyšehrad Castle. Prague's "other" castle area here at Vyšehrad is far more dignified and in its own way more moving than the admittedly more Disneyesque-style Prague Castle downriver. It's less commercial and there's a

feeling of timelessness and place that's increasingly rare in modern-day Prague. Bring a blanket and a bottle of wine and hike up to the castle grounds. If you're lucky, you'll have the place to yourself. *Soběslavová 1.* ☎ *241-410-348. www.praha-vysehrad.cz. Free admission. Metro: Vyšehrad plus a walk.*

3 ★★ kids Renting a Boat on the Vltava. This is great for kids, but it's not bad for grown-ups either. You can rent little pedal- or rowboats from vendors on Žofín island, just across the street from the National Theater (Národní divadlo). You can't pedal far, but far enough that no one can see what you're doing in there. *80 Kč an hour. Metro: Staroměstská plus tram 17 or 18.*

View from Vyšehrad Castle.

Get cozy in a boat as you drift along the Vltava.

4 ★★★ Malá Strana. It's no accident that all those expensive boutique hotels are situated in the Lesser Quarter (Malá Strana). It's the one neighborhood in Prague that truly gives Paris a run for its money. Just about any walk will do, but try in and around the little streets near Kampa Park. *Metro: Malostranská.*

5 ★ Nebozízek. Prague is a city of great views, but there are only a handful of elegant restaurants that can really deliver on this score. Nebozízek stands halfway up Petřín Hill and commands a table view over the sparkling city below. To find it, take the funicular train one stop to Nebozízek station. *Nebozízek.* ☎ 257-315-329. www. nebozizek.cz. *Metro: Malostranská plus tram 12, 20, or 22 to Újezd & then the funicular.* $$$.

6 ★★★ The Charles Bridge at Night. By day, Prague's landmark bridge is thronged with tourists, buskers, sketch artists, touts, and hawkers. The spirit of the place can be totally drowned out. By night, it's a different story. The crowds thin out and the guys selling the cheap jewelry and the old-time photos go home. At the same time, the castle floodlights come on and both the Old Town and Malá Strana sides of the river are caught in the play of light and shadow. Find a spot along the wall of bridge, uncork a bottle of Czech sparkling wine, "Bohemia Sekt," and feel the invigorating breeze over the river.

7 ★ Riegrovy Sady. Prague has plenty of green spaces to stretch out on a bench or blanket, but Vinohrady's beautiful hillside park combines the best attributes of Lovers' Lanes everywhere: a dreamy castle view in the distance and a row of safe and quiet benches perched along a ridge to give you an excuse to linger. Hike up into the park from Vinohradská třída and follow the path to the edge overlooking the train station below and castle beyond. *Best, of course, after dark. Metro: Muzeum plus tram 11 to Vinohradský Pavilon.*

8 Riding the Night Tram. Prague's tram system is like Dr. Jekyll and Mr. Hyde. By day, the trams are a paragon of transportation virtue, ferrying carloads of accountants, shop clerks, dentists, workers, and students to their usual destinations. After midnight, the system lets its hair down. Prague's special night trams take over and the trams become veritable parties on wheels. The central night tram junction is at Lazarská ul. In Nové Město. From here cars fan out in all directions until 5am. Do as the locals do and share a seat—guy on the bottom and girl in his lap. *Metro: Mustek.* ●

Nebozízek is a great place for a romantic dinner.

The Jewish Quarter (Josefov)

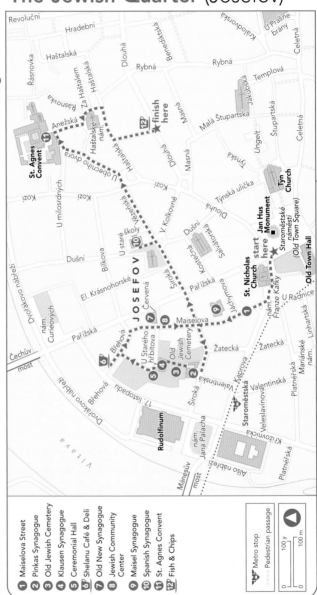

1 Maiselova Street
2 Pinkas Synagogue
3 Old Jewish Cemetery
4 Klausen Synagogue
5 Ceremonial Hall
6 Shelanu Café & Deli
7 Old New Synagogue
8 Jewish Community Center
9 Maisel Synagogue
10 Spanish Synagogue
11 St. Agnes Convent
12 Fish & Chips

Metro stop
Pedestrian passage

0   100 y
0   100 m

Previous page: A quiet street in Malá Strana.

This tour focuses on the remains of the former Jewish ghetto. The Prague Jewish Museum (Židovské muzeum v Praze) maintains four synagogues as well as the most moving remnant, the Old Jewish Cemetery (Starý židovský hřbitov). Another surviving synagogue, the Old New Synagogue (Staronová synagoga), is maintained by the Jewish community of Prague. You can walk the former ghetto for free, but to tour the exhibits you need an entry ticket (see the box "The Jewish Quarter: Practical Matters," below, for details on admissions charges and hours for Jewish Quarter attractions). The Old New Synagogue requires a separate ticket. A combined-entry ticket for all of the sights is also available. **Note:** Many of the sights on this tour are closed Saturdays, the Jewish Sabbath, and on Jewish holidays. Try to get an early start; the area gets very crowded in high season. START: **Old Town Square.**

① **Maiselova Street.** From Old Town Square, walk past St. Nicholas Church (Chrám sv. Mikuláše) and then past the birth house of Franz Kafka (p 27, bullet ①). Maiselova begins here and threads its way through the center of the former ghetto. This was "Main Street" when the ghetto was a walled-in community, and here you'll find some of the most important surviving buildings and the former Jewish Town Hall. ⏱ *10 min.*

② ★★ **Pinkas Synagogue (Pinkasová synagoga).** Continue walking down Maiselova past the Maisel Synagogue (you return to it later), turning left on Široká.

Opposite Široká 4 is the main entrance to the Pinkas Synagogue and the Old Jewish Cemetery. There's a cash desk where you can buy your combined ticket for the Jewish Museum. The Pinkas Synagogue is Prague's second-oldest Jewish house of worship, dating from the 1500s. Following World War II, the names of 77,297 Czech Jews who perished in the Nazi concentration camps were painted on the walls. The names include former U.S. Secretary of State Madeleine Albright's paternal grandparents: Arnošt and Olga Koerbel. The synagogue also holds a deeply moving display of pictures drawn by children held at the

You find this market near Klausen Synagogue and the Ceremonial Hall.

History 101: The Jewish Quarter

For centuries, Prague harbored one of Central Europe's largest and best-educated Jewish communities. The small area just north of the Old Town Square was the center of Jewish life from the 13th to the late 19th century. Although Jews were restricted from living outside the ghetto for much of that time and there were occasional pogroms, the Jewish community enjoyed relatively long periods of peace and tolerance. The high point came in the late 16th and early 17th centuries during the reign of Emperor Rudolf II. The ghetto began to decline in the 19th century after Jews were granted the right of abode and could live wherever they wanted. Many chose to leave the Jewish Quarter, and by the end of the 19th century, the ghetto had become a slum. In an early version of gentrification, the city knocked down many of the buildings, including several synagogues, and built the luxury turn-of-the-20th-century apartment houses you see today.

The Jewish Quarter is not a Holocaust site per se, but World War II did have a devastating effect on the city's Jews. Tens of thousands were deported and murdered in the concentration camps, leaving behind a small community of just a few thousand. The Nazis originally planned to build a museum here of Europe's extinct race of Jews. Ironically, many of the treasures on display are from Jewish towns and villages around the country that were pillaged by the Germans.

Terezín concentration camp during World War II. ⏱ *30 min. Entrance opposite Široká 4.*

❸ ★★★ Old Jewish Cemetery (Starý židovský hřbitov). An absolute must-see, on par with

Detail of a tombstone in the Old Jewish Cemetery.

Prague Castle. The Old Jewish Cemetery is Prague's oldest surviving Jewish burial ground, dating to the middle of the 15th century. Because local laws at the time prohibited Jews from burying their dead outside the ghetto, this tiny graveyard is crammed with some 12,000 visible tombstones and thousands more bodies stacked up in 12 to 15 layers below ground. The last grave dates from 1787. The most prominent grave, in the far corner near the Ceremonial Hall, is that of former Jewish scholar Rabbi Loew, the creator of the legendary Golem (he died in 1609). Across from Rabbi Loew's grave is that of Mordechai Maisel, a former leader

Klausen Synagogue.

of the ghetto for whom the Maisel Synagogue and Maiselova Street are named. Many visitors continue the ancient tradition of placing small pebbles on grave markers or stuffing the graves with small scraps of paper bearing wishes. ⏲ *30 min. Široká 3 (enter through the Pinkas Synagogue).*

❹ ★ Klausen Synagogue (Klausová synagoga).

The Klausen Synagogue is situated behind the Old Jewish Cemetery on U Starého hřbitova. It was the biggest synagogue during the ghetto's heyday and today holds a permanent exhibition of everyday Jewish customs and traditions. ⏲ *20 min. U Starého hř bitova 3a.*

❺ ★ Ceremonial Hall (Obřadní síň).

Just down from the Klausen Synagogue is the former Ceremonial Hall and mortuary of the Old Jewish Cemetery. Appearances can be deceiving: The Ceremonial Hall looks like the oldest building on the street, but in fact it's one of the youngest, dating to just 1912. The exhibition here describes Jewish customs and traditions relating to illness and death. ⏲ *20 min.*

❻ Shelanu Café & Deli.

Follow U starého hřbitova around until it meets Břehová to find this New York–style kosher deli. Choose from a range of classic sandwiches such as pastrami, egg salad, and smoked salmon. Opens early for breakfast. Closed Saturdays. *Břehová 8.* ☎ *221-665-141. www.shelanu.cz. $.*

❼ ★★ Old New Synagogue (Staronová synagoga).

From Břehová, find Maiselova again. You can't miss the Old New Synagogue, still standing and functioning much as it has for some 800 years. The architectural style is early Gothic and the vaulted interior is modeled after a 12th-century synagogue that once stood in the German city of Worms. The synagogue was originally called "New" but took on the name "Old New" in the 16th century when other, newer synagogues were built. The Old New Synagogue is not formally part of the Prague Jewish Museum and requires a separate ticket to enter. ⏲ *30 min.*

❽ Jewish Community Center (Židovská radnice).

Next to the Old New Synagogue, this was once the Jewish town hall. It now houses

Old New Synagogue and the Jewish Community Center.

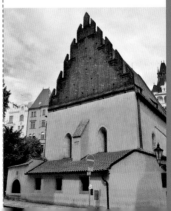

Jewish Quarter: Practical Matters

A ticket to visit the six Prague Jewish Museum sights (the Pinkas, Klaus, Maisel, and Spanish synagogues; the Old Jewish Cemetery; and the Ceremonial Hall) costs 300 Kč per person (200 Kč children). A separate ticket for entering the Old New Synagogue costs another 200 Kč (140 Kč children). A combined admission for all of the sights is available for 480 Kč (320 Kč for children). Tickets are available at cash desks located throughout the former ghetto. All of the major attractions are closed on Saturdays and Jewish holidays, so plan your visit accordingly. For more information, call ☎ 222-317-191 or visit www.jewishmuseum.cz. The museum sights are open Sunday to Friday from 9am to 6pm April through October; from 9am to 4:30pm November through March.

an information and cultural center for locals and visitors. On the tower facing the Old New Synagogue is an old Hebrew clock that keeps time running counterclockwise. *Maiselova 18.*

⑨ ★ Maisel Synagogue. Retrace your steps back up Maiselova, crossing Široká. This is an original Renaissance synagogue dating from the 16th century that underwent extensive renovation and is

now in the neo-Gothic style. It's no longer a functioning synagogue, but it houses the first part of an exhibition on the history of Jews in Bohemia and Moravia. (The exhibition continues in the Spanish Synagogue.) ⏱ *20 min. Maiselova 10.*

⑩ ★★ Spanish Synagogue (Španělská synagoga). The Spanish Synagogue is the last stop on a tour of the Jewish museum. It lies just outside the immediate

Detail of a house in the Jewish Quarter.

Maisel Synagogue.

ghetto area, along Široká. The design is Moorish, a popular style for 19th-century synagogues. Arabesque designs fill the stunning interior. The permanent exhibition continues the history of Jews in Bohemia and Moravia. If you need a quick coffee, there's a small cafe attached to the right of the synagogue. Just outside is a comical statue of the writer Franz Kafka. ⏱ *20 min. Dušní 12.*

⑪ ★★ St. Agnes Convent (Klášter sv. Anežky české). After all that history, decompress with a short stroll through one of the quietest and loveliest corners of the Old Town. Walk first along Vězeňská, then bear to the left on the small street U obecního dvora until you reach Anežská. You can walk the grounds of this former convent, which is made up of early Gothic buildings dating from the 13th century. The National Museum also maintains a fascinating gallery here of Medieval and Gothic art. ⏱ *45 min. U Milosrdných 17.* ☎ *224-810-628. www.ngprague.cz. 150 Kč. Tues–Sun 10am–6pm.*

⑫ Fish & Chips. For something quick and a bit different, try this authentic fish and chips restaurant not far from the Jewish Quarter on Dlouhá street. Not surprisingly, you'll find beer-battered fried cod served with wedge 'chips' (French fries) and 'mushy peas', but the kitchen also turns out a full range of excellent fish dishes. *Dlouhá 21.* ☎ *606-881-414. www.fishandchips prague.cz. $$.*

Window of the Spanish Synagogue.

The Lesser Town (Malá Strana)

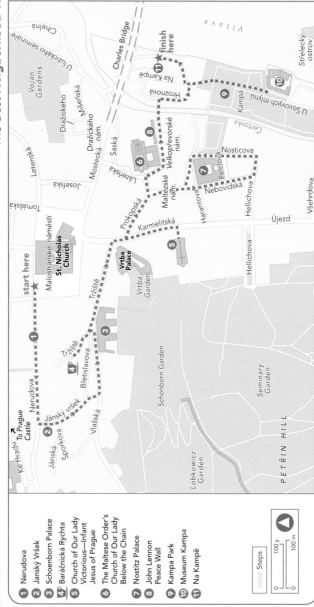

start here

Malostranské náměstí
St. Nicholas Church

Vrtba Palace

Vrtba Garden

To Prague Castle

Nosticova

Na Kampě

finish here

Charles Bridge

Vltava

Střelecký ostrov

PETŘÍN HILL

Seminary Garden

Lobkowicz Garden

Schönborn Garden

1. Nerudova
2. Jansky Vršek
3. Schoenborn Palace
4. Baráčnická Rychta
5. Church of Our Lady Victorious—Infant Jesus of Prague
6. The Maltese Order's Church of Our Lady Below the Chain
7. Nostitz Palace
8. John Lennon Peace Wall
9. Kampa Park
10. Museum Kampa
11. Na Kampě

Steps

0   100 y
0   100 m

In contrast to the Old Town, the Lesser Town feels quieter and more refined. It gives Paris a run for its money in terms of romance. Many of the most important sights in the Lesser Town are covered in the "Best in One Day" tour (p 8), and its gardens and parks are covered in the "Hidden Gardens of Malá Strana" tour (p 90). This tour covers a little bit of familiar territory but is intended to get you off the main drag and onto the quieter cobblestone streets that define the prettiest part of Prague. Feel free to wander off the recommended course if you see a quiet alley, courtyard, or garden that merits exploring. START: **Malostranské nám.**

1 Nerudova. From Malostranské náměstí, follow Nerudova up toward Prague Castle. St. Nicholas Church (Kostel sv. Mikuláše, p 15, bullet **14**) is on your left as you walk uphill. This street takes its name from Czech author Jan Neruda, who was born in this area in the 19th century. The Nobel prize–winning Chilean poet Pablo Neruda admired Jan Neruda's writings so much that he adopted "Neruda" as a pen name. The street is lined with stunning Baroque palaces, many of which have been given cute descriptive names. Look especially at houses at no. 11 (U červeného beránka/"House of the Red Lamb"), no. 12 (U tří housliček/ House of the Three Violins), and no. 16 (U zlaté číše/"House of the Golden Cup"). ⏱ *15 min.*

Nerudova Street.

2 Janský Vršek. Instead of going all the way to the castle, turn left down these inviting stairs. This takes you into the quiet heart of upper Malá Strana. Many of the streets here still bear traces of the days when Prague was bilingual German-speaking. On the corner with Šporková, the street sign reads JOHANNESBERG GASSE, the German name for Janský Vršek. ⏱ *10 min.*

3 Schoenborn Palace (Schoenbornský palác). Continue walking along Janský Vršek, making a left at the intersection with Vlašská. The American flag fluttering in the breeze marks the front of the U.S. embassy, quartered in a 17th-century Baroque palace, the former home of Austro-Hungarian general Count Colloredo-Mansfeld. The U.S. government bought the house in

1925 for the princely sum of $117,000. It has more than 100 rooms and 7 acres of gardens stretching up Petřín Hill. Franz Kafka rented a room here in 1917. The building is not open to the public. ⏱ 10 min. Tržiště 15.

4 **Baráčnická Rychta.** If you're ready for a cold one or quick bite, this rambling Czech pub has great beer and a wonderful atmosphere. To find it, look for the little part of Tržiště that runs up from the Alchymist Grand Hotel. Come back at night for occasional live music downstairs. Tržiště 23. ☎ 257-532-461. www.baracnickarychta.cz. $.

5 ★★ **Church of Our Lady Victorious—Infant Jesus of Prague.** From the U.S. embassy, walk down Tržiště to the bottom of the street, turning right on Karmelitská. This early-Baroque church of the Carmelite order is famous for the wax statue of baby Jesus displayed on an altar on the right wing of the church. The "Infant Jesus of Prague" was presented to the Carmelites in 1628 and commands an almost cultlike status in some countries. Copies of the "bambino" are sold in the church's small museum and at souvenir shops in the area. ⏱ 15 min. Karmelitská 9.

The "Infant Jesus of Prague."

☎ 257-533-646. www.pragjesu.info. Free admission. Mon–Sat 8:30am–7pm, Sun 8:30am–8pm.

6 ★ **The Maltese Order's Church of Our Lady Below the Chain (Kostel Panny Marie pod řetězem).** Cross Karmelitská and walk to the left until you come to Prokopská. Turn down this street and walk into the large Maltézské náměstí, named for this large church off the square belonging to the Knights of Malta. One of the best Romanesque designs in Prague, this church replaced an even older church after it burned in 1420. You can see remnants of the original along the portal and inside the church courtyard. ⏱ 15 min. Lázenská ul. Open during masses.

7 **Nostitz Palace (Nostický palác).** This palace, now home to the Czech Culture Ministry, is a grand, 17th-century Baroque design attributed to Francesco Caratti. A Prague noble family who strongly supported the arts used to own it, and its ornate halls once housed a famed private art collection. You can sometimes hear chamber concerts through its windows. ⏱ 10 min. Maltézské nám. 1. ☎ 257-085-111. www.mkcr.cz. Occasionally open to the public; call or visit website for details.

8 ★★ **John Lennon Peace Wall.** Before seeing the John Lennon Peace Wall, make a small detour down Nebovidská (to the right of the Nostitz Palace), past the luxurious quarters of the Mandarin Oriental Hotel. Walk to the end of the street and turn left on Hellichová. Make another left onto Nosticová. This is one of the quietest and nicest parts of Malá Strana, fully removed from the city. Soon enough, this street will be cleaned up like all the rest, but for the moment enjoy the elegant, faded

Museum Kampa.

feeling. To find the Lennon Wall, walk down Nosticová, returning to Maltézské náměstí and the Knights of Malta Church. Follow Lázenská to the right onto another large square: Velkopřevorské náměstí. The French embassy will be to your right and this half-hidden graffiti wall, a Prague original, to your left. The Lennon Peace Wall came into existence shortly after Beatles musician John Lennon was murdered in New York in 1980. Under Communism, it morphed into an impromptu protest space. The secret police tried to stop the graffiti writers, but every day the wall seemed to be covered with new peace messages extolling the virtues of John Lennon instead of that other "Lenin." Today, the wall has lost its political symbolism but is still a favorite among visitors, and if you've brought some markers or spray paint along, feel free to add your own message. ⏱ *15 min. (20 min. if you plan on writing your own message). Velkopřevorské nám.*

⑨ ★★ **Kampa Park.** Continue walking, crossing a lovely, small bridge over the Čertovká stream to reach Kampa Island and this park, Malá Strana's biggest stretch of green. There are gorgeous views over the Vltava on one side and the charming footbridges and mills over the Čertovká on the other. The big lawn in the middle is the perfect spot to throw down a blanket and open a book. ⏱ *20 min.*

⑩ ★ **Museum Kampa.** Near the Vltava at about the midpoint of the park, you find this very good, relatively new museum dedicated to contemporary Central European art. The permanent collection has works by noted Czech sculptor Otto Gutfreund and Czech painter František Kupka. The museum was hit hard by a flood in 2013, and was closed for cleaning and reconstruction as we went to press. Check the website for updates. ⏱ *1 hr. U sovových mlýnů 2.* ☎ *724-228-838. www.museumkampa.com. 160 Kč. Daily 10am–6pm.*

⑪ ★ **Na Kampě.** Return to the center of the city via this small square, lined with hotels and restaurants on both sides. Take the little street that leads off the square to the right of Na Kampě 15 to walk along the edge of the river and get some great photos of the Charles Bridge. ⏱ *15 min.*

The graffiti-covered John Lennon Peace Wall.

The Castle District (Hradčany)

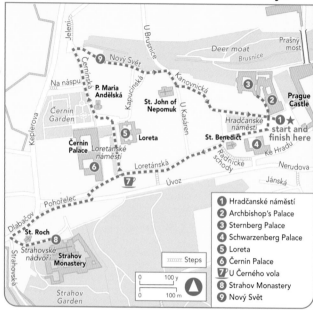

1. Hradčanské náměstí
2. Archbishop's Palace
3. Sternberg Palace
4. Schwarzenberg Palace
5. Loreta
6. Černin Palace
7. U Černého vola
8. Strahov Monastery
9. Nový Svět

The Castle District is quiet and exclusive. Perched on a high hill and lacking good public transportation, it's populated by embassies, institutes, and ministries. The area was leveled by fire in 1541 and rebuilt in Renaissance and Baroque styles. It's easy to combine this tour with the longer tour of Prague Castle on p 31.
START: **Hradčanské nám.**

1 Hradčanské náměstí. One of the city's most beautiful and tranquil squares and a nice place to relax on a bench. The plague column in the center was built in 1726 by the Baroque master Ferdinand Brokoff, creator of several Charles Bridge statues. ⏲ 15 min.

2 Archbishop's Palace (Arcibiskupský palác). The seat of the Prague Archbishop is unfortunately not open to the public, though you can enter the interior chapel once a year, the day before Good Friday. The staid Renaissance exterior was

later remodeled into exuberant late-Baroque Rococo. ⏲ 10 min. Hradčanské nám. 16. No phone. Open 1 day a year.

3 ★★ Sternberg Palace (Šternberský palác). The real treasure here lies just behind the Archbishop's palace. This is home to the National Gallery's excellent collection of European art and includes works by Rembrandt, El Greco, and Goya. ⏲ 2 hr. Hradčanské nám. 15. ☎ 233-090-570. www.ngprague.cz. 150 Kč. Tues–Sun 10am–6pm.

4 Schwarzenberg Palace.

Across the square, the Renaissance sgraffito on the exterior makes this imposing palace easy to recognize. The Schwarzenberg family acquired the property in the early 18th century. It houses a permanent exhibition on Baroque art in the Czech lands. ⏱ 1 hr. Hradčanské nám. 2. ☎ 223-081-713. www.ngprague.cz. 150 Kč. Tues–Sun 10am–6pm.

5 ★★ Loreta.

Follow Loretánská, which leads off the square to the left. This remarkable cloister, church, and Baroque pilgrimage was built in the 17th century after the Habsburg conquest to re-Catholicize the Czechs. It was modeled on the original Santa Casa (Sacred House) in the Italian town of Loreta, brought to Italy from the Holy Lands in the 13th century as the house where the angel Gabriel first told Mary she would bear the baby Jesus. A duplicate Santa Casa stands in the courtyard. Lovers of Baroque will enjoy the ornate interiors and the statuary outside. The Treasury holds a diamond monstrance from 1699 made from some 6,222 diamonds. The carillon of 27 bells is unique in Prague. ⏱ 1 hr. Loretánské nám. 7. ☎ 220-516-740. www.loreta.cz. 130 Kč. Tues–Sun 9am–12:15pm, 1–5pm.

6 Černin Palace (Černinský palác).

Across the street from the Loreta, this forbidding-looking palace is home to the Czech Republic's Foreign Ministry. But its real claim to fame dates from February 1948, following the Soviet-backed Communist coup. It was here that Jan Masaryk, the foreign minister at the time and son of first Czechoslovak president Tomáš G. Masaryk, fell to his death from a high window. He opposed the coup, and it's never been resolved whether he jumped from the window or was pushed. ⏱ 10 min. Loretánské nám. No phone. Closed to the public.

7 U Černého vola.

This is one of the best traditional Czech pubs still standing. Big wooden tables, decent pub grub, and excellent Kozel beer on tap. Loretánské nám. 1. ☎ 220-513-481. $.

8 ★★ Strahov Monastery (Strahovský Klášter).

From Loretánské náměstí, follow Pohořelec. This medieval monastery of the Premonstratensian order goes back to the 12th century. The monks' chambers are off-limits, but visitors can still see the amazing Strahov Library (Strahovská knihovna), laid out in two immense Baroque halls. Also worth visiting are ancient printing presses downstairs and the remains of the order's 10th-century founder, St. Norbert. ⏱ 1 hr. Strahovské nádvoří 1. ☎ 233-107-718. 80 Kč. Daily 9am–noon, 1–5pm.

9 ★ Nový Svět.

The rest of the tour is simply a stroll through the elegant Castle District. Return to Loretánské náměstí and the Černin Palace, making a left on Černinská. Follow this to the end until you come to the remote and lovely cobblestones of quiet Nový Svět street. Make a right at the end of Nový Svět onto Kanovnická, which will take you back to the start of the tour at Hradčanské náměstí. ⏱ 30 min.

Loreta Church.

Old Town (Staré Město)

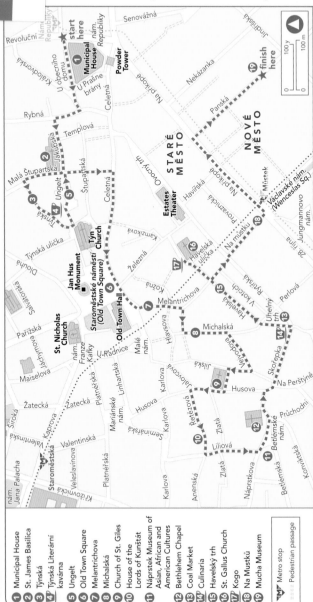

1 Municipal House
2 St. James Basilica
3 Týnská
4 Týnská Literární kavárna
5 Ungelt
6 Old Town Square
7 Melantrichova
8 Michalská
9 Church of St. Giles
10 House of the Lords of Kunštát
11 Náprstek Museum of Asian, African and American Cultures
12 Bethlehem Chapel
13 Coal Market
14 Culinaria
15 Havelský trh
16 St. Gallus Church
17 Kogo
18 Na Mustku
19 Mucha Museum

Ⓜ Metro stop
≡≡≡ Pedestrian passage

Labels on map:
Revoluční
Nám. Republiky
start here
Senovážná
Jindřišská
Municipal House
Powder Tower
nám. Republiky
finish here
U obecního domu
Kralodvorská
U Prašné brány
Na příkopě
Nekázanka
Celetná
Rybná
Templová
Panská
NOVÉ MĚSTO
Malá Štupartská
Jakubská
Štupartská
STARÉ MĚSTO
Ovocny trh
Estates Theater
Ungelt
Celetná
Na příkopě
Můstek
Václavské nám. (Wenceslas Sq.)
Týnská
Týn Church
Havířská
Provaznická
Na mustku
Kamzíkova
Tynská ulička
Jana Palacha
Dlouhá
Jan Hus Monument
Železná
Kožná
Havelská ulička
Jungmannovo nám.
28. října
Salvátorská
Staroměstské náměstí (Old Town Square)
Old Town Hall
Melantrichova
Havelská
V kotcích
Rytířská
Uhelný trh
Perlová
St. Nicholas Church
nám. Franze Kafky
Michalská
Pařížská
Jáchymova
U Radnice
Malé nám.
Hlavsova
Michalská
Skořepka
Na Perštyně
Maiselova
Linhartská
Jilská
Velvarova
Maiselova
Mariánské nám.
Karlova
Husova
Jalovcová
Husova
Na Perštyně
Žatecká
Zatecká
Platnéřská
Seminářská
Řetězová
Zlatá
Betlémské nám.
Průchodní
Siroká
Kaprova
Valentinská
Veleslavínova
Platnéřská
Karlova
Anenská
Zlatá
Náprstkova
Betlémská
Konviktská
nám. Jana Palacha
Křižovnická
Staroměstská
Valentinská
Liliová
0 100 y
0 100 m

The Old Town is the center of Prague and long the seat of commercial power. The main sights of the Old Town, including the Old Town Square, are covered in the "Best in One Day" tour (p 8). This tour snakes in and around the Old Town Square to see some of the lesser attractions off the beaten path. Feel free to wander at will, but be sure to bring a good map—it's easy to get lost. START: **Náměstí Republiky.**

❶ ★★★ Municipal House (Obecní dům).

This turn-of-the-20th-century Art Nouveau building has been an important Czech cultural symbol—the document granting independence to Czechoslovakia was signed here in 1918. The Prague Symphony Orchestra performs in Smetana Hall, the most impressive room. Guided tours through the building are offered year-round but are more frequent in summer. Tours normally begin at odd-numbered hours (11am, 1pm, 3pm), but the exact times vary by the day. Check the website for an up-to-date timetable. ⏱ *15 min. (1 1/2 hr. if you take a tour). See p 9, bullet* ❷.

❷ ★ St. James Basilica (Bazilika sv. Jakuba).

Enter the heart of the Old Town along the small street U obecního domu, to the right of the Municipal House. Take a right on Rybná and then a left on Jakubská to the street Malá Štupartská. The Baroque St. James Basilica is Prague's second-longest church, with 21 altars. When you enter, look up just inside the front door. The object dangling above is the shriveled arm of a 16th-century thief. The church's enormous organ has been restored to its original sound, and St. James regularly hosts organ recitals and concerts (see chapter 8). ⏱ *15 min. Malá Štupartská 6.* ☎ *604-208-490. Mon–Sat 9:30am–noon, 2–4pm.*

❸ Týnská.

As you exit St. James, take a right on Malá Štupartská, then follow it to Týnská, a small

street on your left. This is a beautiful alleyway of Baroque houses—note the barely discernable relief above the door of no. 10. The area has gotten trendy recently, and amid the junk shops (great for browsing) you'll find some high-end antiques dealers and a couple of good bars and restaurants. ⏱ *15 min.*

❹ Týnská Literární kavárna.

If you're starting to flag, stop by this popular student coffeehouse for a coffee or cold drink. Come back later and chill out with a good book—after all, as you can probably tell from the name, this is a "literary" coffeehouse. *Týnská 6.* ☎ *224-827-807. $.*

❺ ★★ Ungelt (Týnský Dvůr).

Round the bend at Týnská to see the back of the magnificent Týn Church (kostel Matky Boží před Týnem). Make a left at the church

Art Nouveau fans should be sure to spend some time at the Municipal House.

The Ungelt.

and enter the Ungelt, the fortified area of the former customs house, once the seat of the city's wealth. It's hard to imagine now, but this area was allowed to fall into appalling disrepair and was restored to its present appearance only in the mid-1990s. Now, the Ungelt holds an appealing mix of upscale shops and restaurants. ⏱ *20 min.*

6 ★★★ Old Town Square (Staroměstské nám.). Continue walking through the Ungelt, exiting through the gate on the other side. Make a right on Malá Štupartská and follow it to the right, connecting with Celetná and eventually entering Old Town Square on the same road used by Bohemian kings 500 years ago. The "Best in One

View of Melantrichova from City Hall Tower.

Day" tour, p 9, covers the square's main sights, so for this tour simply stroll through the square, walking to the left of the Old Town Hall (Staroměstská radnice) and finding Melantrichova, a small street just opposite the Astronomical Clock. ⏱ *15 min.*

7 ★ Melantrichova. This tiny lane connects the city's two main squares (Old Town and Wenceslas) and for that reason is clogged night and day. The usual selection of glass and T-shirt shops lines this street. Don't miss the "House at the Two Golden Bears" (Dům u dvou zlatých medvědů), on the corner with Kožná. It has one of the city's most beautiful Renaissance portals, dating from 1590. ⏱ *10 min.*

8 Michalská. Turn right through an arcade to enter Michalská Street, once one of the main arteries of the Old Town. Art galleries, high-end antiques shops, and the luxurious Iron Gate Hotel (p 144) line this picturesque street. ⏱ *15 min.*

9 ★ Church of St. Giles (Sv. Jilji). Follow Michalská nearly to the end, turning right under an archway onto Vejvodová. Turn right again onto Jilská (unmarked) and follow it to the back of this enormous church. St. Giles was a Hussite church during the 15th-century religious strife, but was given a thorough Baroque makeover after the Austrian Habsburg occupation.

Today, it has perhaps the most opulent interior of any Prague church save St. Nicholas. ○ *15 min. Husová 8. No phone. Daily 9am–5pm (except during masses).*

⑩ House of the Lords of Kunštát (Dům Pánů z Kunštátu).

From St. Giles, walk down Husová until you see a small street running to the left called Řetězová. Look for no. 3, one of the oldest houses in Old Town; it dates from 1200 and has some of the city's best-preserved Romanesque chambers. The house was rebuilt in the 15th century in Gothic style and served as an occasional residence for the Hussite King George of Poděbrady. Unfortunately, it's not often open to the public. ○ *10 min. Řetězová 3. No phone.*

⑪ Náprstek Museum of Asian, African and American Cultures (Náprstkovo Muzeum).

Continue along Řetězová, making a left onto Liliová and following that to Bethlehem Square (Betlémské nám.). On the right side of the square, you see the National Museum's collection of non-European cultures housed in a former brewery. The exhibitions are dry, but the museum has a popular section on North American

Bethlehem Chapel.

Church of St. Giles.

Indians. ○ *30 min. Betlémské nám. 1.* ☎ *224-497-500. www.nm.cz. 80 Kč. Tues–Sun 10am–6pm.*

⑫ ★★ Bethlehem Chapel (Betlémská kaple).

To the left on the square is the real attraction, the Bethlehem Chapel. In the 15th century, this was once home to the fire-brand Czech Protestant theologian Jan Hus. Hus was burned at the stake as a heretic in 1415 in Constanz in what is now Germany, and became a martyr for the Czech Protestant and later nationalist cause. The chapel was completed in 1394 but thoroughly reconstructed in the 1950s. In the main hall you can see the pulpit from where Hus

preached. ⏱ *30 min. Betlémské nám. 4.* ☎ *224-248-595. 60 Kč. Daily 10am–6pm.*

⑬ **Coal Market (Uhelný trh).** Follow Betlémská out of the square, turning right onto Na Perštýně. Be sure to look up at this point to see Czech artist David Černý's "Hanging Man" statue hanging high above Husová. Cross the street and follow Skořepká into what was once the city's main coal market, marked by a tiny statue in the middle. ⏱ *10 min.*

⑭ **Culinaria.** If it's lunchtime and a nice day, pick up some sandwiches-to-go at this popular deli situated on the corner of Skořepká and Uhelný trh. The smoothies and coffee drinks are some of the best in town. Eat at tables outside or on benches around the statue at the center of market. *Skořepká 9.* ☎ *224-231-017. www.culinaria.cz. $.*

⑮ ★ **Havelský trh.** From the Coal Market, walk up busy Havelská Street. The "Havel Market" was the area's commercial center during the Middle Ages and remains a popular market. The stalls here sell everything from fruits and vegetables to drinks, soap, artwork, and leather goods. Prices here are generally lower than in most shops. ⏱ *20 min.*

⑯ ★ **St. Gallus Church (Kostel sv. Havla).** This dignified church, sometimes called St. Havel Church, dominates the end of the square. It dates from the 13th century and is one of the oldest in the Old Town. Jan Hus was an occasional preacher here. The chapel holds the tomb of Bohemian Baroque artist Karel Škréta. ⏱ *10 min. Havelská ul. No phone. Daily 10am–5pm.*

⑰ **Kogo.** This branch of the popular local chain of good pizzas and homemade pastas is perfect for lunch or dinner. The house wine is a dry red called Vranac that's imported from Montenegro. *Havelská 27.* ☎ *224-210-259. www.kogo.cz. $$.*

⑱ **Na Mustků.** From St. Gallus Church, return in the direction of Havelský trh and turn left on Melantrichova. This brings you back to Mustek metro station and the base of Wenceslas Square. The name "Na Mustků" means "on the little bridge" and refers to the days when this was a small bridge crossing a moat, linking the Old Town (Staré Město) and the New Town (Nové Město). You can still see parts of the original foundation downstairs inside the metro station. ⏱ *10 min.*

⑲ ★★ **Mucha Museum.** If you've got the time and energy for one last sight (and especially if you're a fan of lavish Art Nouveau), walk down Na příkopě several blocks until you reach Panská ul. on the right. This museum is dedicated to Czech artist and illustrator Alfons Mucha, who became world famous for his Parisian prints of the actress Sarah Bernhardt. The collection includes some original paintings, drawings, and poster art. ⏱ *45 min. Panská 7.* ☎ *224-216-415. www.mucha.cz. 180 Kč. Daily 10am–6pm.* ●

St. Gallus Church.

Shopping Best Bets

Best for **Architecture Buffs**
★★★ Exlibris, *Veleslavínská 3* (p 74)

Best Place to **Find Old Maps**
★★ Antikvariát Pařížská, *Pařížská 8* (p 74)

Best Place to **Buy a Wooden Rocking Horse**
★★ Rocking Horse Toy Shop, *Loretánské nám. 3 (p 76)*

Best Place to **Buy a Real Puppet**
★★ Marionety, *Týnský dvůr 1* (p 75)

Best **Bohemian Crystal**
★★★ Moser, *Na příkopě 12* (p 77)

Best **Contemporary Glass**
★★ Artěl, *Celetná 29 (p 76)*

Best **1930s Shopping Center**
★★★ Lucerna Pasáž, *Štěpánská 61* (p 78)

Best **Department Store in a Brutalist Building**
Kotva, *Náměstí Republiky 8 (p 77)*

Best Place for **English-Language Books**
★★★ Shakespeare & Sons, *U lužického semináře 10 (p 79)*

Best **Bookstore/Coffeehouse**
★★ The Globe Bookstore and Coffeehouse, *Pštrossová 6 (p 79)*

Best **Czech Clothing Designers**
★★★ Timoure et Groupe, *V kolkovně 6 (p 79)*

Best **Deli**
★★ Culinaria, *Skořepka 9 (p 80)*

Best **Bath Salts & Lotions**
★★ Botanicus, *Týn 3 (p 81)*

Best Place to **Buy a Cubist Couch**
★★★ Kubista, *Ovocný trh 19* (p 82)

Best Place to **Buy a Czech Garnet**
★★ Studio Šperk, *Dlouhá 19* (p 82)

Colorful wooden toys at Manufaktura.

Malá Strana Area Shopping

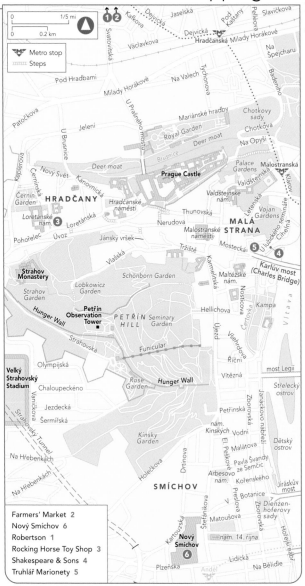

0 ___ 1/5 mi
0 ___ 0.2 km

ᴹᴾ Metro stop
⊓⊓⊓⊓⊓ Steps

Farmers' Market 2
Nový Smíchov 6
Robertson 1
Rocking Horse Toy Shop 3
Shakespeare & Sons 4
Truhlář Marionety 5

Photo p 69: Shop window on Golden Lane.

Staré Město Area Shopping

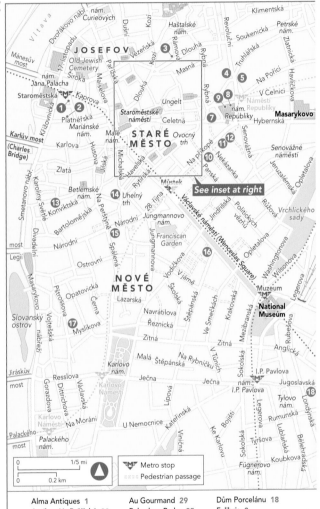

Alma Antiques 1
Antikvariát Pařížská 20
Antikvariát Ztichlá
klika 13
Art Deco Galerie 41
Art Decoratif 8
Artěl 7
Atrium Flora 19

Au Gourmand 29
Bakeshop Praha 25
Boheme 22
Botanicus 33
Bric a Brac 30
Coccinelle 9
Culinaria 14
Dorotheum 42

Dům Porcelánu 18
Exlibris 2
Galerie Art Praha 39
The Globe Bookstore
and Coffeehouse 17
Granát 28
Jiří Švestka 6
Klára Nademlýnská 26

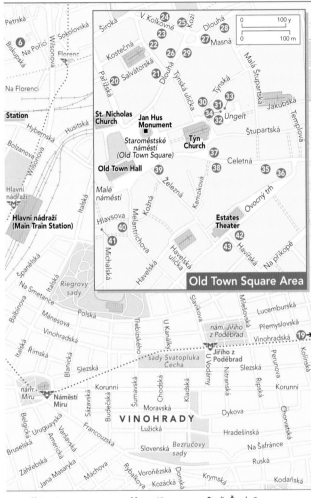

Old Town Square Area

Kotva 4	Moser 10	Studio Šperk 3
Kubista 36	Palladium 5	Swarovski 37
L'Institut Guerlain 27	Report's 23	Tatiana 21
Lucerna Pasáž 16	Sabai 11	Tesco 15
Manufaktura 40	Slovanský dům 12	Timoure et Groupe 24
Marionety 31	Sparky's 43	U zlatého Iva 35
Material 34	Starožitnosti	
Modernista 38	Ungelt 32	

Prague Shopping A to Z

Antiquarian Books & Maps

★★ Antikvariát Pařížská

STARÉ MĚSTO   This small shop lies on one of the most exclusive streets in the city and offers a beautiful selection of older maps and prints. Despite the location, the prices here are not really much higher than elsewhere, and the quality of the goods is among the best you'll find. *Pařížská 8.* ☎ 222-321-442. AE, DC, MC, V. Metro: Staroměstská. Map p 72.

★★ Antikvariát Ztichlá klika

STARÉ MĚSTO   A treasure trove of old books, maps, prints, and postcards, situated in three adjoining shops in a quiet section of Betlémská. One could spend hours browsing these shelves (and believe me, we have). Open Monday to Friday 1 to 7pm. *Betlémská 10–14.* ☎ 222-222-079. AE, DC, MC, V. Metro: Náměstí Republiky. Map p 72.

★★★ Exlibris STARÉ MĚSTO

An absolute must for fans of books on architecture and style from the 1920s to the '60s and '70s. Also stocks vintage prints and posters and a small number of museum-quality paintings from the 1950s–1970s. The only drawback is its limited hours: open Thursday and Friday from 2 until 7pm (or by appointment). *Veleslavínova 3.* ☎ 224-235-451. www.exlibris.cz. MC, V. Metro: Staroměstská. Map p 72.

Antiques & Collectibles

★ Alma Antiques STARÉ MĚSTO

Family-owned and fascinating antiques store/junk shop, with an eclectic range of housewares, bric-a-brac, rugs, clothes, accessories, and just about everything else. If you don't see what you're looking

Antikvariát Pařížská.

for, ask. They have several stores and storage areas around town and can probably find it. *Valentínská 7.* ☎ 222-327-625. www.valentinum.cz. AE, DC, MC, V. Metro: Staroměstská. Map p 72.

★ Art Deco Galerie STARÉ

MĚSTO   Cozy shop on a quiet street in Old Town that focuses on signature pieces from the interwar years, when Czechoslovakia under the First Republic was one of the world's wealthiest countries. Good collections of glass, personal accessories, small pieces of furniture, and secondhand clothing. Note limited opening hours: Monday to Friday from 2 to 7pm. *Michalská 21.* ☎ 224-223-076. www.artdecogalerie-mili.com. MC, V. Metro: Staroměstská. Map p 72.

★★ Bric a Brac STARÉ MĚSTO

The Prague junk shop to end all junk shops. Tens of thousands of used and antique items are crammed into two separate store spaces, located down a hidden alleyway just off of

Týnský dvůr. *Týnská 7.* ☎ *224-815-763. www.bricabrac-antiques. com. MC, V. Metro: Staroměstská. Map p 72.*

★★ Dorotheum STARÉ MĚSTO The local branch of the fabled Austrian auction house of the same name. As you can imagine, the goods on offer—jewelry, furniture, and artwork—are some of the best on the market, at prices to match. Excellent 19th-century collections. Good selection of antique jewelry. *Ovocný trh 2.* ☎ *224-222-001. www. dorotheum.com. AE, DC, MC, V. Metro: Mustek. Map p 72.*

★★ Starožitnosti Ungelt STARÉ MĚSTO Recognized around Prague as one of the best stores for antique glass, ceramics, and jewelry. Prices here are a little higher than most, but the selection is much better. *Týn 1.* ☎ *224-895-454. www.antiqueungelt.cz. MC, V. Metro: Staroměstská. Map p 72.*

Art Galleries
★★ Galerie Art Praha STARÉ MĚSTO Impressive gallery on Old Town Square with a focus on 19th- and 20th-century paintings by Czech and Slovak artists. Always something eye-catching in the window. Strong on Communist-era art.

Galerie Art Praha.

Staroměstské nám. 20. ☎ *224-211-087. www.galerie-art-praha.cz. AE, DC, MC, V. Metro: Staroměstská. Map p 72.*

★ Jiří Švestka NOVÉ MĚSTO Widely considered the leading private gallery in Prague, with a stable of mostly cutting-edge Czech artists and some internationals. There's also a bookshop here with a good selection of art and architecture titles. *Biskupský dvůr 6.* ☎ *222-311-092. www.jirisvestka. com. AE, DC, MC, V. Metro: Náměstí Republiky plus tram 8. Map p 72.*

Children: Toys & Puppets
★★ Marionety STARÉ MĚSTO This shop features handmade wooden marionettes from timeless classic designs, some of which date back 500 years. Pricey, but worth every penny for an authentic souvenir. Open daily from 10am to 8pm. *Týnský dvůr 1.* ☎ *224-895-437. AE, DC, MC, V. Metro: Staroměstská. Map p 72.*

★★ Rocking Horse Toy Shop HRADČANY Excellent collection of vintage, decidedly low-tech Czech toys, including the signature little wooden rocking horse. It feels like it's from a different age entirely, and is sure to be a delight

for little kids. *Loretánské nám. 3.* ☎ *603-515-745. No credit cards. Metro: Hradčanská. Map p 71.*

★ **Sparky's** NOVÉ MĚSTO This modern toy store is reportedly the largest in the city, with a convenient central location. It has a great selection of stuffed animals on the ground floor. Toys for older kids, including lots of model cars, are on the upper floors. Giftwrapping available. *Havířská 2.* ☎ *234-221-402. www.sparkys.cz. AE, DC, MC, V. Metro: Mustek. Map p 71.*

★★ **Truhlář Marionety** MALÁ STRANA A well regarded puppet shop that eschews cheap machine-made marionettes in favor of the handmade, labor-intensive variety. Marionettes have a tradition in Prague going back to the Middle Ages, and many of the witch, king, and nobleman motifs here have been in use for centuries. *U Lužického semináře 5.* ☎ *602-689-918. www.marionety.com. AE, DC, MC, V. Metro: Malostranská. Map p 72.*

★★ **U zlatého lva** STARÉ MĚSTO This quaint and atmospheric toy shop is an antidote to touristy Celetná street and an excellent place to seek out traditional Czech wooden toys, puppets, stuffed animals, and the like. Everything is fairly priced and locally made. *Celetná 32.* ☎ *224-239-469. www. czechtoys.cz. AE, DC, MC, V. Metro: Náměstí Republiky. Map p 72.*

China, Crystal & Porcelain

★★ **Artěl** STARÉ MĚSTO American expat Karen Feldman has almost single-handedly revived international interest in classic Czech glass and stemware design from the 1920s and '30s. Her high-end reproductions are now sold around the world. The flagship store on Celetná features the signature glass lines as well as retro gifts, books, and found objects. *Celetná 29 (entrance on Rybná).* ☎ *224-815-085. www.artelglass.com. AE, DC, MC, V. Metro: Náměstí Republiky. Map p 72.*

★ **Dům Porcelánu** VINOHRADY In addition to crystal, the Czech Republic is renowned for porcelain, much of it made in or near the spa town of Karlovy Vary. At this large shop in Vinohrady, you'll find designs from all of the leading Czech producers—at prices that haven't been marked up for tourists. Look out especially for traditional Czech "onion" *(cibulák)* china.

Marionety.

Dům Porcelánu.

Jugoslávská 16. ☎ 221-505-320. www.dumporcelanu.cz. AE, DC, MC, V. Metro: Náměstí Miru. Map p 72.

★★ Material STARÉ MĚSTO
This small, locally owned outfit specializes in designer glassware, chandeliers, candleholders, vases, and decorative objects of all sorts. The company combines traditional Czech glassblowing and glassworking skills with eye-catching modern designs, shapes, and colors. Týn 1. ☎ 608-664-766. www.i-material.com. AE, DC, MC, V. Metro: Staroměstská. Map p 72.

★★★ Moser NOVÉ MĚSTO
The leading Bohemian producer of luxury cut class, crystal, stemware, and vases for 150 years. The company's gorgeous 1920s showroom on Na příkopě in central Prague is worth a visit on its own just to see the glass in its proper setting. A perfect gift for someone special back home. Na příkopě 12. ☎ 224-211-293. www.moser-glass.com. AE, DC, MC, V. Metro: Mustek. Map p 72.

★★ Swarovski STARÉ MĚSTO
The "Austrian" glassmaker who originally founded this world-famous lead crystal maker, Daniel Swarovski, was actually born in a small town in Bohemia. So in a way it's fitting to

have such a beautiful store in the center of Prague. The selection here is excellent, but the prices are similar to or higher than what you'll find anywhere else in the world. Celetná 7. ☎ 222-315-585. www.swarovski.com. AE, DC, MC, V. Metro: Staroměstská. Map p 72.

Department Stores & Shopping Centers
★ Atrium Flora VINOHRADY
Similar to Nový Smíchov (see below), with more than 100 stores and a large multiplex cinema. It has the city's only 3D IMAX theater, and is convenient to the metro

Crystal pieces from Moser.

The unusual upside-down horse sculpture at Lucerna Pasáž.

(A line). *Vinohradská 151.* ☎ *255-741-712. www.atrium-flora.cz. Metro: Flora. Map p 72.*

Kotva STARÉ MĚSTO This Communist-era department store still feels stuck in the 1970s—and might be more interesting because of it. It's adequate for basic purchases such as housewares, toiletries, and stationery, but give the clothes and shoes a miss. The Brutalist-style building from the 1970s is protected as a cultural monument. *Náměstí Republiky 8.* ☎ *224-801-111. www.od-kotva.cz. AE, MC, V. Metro: Náměstí Republiky. Map p 72.*

★★★ Lucerna Pasáž NOVÉ MĚSTO Funky 1930s-era shopping center stuffed with an indescribable mix of stores. There are shops selling high Czech fashion, wines, gifts, and even vintage cameras. The main attractions here are the early-modern interior, the elegant Lucerna cinema and cafe, and the wacky David Černý statue of St. Wenceslas riding on an upside-down horse. One of a kind. *Štěpánská 61.* ☎ *224-224-537. www.lucerna.cz. Metro: Mustek. Map p 72.*

★ Nový Smíchov SMÍCHOV Big American-style shopping mall with more than 100 stores. The highlights here are a large Tesco supermarket (one of the best in the city) on the ground floor, a big food court on top, and a multiplex cinema that's heavy on Hollywood blockbusters (usually shown in English with Czech subtitles). *Plzenská 8.* ☎ *251-511-151. www.novy smichov.eu. Metro: Anděl. Map p 71.*

★★★ Palladium NOVÉ MĚSTO The biggest and splashiest shopping mall in the Czech Republic is just off of Náměstí Republiky (across from Kotva). There are several floors of high-end stores, with a huge, elaborate—and very expensive—food court on top and a handy Starbucks below ground. *Náměstí Republiky 1.* ☎ *225-770-250. www.palladiumpraha.cz. AE, DC, MC, V. Metro: Náměstí Republiky. Map p 72.*

★★ Slovanský dům NOVÉ MĚSTO A convenient, centrally located shopping center with a number of leading-brand clothing and accessories stores like Max Mara, Ralph Lauren, and Geox. The 10-screen multiplex cinema is committed to showing films in English, and is one of the few cinemas in town to carry Czech movies subtitled in English. The Kogo restaurant at the back is a local favorite for a pre- or post-film repast. *Na příkopě 22.* ☎ *221-451-380. www.slovanskydum.com. Metro: Mustek. Map p 72.*

Tesco NOVÉ MĚSTO Local outlet of the British retailer that's housed in another noteworthy 1970s Brutalist building (designed loosely—*very loosely*—on the Centre Pompidou in Paris). Despite a recent remodeling in which the name of the store was changed to "My Tesco," the goods on offer are a bit of a disappointment. Like Kotva, it's fine for basics, but you'll look high and low for really decent quality. The big grocery store in the basement is handy for picnic provisions. *Národní třída 26.* ☎ *222-815-111. www.itesco.cz. MC, V. Metro: Mustek. Map p 72*

English Books & Magazines

★★ The Globe Bookstore and Coffeehouse NOVÉ MĚSTO

This venerable expat institution has been going strong since 1993. The Nové Město location has books on two levels, with a good stock of new fiction and Czech and Eastern European authors in translation. There's a big cafe in the back, with excellent light-lunch and dinner offerings as well as a full range of coffee drinks. The shop frequently hosts readings, music nights, and films. *Pštrossová 6. ☎ 224-934-203. www.globebook store.cz. AE, DC, MC, V. Metro: Karlovo náměstí. Map p 72.*

★★★ Shakespeare & Sons

MALÁ STRANA A wonderfully eclectic bookstore on several levels that's worth making a special trip to Malá Strana. There are thousands of books in all categories and a laid-back atmosphere highly conducive to browsing. Recommended. *U lužického semináře 10. ☎ 257-531-894. www.shakes.cz. MC, V. Metro: Malostranská. Map p 71.*

Fashion

★★ Boheme STARÉ MĚSTO

Simple yet fashionable women's clothing designed with younger women in mind. You'll find skirts, tops, jackets, boots, and accessories at decent prices. The staff is friendly and accommodating. *Dušní 8. ☎ 224-813-840. www.boheme.cz. AE, DC, MC, V. Metro: Staroměstská. Map p 72.*

★★ Coccinelle STARÉ MĚSTO

The city's top address for beautifully constructed high-end women's handbags and other leather items. *U Obecního domu 2. ☎ 222-002-340. www.coccinelle.com. AE, DC, MC, V. Metro: Náměstí Republiky. Map p 72.*

★★ Klára Nademlýnská STARÉ MĚSTO The main sales outlet for a popular and well-respected local

designer whose clothing and accessories are favored by Czech models and actresses. Nademlýnská's lines are suitable for both office and evening and feature high-quality materials and crisp, tailored cuts. *Dlouhá 7. ☎ 224-818-769. www. klaranademlynska.cz. AE, DC, MC, V. Metro: Staroměstská. Map p 72.*

★★ Report's STARÉ MĚSTO

Exclusive, well-made, mostly Italian clothing for men. Everything from top-of-the-line suits and jackets to shoes, sweaters, belts, and accessories. The showroom is reminiscent of a posh men's club and the service is excellent. *V kolkovně 5. ☎ 732-451-780. www.reports.cz. AE, DC, MC, V. Metro: Staroměstská. Map p 72.*

★★ Tatiana STARÉ MĚSTO

High-end women's fashion by a local designer with an eye for elegance and originality. Browsers are welcome, but be forewarned that the staff may not be able to speak much English. *Dušní 1. ☎ 224-813-723. www.tatiana.cz. AE, DC, MC, V. Metro: Staroměstská. Map p 72.*

★★★ Timoure et Groupe (TEG)

STARÉ MĚSTO The name sounds French, but this is the creation of two Czech designers who make sophisticated, wearable women's

The Globe Bookstore and Coffeehouse

clothing that transitions beautifully from the office to dinner afterwards. *V kolkovně 6.* ☎ *222-327-358. www.timoure.cz. AE, DC, MC, V. Metro: Staroměstská. Map p 72.*

Food

★★ Au Gourmand STARÉ MĚSTO
Similar to Bakeshop Praha (see below), but more akin to a French bakery, with classic French pastries as well as light sandwiches, salads, quiches, and cakes that you can eat in or take away for a picnic lunch. The back garden is something of a local secret and is a lovely spot to have a coffee and some of Au Gourmand's signature homemade ice cream. *Dlouhá 10.* ☎ *222-329-060. www.augourmand. cz. MC, V. Metro: Staroměstská. Map p 72.*

★★★ Bakeshop Praha STARÉ MĚSTO
An American-inspired bakery featuring freshly prepared sandwiches, soups, and salads, as well as some of the city's best cookies, cakes, and brownies. The coffee drinks are very good. You can eat in or take away for a picnic. *Kozí 1.* ☎ *222-316-823. www.bakeshop.cz. MC, V. Metro: Staroměstská. Map p 72.*

TEG

★★ Culinaria STARÉ MĚSTO
The most enticing deli case in Prague, filled with goodies like beef Wellington and grilled salmon that make for an inspired choice for a quick lunch. Also offers made-to-order sandwiches and salads, as well as fresh smoothies and coffee drinks. There's a small retail business where homesick Americans can stock up on goodies such as Oreo cookies and Pop-Tarts at about double the price of what they'd pay back home. *Skořepká 9.* ☎ *224-231-017. www.culinaria.cz. AE, DC, MC, V. Metro: Mustek. Map p 72.*

★★ Farmers' Market DEJVICE
This popular market, held on Saturdays from 8am to 2pm (Mar–Oct), makes for a great family outing, plus it's a wonderful chance to pick up organic, locally sourced fruits and vegetables, as well as breads, cheeses, wines, and honey. The market takes place in an open field just near the metro station entrance. Exit the station and follow the crowds. *Vítězné náměstí.* ☎ *605-260-309. www.farmarske-trhy.cz. No credit cards. Metro: Dejvická. Map p 71.*

★ Robertson DEJVICE
An English-style butcher that's evolved into an all-purpose refuge for homesick Brits and Americans. Excellent steaks and chops are cut to suit foreign tastes, but there's also an excellent range of familiar items like cake mixes, breakfast cereals, hard-to-find baking ingredients, snacks, and beverages. It's probably not worth a stop if you're just passing through town, but a must if you plan on staying a while. This branch is in the western suburb of Dejvice; there are also branches in Vinohrady and Nusle (see website for locations). *Jugoslávských partyzánů 38.* ☎ *233-321-142. www.robertson.cz. MC, V. Metro: Dejvická plus tram 8 to Zelená. Map p 71.*

All This and a Burberry Too

During the past few years, Prague has become a [...] interesting city for buying clothes and accessories—e[...] you're a woman. Credit for that goes mainly to the international chains, which have come here to capitalize on both Czechs' rising personal incomes and—of course—the thousands of tourists. Pařížská, just off of Old Town Square, is home to the ultra-high-end. Here you'll find **Hermès** (Pařížská 12; ☎ 224-817-545), **Prada** (Pařížská 16; ☎ 222-890-380), **Louis Vuitton** (Pařížská 13; ☎ 224-812-774), and other similarly vaunted names. If you're looking for something with a little more street smarts, head to Na příkopě, the pedestrian zone between Old Town (Staré Město) and New Town (Nové Město). This is where you'll find **Zara's** big flagship store (Na příkopě 15; ☎ 224-239-861), with separate floors for men's, women's, and children's clothing, as well as several other well-known international chains. Europe's hottest high-street fashion outlet, **H&M** (Václavské nám. 19; ☎ 234-656-051), is just a short walk up Václavské náměstí.

Gifts & Souvenirs

★★ **Botanicus** STARÉ MĚSTO
A Czech original that's as impressive as it is hard to describe. It sells all-natural products for the bath and kitchen such as bath oils, soaps, shampoos, and cooking oils—all made from natural ingredients grown locally. You'll probably fall in love with everything and want to stuff your suitcase until it can no longer close. *Týn 3.* ☎ *234-767-446. www.botanicus.cz. AE, DC, MC, V. Metro: Staroměstská. Map p 72.*

★ **Manufaktura** STARÉ MĚSTO
This shop is similar to—and probably inspired by—Botanicus, but there's less of a focus here on bath and food items and more on traditional Czech crafts like lace, wooden toys, coffee mugs, textiles, and even pieces of clothing, like scarves and sweaters. Everything feels all-natural and environmentally friendly. The packaging is so nice, it's like it's been gift-wrapped for you. *Melantrichova 17.* ☎ *221-632-480. www.*

manufaktura.cz. AE, DC, MC, V. Metro: Staroměstská. Map p 72.

Home Furnishings

★★ **Art Decoratif** STARÉ MĚSTO
This small shop on the back side of the Municipal House (Obecní dům) sells high-end Art Nouveau and Art

Botanicus.

Garnet necklace from Český Granát.

Deco replica household accessories, vases, clocks, lamps and figures. *U Obecního domu 2.* ☎ *222-002-350. www.artdecoratif.eu. AE, DC, MC, V. Metro: Náměstí Republiky. Map p 72.*

★★★ **Kubista** STARÉ MĚSTO Fans of Bauhaus, Cubism, and early-Modern design will think they died and went to heaven. The home furnishings, textiles, glassware, and jewelry are a mix of originals and reproductions, but everything here looks classy. It's right next to the Cubist **House of the Black Madonna** to get you in the proper mood. *Ovocný trh 19.* ☎ *224-236-378. www.kubista.cz. AE, DC, MC, V. Metro: Náměstí Republiky. Map p 72.*

★★ **Modernista** STARÉ MĚSTO An eye-catching collection of furniture extolling Cubism, functionalism, and mid-century modern. You'll find a mix of antiques and reproductions. Many of the items here are too large to fit in a suitcase, but it's certainly worth a look. You'll find the showroom near the back of a small passageway. *Celetná 12.* ☎ *224-241-300. www.modernista.info. AE, DC, MC, V. Metro: Náměstí Republiky. Map p 72.*

Jewelry

★ **Granát** STARÉ MĚSTO You'll see lots of amber outlets in the touristy parts of Prague, but the *echt* Czech gemstone is a deep red garnet, mined in the northern and eastern parts of the country. This centrally located shop has an excellent selection of rings, necklaces, bracelets, and broaches. *Dlouhá 28–30.* ☎ *222-315-612.www.granat. eu. AE, DC, MC, V. Metro: Staroměstská. Map p 72.*

★★ **Studio Šperk** STARÉ MĚSTO This little studio/boutique off of Old Town Square takes chances with more contemporary settings and unique designs. The store takes pride in offering only the highest-quality, genuine Bohemian garnets. *Dlouhá 19.* ☎ *224-815-161. www.drahonovsky.cz. AE, DC, MC, V. Metro: Staroměstská. Map p 72.*

Personal Care Salons

★★ **L'Institut Guerlain** STARÉ MĚSTO This high-end beauty salon offers a full range of facials, manicures, pedicures, and hair care. Reserve in advance. *Dlouhá] 16.* ☎ *227-195-330. www.guerlain. cz. AE, DC, MC, V. Metro: Staroměstská. Map p 72.*

★ **Sabai** NOVÉ MĚSTO This is the best of many shops around town offering relaxing and de-stressing Thai massage and other relaxation services like hot-oil or therapeutic massage. Best to make an appointment in advance, but occasionally they can handle walk-ins. Located inside the Slovanský dům shopping center. *Na Příkopě 22.* ☎ *221-451-180. www.sabai.cz. AE, DC, MC, V. Metro: Mustek. Map p 72.* ●

A Walk Across **Petřín Hill**

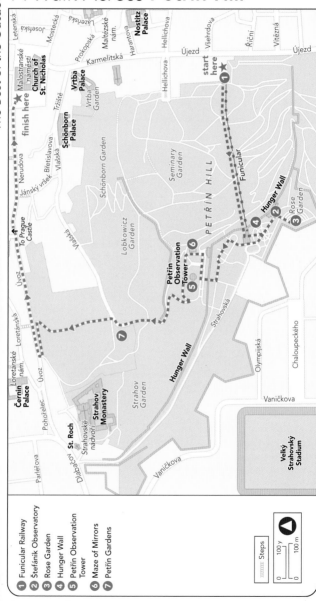

1. Funicular Railway
2. Štefánik Observatory
3. Rose Garden
4. Hunger Wall
5. Petřín Observation Tower
6. Maze of Mirrors
7. Petřín Gardens

Previous page: The Rose Garden.

There are lots of lookout spots in this city of a hundred spires that boast of having the best views. Certainly, the beer garden at Letenský zámeček, in Letná (see below), has a legitimate claim. But for our money, nothing beats the Prague panorama as seen from the top of the long, sloping valley that runs from the top of Petřín Hill down toward the banks of the Vltava river. This walk begins with a funicular train ride to the top of the hill. The smattering of interesting sights up here includes a miniature Eiffel Tower built for the 1891 Prague Jubilee exhibition. After that it's a peaceful stroll through a lovely park and then out across a long meadow, with those vaunted views over Prague Castle and the city below.

START: The funicular station at the Újezd tram stop. From Malostranská metro station, take tram no. 12, 20, or 22 three stops (to Újezd). On exiting the tram, walk back toward Malostranské nám. about 15m (50 ft.).

1 ★★ kids **Funicular Railway (lanová dráha).** This 488m (1,600-ft.) cable railway is part of the city's public transportation system; you'll need a full-price 32 Kč ticket to ride it (1- and 3-day metro passes work too). The funicular was originally built to ferry passengers to the 1891 exhibition. Now it's a mainstay of the tourist industry, taking visitors up to the "Eiffel Tower" or hauling concertgoers or sports fans up to an event at giant Strahov Stadium on top of the hill. The line has two stops; take it to the top, Petřín station. If you'd rather walk up the hill, follow any of the paths leading upward. Figure on a moderately demanding hike of 20 to 30 minutes. ⏱ *15 min. Daily 9am–11:20pm.*

2 ★ kids **Štefánik Observatory (Štefánikova hvězdárna).** As you exit the funicular station, walk to your left to see this still-functioning observatory with a classic Zeiss telescope from the 1920s. In good weather, you can look through the telescope for views of the sun during the day and of the moon, planets, and stars at night. ⏱ *10 min.; 1 hr. if you stop to observe. Petřín 205.* ☎ *257-320-540. www.observatory.cz. 65 Kč, 45 Kč children 3–15. Mon–Fri 2–7pm,* 9–11pm; Sat–Sun 10am–noon, 2–7pm, 9–11pm.

3 **Rose Garden.** This sprawling, very pretty rose garden stands just in front of the Štefánik Observatory and meanders in and around Petřín Hill. Take some time to relax on a bench with a book and

Enjoy the views from a funicular ride to the top of Petřín Hill.

The Rose Garden.

people-watch. Popular with seniors on Sunday afternoons. ⏱ *15 min. Free admission. Daily 8am–8pm.*

④ Hunger Wall (Hladová zeď). From the Rose Garden, walk back toward the funicular train station and you'll see this tall, snaggle-tooth-topped wall running to your left. The wall dates from the

The mini Eiffel Tower at the top of Petřín Hill.

mid–14th century and was part of Prague's original medieval defenses—the last thing Prague needed at that time was for Mongol invaders to come pouring in over the hill. The origin of the name "Hunger Wall" is disputed, but the best theory is that the wall was built by the city's poor during a time of famine; workers received food in exchange for their labors. ⏱ *10 min.*

⑤ ★★ kids Petřín Observation Tower (Petřínská rozhledna). Walk along the Hunger Wall for about 30m (100 ft.) beyond the funicular station, looking for signs to the "Petřínská rozhledna." It's hard to miss this 61m (200-ft.) "Eiffel Tower," which was built in 1891 to resemble the original in Paris (though just one-third the size). The unbeatable views from the top make the long climb up 299 steps worthwhile (or save the hassle and take the lift). On a clear day you can see all the way north to the mountains on the Polish border. ⏱ *30 min. Petřínské sady.* ☎ *224-816-772. www.petrinska-rozhledna.cz. 105 Kč, 55 Kč for children 6–15 and seniors, 25 Kč under 6. Apr–Sept daily 10am–10pm, Oct–Mar daily 10am–6pm.*

⑥ ★ kids Maze of Mirrors (Bludiště). Another oddity built for the 1891 exhibition, this "House of Mirrors" is just like one you might see at a carnival. To find it, just walk about 30m (100 ft.) to the right of the Petřín Observation Tower. It's great fun for kids (and highly disorienting for adults!). ⓘ 20 min. ☎ 724-911-497. *75 Kč, 55 Kč children 6–15 and seniors, 25 K č under 6. May–Aug daily 10am– 10pm, Sept–Apr daily 10am–6pm.*

⑦ ★★ Petřín Gardens (Petřínské sady). From the Maze of Mirrors, walk back toward the Petřín Observation Tower and follow the path to the left of the tower running downhill. About 15m (50 ft.) along the path, turn left onto another path and walk toward Prague Castle. Don't worry if you get a little bit lost; all of the paths lead in the same general direction. The first 10 minutes of the walk take you through some quiet woods and the last 15 to 20 minutes through an apple orchard and across a long meadow, with the castle out in the distance and the town spread out in all its glory below. This is our favorite walk in Prague. Follow the trail across the meadow until you reach the top of Malá Strana on the other side. From here, you can turn right and walk down to Malostranské náměstí.

Take some time to stroll the quiet lanes of Petřín Gardens.

Lounging in Letná (Letenské sady)

- ☐☐☐☐ Steps
- Milady Horákové
- Nad Štolou
- Letohradská
- Kamenická
- Kostelní
- **finish here**
- LETNÁ PARK
- To Prague Castle
- nábřeží Edvarda Beneše
- Vltava
- Štefánikův most
- nábřeží Edvarda Beneše
- Kosárkovo nábřeží
- Čechův most
- Dvořákovo nábřeží
- St. Agnes Convent
- **start here** nám. Curieových
- U milosrdných
- Kozí
- Revoluční
- STARÉ MĚSTO
- Dvořákovo nábřeží
- 17. listopadu
- Pařížská
- Dušní
- Vězeňská
- Rudolfinum
- Old Jewish Cemetery JOSEFOV

1 Metronome
2 Hanavský pavilion
3 Letná Plain
4 Letenský Zámeček

Whenever I come to Letná, it's hard not to think of Woody's Allen's movie *Manhattan*. Not the movie so much, but that famous poster of Woody and Diane Keaton sitting on a bench in Brooklyn looking out toward the Manhattan skyline. If they ever came to Prague, this is where they'd sit and look. It's that classic. Letná offers something to everyone. Rollerbladers love it for the smooth paths (and you can even rent blades here). Naturally, it's a favorite among dog walkers. It's nice, easy jogging terrain, with relatively clean air because of the elevation. It also happens to have one of the best open-air beer gardens in the city. START: **Čechův most (Čechův bridge), which crosses the river from the Intercontinental Hotel in Old Town.**

1 ★ **Metronome.** Walk across the Čechův most and climb the stairs in either direction up to the top of the hill. In the 1950s, the Communist government erected the biggest-ever statue of Soviet dictator Josef Stalin here (see p 42, bullet 8). Since 1991, the space

has been given over to a giant metronome, apparently marking time since the 1989 Velvet Revolution. It's an interesting idea, but in truth this space is wasted and neglected. The views out over the city are great, though, and worth the climb. ⏲ 10 min.

2 Hanavský Pavilon. Facing away from the town below, walk to your left in the general direction of Prague Castle. The path skirting the edge of the hill here affords some picture-perfect views over the Vltava River, with Charles Bridge in the background. The Hanavský Pavilon was built for the 1891 Prague Jubilee Exhibition in a neo-Baroque style. Today, it houses a cute cafe and restaurant overlooking the Old Town. ⓘ *10 min.; 1hr. if you stop for coffee or a bite to eat. Letenské sady 173.* ☎ *233-323-641. www.hanavsky pavilon.cz. Daily 11am–11pm.*

3 ★ Letná Plain. What you do from here depends on your time and interests. If you continue walking in the same direction, you'll eventually come to a footbridge that takes you on toward Prague Castle. If you'd like to see more of Letná, walk toward the interior of the park, choosing any of the trails that strike your fancy. Much of Letná is a giant plain, and in the very earliest years of aviation, this area functioned as Prague's makeshift airport. Much later, the open space was used by the Communists to hold their massive May Day rallies on May 1. Hundreds of thousands of people gathered here during the Velvet Revolution in 1989. And in more recent times, it's been the site of an open-air mass by Pope John Paul II, and in 2003 even hosted the Rolling Stones for a massive alfresco concert. On a typical summer day, it's great for tossing a football or a Frisbee. Note that at press time, part of the plain has been turned into a massive construction zone as road workers dig out below the park to build a highway tunnel. ⓘ *20 min.*

4 ★★ Letenský Zámeček. Once you've had your fill of fresh air and sunshine, it's time for liquid refreshment. In the Czech Republic, that usually means beer. This complex of restaurants, terraces, and a comfortably down-market beer garden is one of the city's most popular places to meet up after work or on a weekend afternoon. To find it, walk to the extreme eastern end of the park (in the direction away from Prague Castle). The *zámeček* (little castle) is actually a 19th-century neo-Renaissance chateau, housing a decent but expensive restaurant inside and a cheaper pizza-and-barbecue joint on the terrace. Opposite the restaurant, and with gorgeous views out over the city, are picnic tables where you're free to consume your own food and drinks. Do as the locals do and buy some beers in plastic cups (35 Kč per half-liter) from the little stand out front and relax in the open air. Highly recommended. ⓘ *1 hr. Letenské sady 341.* ☎ *233-378-208. www.letenskyzamecek.cz. Daily in summer 11am–11pm.*

Letná Plain.

The **Hidden Gardens of Malá Strana**

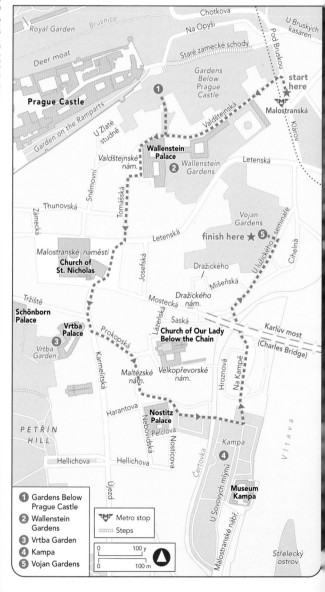

Royal Garden
Brusnice
Chotkova
Na Opyši
U Bruských kasáren
Deer moat
Staré zámecké schody
Pod Bruskou
Gardens Below Prague Castle
start here ★
Prague Castle
Garden on the Ramparts
Valdštejnská
Malostranská
U Zlaté studně
Klárov
1
Valdštejnské nám.
Wallenstein Palace
2
Wallenstein Gardens
Letenská
Sněmovní
Tomášská
Thunovská
Zámecká
Vojan Gardens
finish here ★ 5
Letenská
Malostranské náměstí
Church of St. Nicholas
Josefská
Dražického
Mišeňská
U lužického semináře
Cihelná
Tržiště
Mostecká
Dražického nám.
Schönborn Palace
Vrtba Palace
3
Prokopská
Lázeňská
Saská
Church of Our Lady Below the Chain
Karlův most
(Charles Bridge)
Vrtba Garden
Karmelitská
Maltézské nám.
Velkopřevorské nám.
Hroznová
Na Kampě
Harantova
Nostitz Palace
Nebovidská
Pelclova
Nosticova
Kampa
Vltava
PETŘÍN HILL
Hellichova
Hellichova
Čertovka
4
Újezd
U Sovových mlýnů
Museum Kampa
Malostranské nábř.
Střelecký ostrov

1 Gardens Below Prague Castle
2 Wallenstein Gardens
3 Vrtba Garden
4 Kampa
5 Vojan Gardens

Ⓜ Metro stop
▦▦▦ Steps

0 ——— 100 y
0 ——— 100 m

From street level, Malá Strana looks like an impenetrable collection of walls, cobblestones, bricks, and mortar. Beautiful to be sure, but nary a tree or bush in sight. This is only an illusion. Behind every Baroque *palais*, towering wall, or imposing gate, there lurks a beautifully manicured garden. Many of the mainly Italian masters who laid out these green oases more than 300 years ago were every bit as famous—and meticulous—in their day as the architects and craftsmen who built the lovely residential palaces. Some of the gardens remain closed to the public, but several have been converted to public parks or gardens. Many bear the names of the aristocratic families that once owned them. But be forewarned that most of the parks are open only from April to October.

START: The Malostranská metro station (Line A).

① ★★ Gardens Below Prague Castle (Zahrady pod Pražským hradem). Exit the metro station and walk to the left to Valdštejnská ul. At Valdštejnská 12, walk through an iron gate and a small courtyard. This leads you to five beautifully terraced Baroque gardens that front the side of the hill rising up to Prague Castle. One ticket buys entry into all five, and you're free to spend as long as you wish walking and climbing along the walls and steps from garden to garden. It's confusing keeping track of exactly which garden is which, but you can get a map at the ticket window. The Kolowrat Garden (Kolovratská

zahrada) is considered the most valuable from an architectural point of view, with its lookout garden house. The others include the Ledeburg Garden (Ledeburská zahrada), the Small and Big Palffy Gardens (Malá a Velká Pálffyovská zahrada), and the Furstenberg Garden (Furstenberská zahrada). ⏱ *40 min. Valdštejnská 12.* ☎ *257-214-817. www.palacove-zahrady.cz. 80 Kč. Apr–Oct daily 10am–8pm. Metro: Malostranská.*

② ★★ Wallenstein Gardens (Valdštejnská Zahrada). Continue walking along Valdštejnská ul. until you come to Valdštejnské nám. (Wallenstein Square). The

Kolowrat Garden, one of the Palace Gardens.

imposing Baroque Wallenstein Palace at no. 4 hides an amazing garden in the back, with an even more amazing limestone drip wall—a grotto—that you have to see to believe. The *palais* itself was the creation of Albrecht von Wallenstein, a brilliant general during the Thirty Years' War of the 17th century, and was meant to rival Prague Castle in terms of pure shock and awe. Wallenstein's ambitions cost him his life when he was assassinated in 1634 in the western Bohemian town of Cheb (probably on orders of Emperor Ferdinand II). The main building now houses the Czech Senate. The garden follows a formal geometric design and is dotted with ponds and bronze statues. Look closely at the limestone grotto to see animal heads, snakes, and other grotesque figures peeking out. ⏱ *20 min. Valdštejnské nám. 4.* ☎ *257-072-759. Free admission. Daily June–Oct 10am–6pm.*

③ ★★★ Vrtba Garden (Vrtbovská Zahrada). From Valdštejnské náměstí, follow Tomášská ul. to Malostranské nám., cross the square diagonally, and walk down Karmelitská ul. to the unassuming door at no. 25. Inside

Vrtba Garden.

lies a meticulously manicured 18th-century terraced garden that truly sets the standard for Baroque gardens. The brilliant statuary, including an eye-catching Atlas as you walk through the door, is the work of Matyáš Bernard Braun. It's a steep hike to the top, but worth it for the views over Malá Strana and the perfect photo op of St. Nicholas Church. ⏱ *30 min. Karmelitská 25.* ☎ *272-088-350. www.vrtbovska. cz. 60 Kč, 40 Kč children 6–15. Apr– Oct daily 10am–6pm.*

④ ★★ Kampa. From the Vrtba Garden, walk back a few steps in the direction of Malostranské nám., cross the street, and walk down Prokopská ul. Cross Maltézké nám. and then bear left at the far end of the square onto Nosticová ul. Here you'll find the opening to Kampa Park, the largest expanse of green in Malá Strana. This is one of Prague's prettiest parks, with gorgeous views over the Vltava on one side and the charming Čertovka stream (with its footbridges and water mills) on the other. The big lawn in the middle is the perfect spot to throw down a blanket and open a book. ⏱ *30 min.*

⑤ Vojan Gardens (Vojanovy Sady). If you have time for one more park, walk through Na Kampě (Kampa Square) in the direction of Charles Bridge. Continue straight, going underneath the bridge, and then bear right on U lužického semináře. The Vojan Gardens is a sprawling series of walkways, benches, lawns, and fountains in the middle of the city, well hidden from the masses behind formidable walls. It began life in the 13th century as a fruit garden, and now mostly functions as an urban idyll for office workers looking to escape modern life for half an hour. ⏱ *20 min. U lužického semináře 17. Free admission. Daily sunrise–sundown.* ●

Dining Best Bets

Best for Kids
★★ Rugantino $$ *Dušní 4 (p 103)*

Best Vegetarian
★★ Lehká Hlava $ *Boršov 2 (p 101)*

Best View of the Castle
★★ Bellevue $$$$ *Smetanovo nábř. 18 (p 98)*

Best View of the Bridge
★★ Hergetova Cihelna $$$ *Cihelna 2b (p 99)*

Best Italian Hideaway
★★ Peperoncino $$ *Letohradská 34 (p 103)*

Best for a Hearty Bowl of Pho
★★ Pho Vietnam Tuan & Lan $ *Anglická 15 (p 103)*

Best Sushi
★★ Sushi Bar $$$$$ *Zborovská 49 (p 104)*

Best Meal for the Money
★★★ Kofein $$ *Nitranská 9 (p 100)*

Best Czech-Mex
★★ Las Adelitas $ *Americká 8 (p 101)*

Best Beer and Burger Joint
★★ The Tavern $ *Chopinová 26 (p 104)*

Best for Celeb Sightings
★ Kampa Park $$$ *Na Kampě 8b (p 99)*

Best Eight-Course Meal
★★★ La Degustation $$$$$ *Haštalská 18 (p 100)*

Best Czech Pub Food
★★ Lokál $ *Dlouhá 33 (p 101)*

Best if Price is No Object
★★★ Aromi $$$ *Mánesova 78 (p 98)*

Best Meal Near the Opera
★★ Čestr $$$ *Legerová 75 (p 98)*

Best Pork Knee
★★ V Kolkovně $ *V Kolkovně 8 (p 105)*

Maitrea.

Malá Strana Area Dining

Café Savoy 8	Peperoncino 2
Cukrkávalimonáda 6	SaSaZu 1
Hergetova Cihelna 4	Sushi Bar 7
Ichnusa Botega 9	Villa Richter 3
Kampa Park 5	

Photo p 93: V Zátiši restaurant.

Staré Město Area Dining

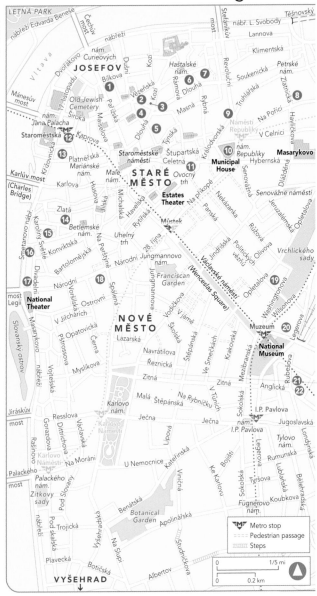

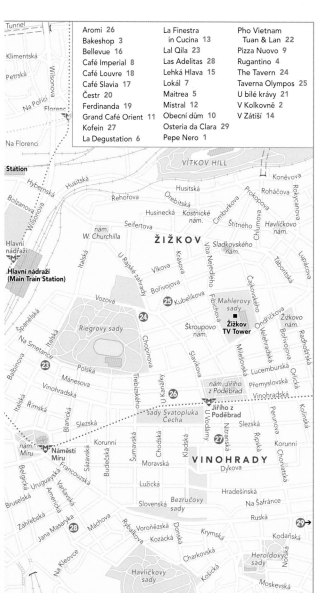

Aromi **26**
Bakeshop **3**
Bellevue **16**
Café Imperial **8**
Café Louvre **18**
Café Slavia **17**
Čestr **20**
Ferdinanda **19**
Grand Café Orient **11**
Kofein **27**
La Degustation **6**

La Finestra
  in Cucina **13**
Lal Qila **23**
Las Adelitas **28**
Lehká Hlava **15**
Lokál **7**
Maitrea **5**
Mistral **12**
Obecní dům **10**
Osteria da Clara **29**
Pepe Nero **1**

Pho Vietnam
  Tuan & Lan **22**
Pizza Nuovo **9**
Rugantino **4**
The Tavern **24**
Taverna Olympos **25**
U bílé krávy **21**
V Kolkovně **2**
V Zátiší **14**

Prague Restaurants A to Z

★★★ Aromi VINOHRADY

ITALIAN This upscale Italian restaurant in residential Vinohrady remains a tough table to book on a Friday or Saturday night. The secret: arguably the city's best high-end Italian cooking matched with excellent service. We have lots of favorites on the menu, including the homemade ravioli stuffed with either wild mushrooms or sea bass. Sticking to the pastas can keep the bill manageable. Book in advance. *Mánesová 78.* ☎ *222-713-222. www.aromi.cz. Entrees 350 Kč –600 Kč . AE, DC, MC, V. Lunch & dinner daily. Metro: Jiřího z Poděbrad. Map p 96.*

★★ Bakeshop STARÉ MĚSTO

SANDWICHES We love this American-style bakery, which serves a wide array of soups, salads, and sandwiches (packed to go) as well as amazing cakes, cookies, and brownies. Prices are high when you add everything up (salad, sandwich, coffee, and dessert), but no higher than a restaurant meal nearby (and usually much better). Choose your meal at the counter and then sit at the bar stools that line the windows, or order everything to go for a picnic lunch. *Kozí 1.* ☎ *222-316-823. www.bakeshop.cz. Salads and sandwiches 90 Kč–180 Kč. AE, DC, MC, V. Lunch & dinner (till 7pm) daily. Metro: Staroměstská. Map p 96.*

★★ Bellevue STARÉ MĚSTO

CONTINENTAL With its excellent views of Prague Castle, the Bellevue is a perennial top choice. The ambitious owners have put all their energy into the intelligent menu: beef, nouvelle sauces, well-dressed fish and duck, delicate pastas, and artistic desserts. For a tamer but extraordinary treat, try the pan-fried sea bass in a sauce of squid and caper. Desserts feature a vanilla-bean *créme brûlée.* Reserve in advance to snag a coveted table with a castle view. *Smetanovo nábř. 18.* ☎ *222-221-443. www.bellevue restaurant.cz. Entrees 600 Kč–800 Kč. AE, DC, MC, V. Lunch & dinner daily. Metro: Staroměstská. Map p 96.*

★★ Čestr VINOHRADY *STEAK-HOUSE*

Ignore the noisy location, just off the highway next to the National Museum, and rest assured that this is one of the best meals in Prague for the money. The specialty here is beef from locally raised cattle. Servings are on the small side, but the quality of the meat is the best in town. We love the fries, too. The atmosphere is dressy-casual, and the location next to the State Opera makes it a convenient spot for a pre- or post-performance bite. *Legerová 75.* ☎ *222-727-851. www.ambi.cz. Entrees 220 Kč–500 Kč. AE, DC, MC, V. Lunch & dinner daily (last orders 10pm). Metro: Muzeum. Map p 96.*

Bellevue.

★★ **Cukrkávalimonáda** MALÁ STRANA *INTERNATIONAL* This cozy spot serves simple but excellent salads, sandwiches, and pasta dishes in a warm atmosphere accentuated by wooden floors and exposed ceiling beams. Perfect for a quick and easy lunch. It's ideal for coffee on the go or a super-rich hot chocolate on a cold day. *Lázeňská 7.* ☎ *257-225-396. www.cukrkavali monada.com. Entrees 140 Kč–220 Kč. No credit cards. Lunch & dinner Mon–Sat. Metro: Malostranská plus tram 12, 20, 22 to Malostranské nám. Map p 95.*

★ **Ferdinanda** NOVÉ MĚSTO *CZECH* This popular Czech pub right off of Wenceslas Square serves decent local fare plus beers from the small Ferdinand brewery located in Benešov, about 48km (30 miles) south of Prague. Goulash gets top billing here; it's served Czech-style, cooked with cumin and sweet paprika and served with fresh grated onions on top. The beers are excellent. Try the sweetish dark beer (*tmavé*), or a stronger semi-dark, Sedml kuli. *Opletalová 24.* ☎ *222-244-302. www.ferdinanda.cz. Entrees 100 Kč–160 Kč. MC, V. Lunch & dinner daily. Metro: Muzeum. Map p 96.*

★★ **Hergetova Cihelna** MALÁ STRANA *CONTINENTAL* This might be Prague's best riverside restaurant, with a view to the Charles Bridge that even Charles IV would appreciate. The dining concept here is high-end casual: pastas, sandwiches, and burgers, but the menu also has a nice range of salads and grilled meats. Call well in advance to book a terrace table. This restaurant is managed by the same company that owns Kampa Park. *Cihelna 2b.* ☎ *296-826-103. www.kampagroup.com. Entrees 400 Kč–600 Kč. AE, DC, MC, V. Lunch & dinner daily. Metro: Malostranská. Map p 95.*

Hergetova Cihelna.

★★ **Ichnusa Botega** MALÁ STRANA *ITALIAN* More like visiting an Italian friend's kitchen than a restaurant—and a small kitchen at that. Only a handful of tables, meaning that reservations are essential but worth the effort. Start off with an appetizer plate of fresh cheeses and prosciutto, followed by mains like gnocchi with boar or duck confit. Expect the chef to come over several times during the evening to ask how everything tastes. *Plaská 5.* ☎ *605-375-012. www.ichnusabotegabistro.cz. Entrees 240 Kč–400 Kč. AE, DC, MC, V. Lunch & dinner Mon–Fri, dinner only Sat. Metro: Malostranská plus tram 12, 20, or 22 to Malostranské nám. Map p 95.*

★ **Kampa Park** MALÁ STRANA *CONTINENTAL* Year after year, a table here is widely considered the best in town, even if the cooking has slipped a notch and the prices have gone through the roof. The list of who's dined here reads like the Hollywood Walk of Fame: Johnny Depp, Matt Damon, Bruce Willis, Brad Pitt, Bruce Springsteen, and Bill and Hillary Clinton (to name a few). In nice weather, definitely book early to try to snag a table on the terrace overlooking

La Degustation.

the river. *Na Kampě 8b.* ☎ *296-826-102. www.kampagroup.com. Entrees 600 Kč–900 Kč. AE, DC, MC, V. Lunch & dinner daily. Metro: Malostranská. Map p 95.*

★★★ Kofein VINOHRADY

SPANISH This popular tapas bar in Vinohrady is full to bursting every night, making advance reservations essential. The menu is divided into cold and warm tapas dishes, with three dishes usually enough to make for a satisfying meal. Our favorites include homemade pate with caramelized onion and pan-fried calamari served on baby spinach, but everything is good. Excellent Spanish wines by the glass. *Nitranská 9.* ☎ *273-132-145. www.ikofein.cz. Tapas dishes 65 Kč–75 Kč. AE, DC, MC, V. Lunch & dinner Mon–Fri, dinner only Sat–Sun. Metro: Jiřího z Pod ě brad. Map p 96.*

★★★ La Degustation STARÉ

MĚSTO *CZECH/CONTINENTAL* A veritable orgy of fine food. Diners are offered a choice of two elaborate, 6- to 8-course set menus, featuring either Czech or Continental classics. The meal unfolds over 3 hours, and sommeliers are on hand to suggest wines to match the dishes. Not cheap, but a one-of-a-kind culinary adventure. Reservations

are essential. *Haštalská 18.* ☎ *222-311-234. www.ladegustation.cz. Fixed-price menu 2,150 Kč–3,150 Kč, not including wine. AE, DC, MC, V. Daily dinner only. Metro: Staroměstská. Map p 96.*

★★ La Finestra in Cucina

STARÉ MĚSTO *ITALIAN* This Italian-style steak and seafood house is run by the same people who created the popular Aromi (see above) in Vinohrady, and many of the same virtues—fresh ingredients, excellent meats and seafood, and attentive service—are on display here. Sit back and allow the waiters to advise on what looks best. It's a good choice for a splurge and the Old Town location is convenient. *Platnéřská 13.* ☎ *222-325-325. www.lafinestra.cz. Entrees 400 Kč–600 Kč. AE, DC, MC, V. Lunch & dinner daily. Metro: Malostranská. Map p 96.*

★★ Lal Qila VINOHRADY

INDIAN This Indian mom-and-pop is ideal if you're looking for a good-value alternative to Czech cooking. The engaging staff will ask you how much spice you want, but watch yourself: Unlike many other Prague Indian restaurants, they are not afraid to add heat here. All the classics, including fresh naan and flavored yogurt drinks, stand out. Be sure to reserve, especially on a Friday or Saturday night, because there are only a handful of tables and they fill up quickly. *Italská 30.* ☎ *774-310-774. www.lalqila.cz. Entrees 175 Kč–350 Kč. AE, DC, MC, V. Lunch & dinner daily. Metro: Muzeum. Map p 96.*

★ **Las Adelitas** VINOHRADY *MEXICAN* Authentic Mexican food served in a small, informal space in Vinohrady and run by a group of friends from Mexico City. The tacos, tostadas, burritos, and other items are prepared fresh with home-baked tortillas. Eat in or take away. *Americká 8.* ☎ *222-542-031. www.lasadelitas.cz. Entrees 150 Kč–210 Kč. No credit cards. Lunch & dinner daily. Metro: Náměstí Miru. Map p 96.*

★★ **Lehká Hlava** STARÉ MĚSTO *VEGETARIAN* Arguably the best vegetarian restaurant in Prague, and one of the few places that manage to make a virtue of tofu. The eclectic menu borrows from Spanish, Mexican, Middle Eastern, and Asian cooking. Try the veggie tofu stir-fry with fresh ginger or the baked quesadillas with cheddar

Lekhá Hlava.

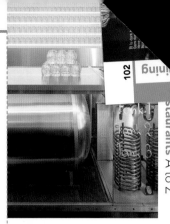

Lokál.

cheese and jalapeños. The whole place is nonsmoking, and the casual, funky interior makes it a fun place to hang out. *Boršov 2.* ☎ *222-220-665. www.lehkahlava.cz. Entrees 120 Kč–220 Kč. No credit cards. Lunch & dinner daily. Metro: Staroměstská. Map p 96.*

★★ **Lokál** STARÉ MĚSTO *CZECH* Every so often a restaurant comes along that fills a void so obvious, it's a wonder the place hasn't existed for years. In this case, excellent traditional Czech pub food and the best beer from the Pilsner Urquell brewery—within walking distance of Old Town Square. The setting is a modern rendition of a Czech pub in the 1970s—and the low prices (for the quality) feel retro too. On the downside, it's packed night and day. Give it a go, but book a table in advance or try to time your arrival a little before the lunch or dinner rush. *Dlouhá 33.* ☎ *222-316-265. www.ambi.cz. Entrees 110 Kč–200 Kč. AE, DC, MC, V. Lunch & dinner daily. Metro: Staroměstská. Map p 96.*

★★ **Maitrea** STARÉ MĚSTO *VEGETARIAN* Vegetarians have it rough in Prague. The practice of

Peperoncino.

going meatless has been slow to catch on, and to add insult to injury, even items in the *bez masa* (without meat) section of restaurant menus often contain small bits of ham or bacon. This restaurant combines good cooking with a touch of dining sophistication, just a stone's throw from Old Town Square. Entrees focus on meatless versions of popular foods like chili, burritos, and quesadillas. Also features meatless versions of Czech specialties like "Bohemian platter"—red beets, polenta, and smoked tofu. *Týnská 6.* ☎ *221-711-631. www. restaurace-maitrea.cz. Entrees 130 Kč–160 Kč. AE, DC, MC, V. Lunch & dinner daily. Metro: Starom ě stská. Map p 96.*

★★ Mistral STARÉ MĚSTO

CZECH   This unpretentious restaurant, almost an upscale diner in its simplicity, is a godsend. Just a couple of blocks off the Old Town Square, yet serves much better Czech specials like *ř ízek* (Wiener schnitzel) and *svičková* (braised beef tenderloin in cream sauce) than most of the restaurants closer to the square (and it's cheaper too). Good and creative soups and a full breakfast menu round out its charms. *Valentínská 11.* ☎ *222-317-737. www.mistralcafe.cz. Entrees*

140 Kč–240 Kč. AE, DC, MC, V. Breakfast, lunch & dinner daily. Metro: Staroměstská. Map p 96.

★★★ Osteria da Clara

VRŠOVICE ITALIAN   This excellent, family-run Italian restaurant is situated outside the center in the neighborhood of Vršovice. The menu features innovative pastas with items like zucchini and calamari, while the main courses rotate depending on what's fresh in the market. Booking ahead is essential, and you'll need to bring a good map to find this place, but it's worth the effort. *Mexická 7.* ☎ *271-726-548. www.daclara.com. Entrees 260 Kč–330 Kč. AE, DC, MC, V. Lunch & dinner Mon–Sat, lunch only Sun. Metro: Námě stí Miru plus tram 4, 22. Map p 96.*

★ Pepe Nero STARÉ MĚSTO

PIZZA   Perennial contender for best pizza in Prague. Pies here have a thicker, breadier crust, but the sauces and toppings make ample covering. The house pizza is a fiery mix of sausage and peppers. Service is efficient but can be on the gruff side. A convenient stop while exploring the former Jewish quarter. *Bílkova 4.* ☎ *222-315-543. www. pepenero.cz. Entrees 130 Kč–250 Kč. AE, DC, MC, V. Lunch & dinner daily. Metro: Staroměstská. Map p 96.*

★★ **Peperoncino** LETNÁ *ITAL-IAN* Good Italian food in Prague is expensive, which is why we love this hideaway in Letná. Appetizers like octopus in bean sauce and entrees like seared tuna are cooked to perfection. There's an excellent wine list and a big garden out back during the summer months. Call in advance to reserve a table before making the trek out here. *Letohradská 34.* ☎ *233-312-438. www.restaurant-peperoncino.cz. Entrees 200 Kč–300 Kč. AE, DC, MC, V. Lunch & dinner daily. Metro: Hradčanská plus tram 1, 8, 26. Map p 95.*

★★ **Pho Vietnam Tuan & Lan** VINOHRADY *VIETNAMESE* Vietnamese immigrants make up the largest non-European ethnic group in the Czech Republic, but there have not been very many good Vietnamese restaurants. Now, places like Pho Vietnam are taking the city by storm and residents have really warmed to Vietnamese specialties, especially the fresh spring rolls and hearty beef noodle soup known as *pho. Anglická 15.* ☎ *773-688-689. http://photuanlan.com. Entrees 100 Kč–200 Kč. No*

credit cards. *Lunch & dinner daily. Metro: I.P. Pavlova. Map p 96.*

★★ kids **Pizza Nuovo** STARÉ MĚSTO *PIZZA* The local Ambiente restaurant chain has brought the concept of "tasting restaurant" to Prague. Here, you pay a set price and then you taste and eat what you want (or are able to). Your choice is the exquisite antipasto salad bar with a wide selection of meats, cheeses, and fish, or the Pasta & Pizza "degustation"—basically unlimited servings of surprisingly good pizza and pasta brought to your table until you burst. The restaurant is on the first floor of the corner building next to the Kotva department store. For smaller kids there is a play corner with toys and activities, so you will have a better chance to fully enjoy the tasting. *Revoluční 1.* ☎ *221-803-308. www.ambi.cz. All you can eat antipasti buffet 300 Kč; entrees 265 Kč. AE, DC, MC, V. Lunch & dinner daily. Metro: Náměstí Republiky. Map p 96.*

★★ kids **Rugantino** STARÉ MĚSTO *PIZZA* Easily the most family-friendly restaurant in all of Prague, with highchairs at the ready

SaSaZu.

and staff who seem oblivious to hordes of little tykes scurrying between the tables. It also happens to have (arguably) the best thin-crust pizza in town, with Italian-imported olive oils and mozzarella. Pizza Calabrese, a spicier version of American-style pepperoni pizza, is a local classic. A more spacious Rugantino II is located at Klimentská 40, Prague 1 (☎ 224-815-192; Metro: Florenc or Náměstí Republiky), with a children's corner and plasma TV. *Dušní 4.* ☎ *222-318-172. www.rugantino.cz. Entrees 160 Kč–260 Kč. AE, DC, MC, V. Lunch & dinner daily. Metro: Starom ě stská. Map p 96.*

★★ SaSaZu HOLEŠOVICE

ASIAN This trendy, upscale Asian restaurant shares space with a popular dance club of the same name. Although the prices are not extreme for the high quality of the cooking, the portions are small, so they tend to add up. The setting is a remodeled warehouse in the vast expanse of the Holešovice market, but the crowd tends to be glamorous, so dress up. *Bubenské nábřeží 306.* ☎ *284-097-455. www.sasazu. com. Entrees 200 Kč–400 Kč. MC, V. Lunch & dinner daily. Metro: Vltavská plus tram to Pražská tržnice. Map p 95.*

★★ Sushi Bar MALÁ STRANA

JAPANESE Sushi restaurants in Prague tend to be sterile and a little lifeless. This Czech-run place is tiny, intimate, and always hopping. Prices have climbed in recent years, but the fish is the freshest in Prague. Standard sushi and maki sets. The eight-piece "Dragon Roll" is made from grilled eel, avocado, and sesame. *Zborovská 49.* ☎ *603-244-882. www.sushi.cz. Sushi menu 999 Kč, exclusive maki 1,190 Kč. AE, DC, MC, V. Lunch & dinner daily. Metro: Malostranská plus tram 12, 22. Map p 95.*

Sushi Bar.

★★ The Tavern VINOHRADY

BURGERS Burger love has taken the Czech Republic by storm in the past few years, and this cozy place on a quiet corner in Vinohrady makes the best burgers in Prague. The owners are an expat American couple, but the clientele is a healthy mix of Czechs and expats. Book in advance to secure a table (online only; no reservations taken on Tues–Wed). *Chopinova 26. No phone. www.thetavern.cz. Burgers 129 Kč–185 Kč. No credit cards. Lunch & dinner Tues–Sat. Metro: Jiřího z Podě brad. Map p 96.*

★★ Taverna Olympos ŽIŽKOV

GREEK This convivial Greek restaurant is a local favorite. It's located in Žižkov, just on the Vinohrady line. In summer, sit out in the garden; in winter, bask in the enclosed winter garden. The highlights here are appetizers like *tzatziki* and baked cheese in foil. The calamari is fresh; our favorite is the baked calamari stuffed with cheese and red pepper. House wine flows from carafes and the staff is cheerful, if occasionally forgetful. *Kubelíkova 9.* ☎ *222-722-239. www.taverna-olympos.eu.*

Entrees 180 Kč–300 Kč. AE, DC, MC, V. Lunch & dinner daily. Metro: Jiřího z Poděbrad. Map p 96.

★★ **U bílé krávy** VINOHRADY *FRENCH/STEAKHOUSE* This French-owned (or at least French-themed) steakhouse feels more like an inviting tavern, where you are whisked inside like an old friend and treated to some of the best steaks and wines in the city, at prices roughly half those at the fanciest places. The "White Cow" in the name refers to a special breed of French cattle, from which the meat is sourced. *Rubešova 10.* ☎ *224-239-570. Entrees 160 Kč–420 Kč. AE, DC, MC, V. Lunch & dinner Mon–Fri, dinner only Sat. Metro: Muzeum. Map p 96.*

★ **Villa Richter** HRADČANY *CONTINENTAL* Come here in nice weather for the stunning castle setting overlooking Malá Strana and the Old Town. This luxury vineyard, just as you exit the Prague Castle complex on the eastern end, houses three restaurants, including a relatively inexpensive wine bar that has tastings for 50 Kč a glass. The big culinary draw is the "Piano Nobile," a gourmet restaurant offering very good Czech and international cooking and a wine vault with some 2,000 bottles. *Staré zámecké schody 6.* ☎ *257-219-079. Entrees 340 Kč–580 Kč. AE, DC, MC, V. Lunch & dinner daily. Metro: Malostranská plus a walk up the stairs. Map p 95.*

★★ **V Kolkovně** STARÉ MĚSTO *CZECH* This classic Czech pub is part of a chain owned by the Pilsner Urquell brewery, but don't let that deter you. The standards for food and service are high, and it's even worth stopping in for the beer alone. This is a good place to sample a massive pork knee *(koleno)*, served on a wooden board with slices of bread, plus mustard and

Prague Cafes: Kafka, Havel, and You

The Czech Republic spent 4 centuries under Austrian rule, and more than a little bit of Vienna's famed cafe culture has rubbed off on Prague. As in Vienna, over the years, cafes served as a kind of public living room for the city's intellectual elite, including writers, journalists, essayists, and playwrights. Franz Kafka, in his heyday, was a denizen of several city cafes, including the Louvre (see below), which still exists. Later, Václav Havel and his dissident buddies would hang out over a coffee at the Slavia (below), another jewel that is still going strong. Unfortunately, only a handful of the most famous cafes survived the Communist period unscathed. We've listed some of the best below.

The word "cafe" can mean many things in Prague. Naturally, cafes are places where people meet for coffee or tea and chit-chat. In Prague, cafes also usually serve alcoholic beverages, including beer and wine. There's almost always food on hand too. Indeed, some of the city's best restaurants call themselves "cafes."

V Kolkovně.

horseradish. You won't eat again for 2 days. Crowded at meal times, so book in advance. *V Kolkovně 8.* ☎ *224-819-701. www.vkolkovne.cz. Entrees 160 Kč–280 Kč. MC, V. Lunch & dinner daily. Metro: Staroměstská. Map p 96.*

★★ **V Zátiší** STARÉ MĚSTO *CONTINENTAL* The "Still Life" restaurant is the jewel in local restaurateur Sanjiv Suri's crown of high-end restaurants (which also includes the Bellevue, above). The quiet location, just off Betlémské nám., makes it a favorite for intimate dinners or important business engagements. Like Suri's other restaurants, the menu holds few surprises (it favors standards such as grilled salmon, pork tenderloin, and roast lamb), but the quality of the ingredients and presentation is flawless. *Liliová 1.* ☎ *222-221-155. www.vzatisi.cz. Entrees 400 Kč–700 Kč. AE, DC, MC, V. Lunch & dinner daily. Metro: Staroměstská. Map p 96.*

Cafes

★★ **Café Imperial** NOVÉ MĚSTO *TRADITIONAL CAFE* This eclectic, Art Nouveau cafe dates from 1912, but was thoroughly renovated about 5 years ago. The signature tiled pillars and mosaics remain intact, but the renovation brought in nicer tables and chairs and a revamped menu of well-prepared Czech and international dishes. There's also an excellent American breakfast with eggs, sausage, and bacon. It's a perfect spot for lunch or a midday coffee and cake. *Na Poříčí 15.* ☎ *246-011-440. www.cafeimperial.cz. Entrees 200 Kč–400 Kč. MC, V. Breakfast, lunch & dinner daily. Metro: Náměstí Republiky. Map p 96.*

★★ **Café Louvre** NOVÉ MĚSTO *TRADITIONAL CAFE* This former intellectual heavyweight was a favorite hangout of German-speaking students in the early years of the 20th century, including—for a time—a visiting professor named Albert Einstein. Even Kafka dropped by for a debate or two. There's nothing remotely cerebral about the place today; it's just a bright, bustling cafe, serving decent coffee drinks and a full (and delicious) menu of Czech and international dishes. Great lunch spot. *Národní 22.* ☎ *224-930-949. www. cafelouvre.cz. Entrees 100 Kč–300 Kč . MC, V. Breakfast, lunch & dinner daily. Metro: Mustek. Map p 96.*

★★ **Café Savoy** MALÁ STRANA *CZECH* A beautifully restored 19th-century coffeehouse, with an eclectic menu running from Czech classics like *svičková* to full-on English and American breakfasts, including a great weekend brunch. Ideal for lunch or for coffee and cakes between meals. At meal times, reservations are recommended. *Vítězná 1.* ☎ *257-311-562. www.ambi.cz. Entrees 150 Kč–300 Kč. AE, DC, MC, V. Lunch &*

dinner daily. Metro: Malostranská plus tram 12, 20, 22. Map p ###.

★ **Café Slavia** STARÉ MĚSTO *TRADITIONAL CAFE* This legendary dissident cafe has the added advantage of a perfect view out over the river toward Prague Castle. The Slavia was once a meeting point for Václav Havel and other dissident intellectuals from the theater and film worlds; it was remodeled in the 1990s and never fully recaptured its former cachet. Now, it's mostly filled with tourists perched at the window admiring the castle. Both the coffee and the food are hit-and-miss, but it's still a must visit for Havel fans. *Smetanovo náb. 2.* ☎ *224-218-493 www.cafeslavia.cz. Entrees 140 Kč–200 Kč. MC, V. Lunch & dinner daily. Metro: Staroměstská plus tram 17, 18. Map p 96.*

★★★ **Grand Café Orient** STARÉ MĚSTO *TRADITIONAL CAFE* A beautifully refurbished flapper-era 1920s cafe that lays

V Zátiši.

Café Imperial.

claim to being the only Cubist cafe in the world. It's delightfully free from the tour-bus crowd and an excellent spot for a quiet coffee and cake or a glass of wine during the day. *Ovocný trh 19 (at the corner of Celetná).* ☎ *224-224-240. www. grandcafeorient.cz. Entrees 100 Kč–230 Kč. MC, V. Breakfast, lunch & light dinner daily. Metro: Mustek. Map p 96.*

★★★ Obecní dům STARÉ MĚSTO *TRADITIONAL CAFE* It's a pity this incredible space seems frequented only by tourists; we consider it a serious contender for a list of the world's top 10 most beautiful cafes. The Art Nouveau details, such as the ornamented chandeliers and tiled mosaics, the evening piano music, and even the beautiful lavatories, overwhelm the comparatively humdrum business of serving coffees and cakes. You can sit on the terrace in nice weather, but who would want to when it's this nice inside? Also serves beer, wine, and light food items. *Náměstí*

Republiky 5. ☎ *222-002-763. www. kavarnaod.cz. Entrees 100 Kč –300 Kč . Breakfast, lunch & light dinner daily. Metro: Náměstí Republiky. Map p 96.* ●

Obecní dům.

Malá Strana Area Nightlife

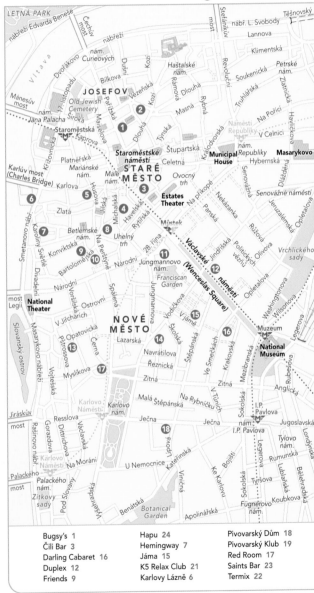

Bugsy's 1
Čili Bar 3
Darling Cabaret 16
Duplex 12
Friends 9

Hapu 24
Hemingway 7
Jáma 15
K5 Relax Club 21
Karlovy Lázně 6

Pivovarský Dům 18
Pivovarský Klub 19
Red Room 17
Saints Bar 23
Termix 22

Previous page: Karlovy Lázně dance club.

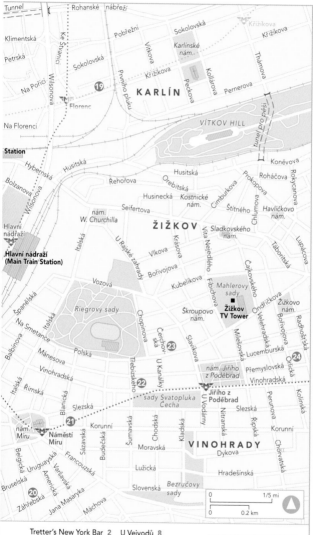

Tretter's New York Bar 2
U Fleků 13
U Medvídků 10
U Pinkasů 11
U Sudu 14

U Vejvodů 8
U Zlatého tygra 5
Vodka Bar/
  Propaganda Club 4
Žlutá Pumpa 20

Metro stop
Pedestrian passage
Steps

Staré Město Area Nightlife

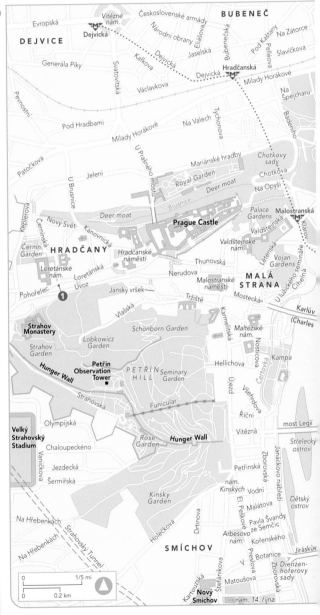

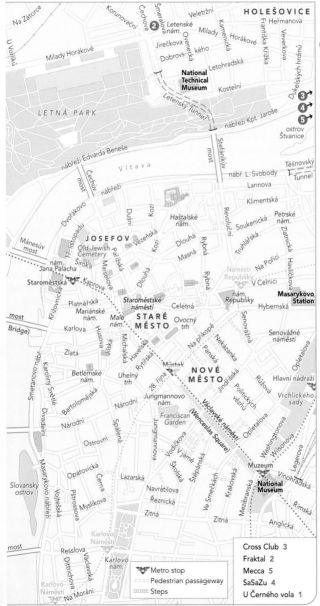

Cross Club 3
Fraktal 2
Mecca 5
SaSaZu 4
U Černého vola 1

Nightlife Best Bets

Best **Microbrew**
★★★ Pivovarský Klub, *Křižíkova 17 (p 117)*

Best **Traditional Hospoda (Pub)**
★★ U Černého vola, *Loretánské nám. 1 (p 117)*

Best **Classy Cocktail Bar**
★★★ Hemingway, *Karolíny Světlé 26 (p 115)*

Best **Martini**
★★ Hapu, *Orlická 8 (p 115)*

Best **Shot of Spiced Rum**
★★★ Čili Bar, *Kožná 8 (p 115)*

Best **Wine Bar**
★★ U Sudu, *Vodičková 10 (p 116)*

Best for **Celeb Spotting**
★★ Tretter's New York Bar, *V kolkovně 3 (p 116)*

Best **Place to Dance if You're Over 30**
★★★ SaSaZu, *Bubenské náb. 306 (p 120)*

Best **Place to Dance for Twentysomethings**
★★★ Cross Club, *Plynární 23 (p 119)*

Best **Cheesy Dance Club**
★ Vodka Bar/Propaganda Club, *Michalská 12 (p 120)*

Best **Gay Bar**
★★ Friends, *Bartolomějská 11 (p 119)*

Karlovy Lázně.

Bars

★★ **Bugsy's** STARÉ MĚSTO
This calm and classy cocktail and cigar bar lies just off fashionable Pařížská. A perfectly refined spot to get the evening rolling or to say goodnight over a nightcap. The bartenders know their drinks, and will gladly make one to order if you want something that's not on the menu. Open daily from 7pm to 2am. *Pařížská 10.* ☎ *840-284-797. www.bugsysbar.cz. Metro: Staroměstská. Map p 110.*

★★★ **Čili Bar** STARÉ MĚSTO
Full disclosure here: I like this place and come here frequently. Not only are the Latin and rum-based cocktails (*mojitos* and the like) the best around, but the owner is also a friendly guy and the service is prompt and polite. The only drawback I can see is this establishment's tiny size. There are only about a dozen tables and a bar that accommodates just six drinkers at a time. Open daily 6pm to 2am. *Kožná 8.* ☎ *724-379-117. www.cilibar.cz. Metro: Staroměstská. Map p 110.*

★★ **Fraktal** LETNÁ   Not so long ago, this was a scruffy basement joint reserved exclusively for hardcore partiers. The owners cleaned up their act and took Fraktal slightly more upmarket. The result is the friendliest and most enjoyable pub in this part of town, across the river north of the Old Town. Decent pub-style food and an English-speaking staff round out the charms. Open daily 11am to midnight. *Šmeralová 1.* ☎ *777-794-094. www.fraktalbar.cz. Metro: Hradčanská plus tram 1, 8, 25, or 26. Map p 112.*

Almond cigar cocktail at Bugsy's.

★★ **Hapu** ŽIŽKOV   This modest neighborhood speakeasy–type place is perfect for people who enjoy well-made cocktails, but don't like the pretension that's sometimes associated with "cocktail bars." Comfortably down-market surroundings, such as amiably frayed rugs and thrift-store couches, contribute to the relaxed vibe. Call in advance to reserve a table. Open Monday to Saturday 6pm to 2am. *Orlická 8.* ☎ *775-109-331. Metro: Flora plus tram 11. Map p 110.*

★★★ **Hemingway** STARÉ MĚSTO   This is my vote for the best cocktail bar in town. The drinks are excellent, the service is polite but restrained, and the atmosphere is civilized without being stuffy in the slightest. Hemingway is very popular, so reserve ahead. Open daily 7pm to 1am. *Karolíny Světlé 26.* ☎ *773-974-764. www.hemingwaybar.cz. Metro: Staroměstská plus tram 17, 18. Map p 110.*

★★ **Jáma** NOVÉ MESTO This fun, college-town-hangout type of place draws an eclectic crowd of Czechs, expats, and tourists from all walks of life. The bar area—with English-speaking bartenders (usually female)—is great for solo travelers. After a few drinks, you'll have a roomful of new friends. The beer list features hard-to-find regional brews; the hamburgers and other bar-food offerings are some of the best in town. Open daily 11am to 1am. *V jámě 7.* ☎ *222-967-081.* *www.jamapub.cz. Metro: Mustek. Map p 110.*

★ **Red Room** NOVĚ MĚSTO This small bar is a great place to repair to for a few late-night beers and is popular with students and travelers. The expat owners are musicians, so there's a tiny stage in the corner for occasional live music and open-mic nights on Sundays. Open Wednesday to Sunday 8pm to 1am. *Myslíkova 28.* ☎ *222-520-084. Metro: Karlovo náměstí. Map p 110.*

★★ **Tretter's New York Bar** STARÉ MĚSTO This elegant Old Town cocktail bar attracts the glamour set as well as a fair number of Hollywood celebrities in town for a movie shoot. Arrive before 9pm to snag a coveted table along the wall opposite the bar (or phone in advance to book a table). Dress up after 11pm in order to get past the doorman out front. Open daily 7pm to 2am. *V kolkovně 3.* ☎ *224-811-165. www.tretters.cz. Metro: Starom ě stská. Map p 110.*

★★ **U Sudu** NOVÉ MĚSTO You'll find this labyrinthine wine bar just a short walk from Václavské náměstí. People come here not for the wines—the drink card contains mostly ordinary Czech whites and reds—but for the all-important social aspect of drinking. If at first you don't find a seat, keep on walking down and down. In the fall, look out for *burčák,* a cloudy young wine with a sour-sweet taste and deceptively high potency. Open daily 10am to 2am. *Vodičková 10.* ☎ *222-232-207. www.usudu.cz. Metro: Mustek. Map p 110.*

★ **Žlutá Pumpa** VINOHRADY Students are in the majority at this informal watering hole in Vinohrady. It gets impossibly crowded after midnight, so come early or content yourself with standing at the bar. They serve passably good Mexican food, but most people are here for the beer and the party vibe. Open daily 11:30am to 12:30am. *Belgická 12.* ☎ *608-184-360. www.zluta-pumpa.info. Metro: Náně sti Miru. Map p 110.*

Cabarets & Adult Entertainment

★ **Darling Cabaret** NOVÉ MĚSTO Probably the biggest and best-known of Prague's many "cabarets"—in this instance, a polite word for strip club. It advertises more than 150 girls nightly, with all kinds of dances and entertainment. Highly popular with the many British

U Sudu.

Pivovarsky Klub.

guys who come to Prague for a relatively cheap bachelor-party stag. Open until 5am. *Ve Smečkach 32.* ☎ *732-248-082. www.kabaret.cz.* Metro: Muzeum. Map p 110.

★★ **K5 Relax Club** VINOHRADY This high-end gentlemen's club caters to a mostly corporate clientele. It occupies three floors of a Vinohrady town house, with a restaurant, a bar, and a large area for sauna, massage, and steam baths. *Korunní 5.* ☎ *224-250-505. www. k5relax.cz.* Metro: Náměstí Miru. Map p 110.

Czech Pubs (Hospody)

★★ **Pivovarský Dům** NOVÉ MĚSTO One of a growing number of popular microbreweries in Prague. Purists may turn their noses up at oddities like sour-cherry beer and banana beer, but the fact remains that this is one of the most crowded pubs in town. They must be doing something right. You'll also find a full menu of very good Czech classics, like the ever-present *vepřo-knedlo-zelo* (roast pork, dumplings, and sauerkraut). Reservations highly recommended. Non-smoking throughout. Open daily 11am to 11:30pm. *Lípová 15.* ☎ *296-216-666. www.gastroinfo.cz.* Metro: I.P. Pavlova. Map p 110.

★★★ **Pivovarský Klub** KARLÍN A beer-lover's nirvana, bar none. There's a daily selection of the best regional Czech lagers, dark beers,

and wheats, plus bottled beers from around the world. It's non-smoking throughout, and the food, traditional Czech pub grub, is worth a trip on its own. Settle back and get your beer education over the course of an evening. Open daily 11am to 11:30pm. *Křižíkova 17.* ☎ *222-315-777. www.pivovarsky-klub.com.* Metro: Florenc. Map p 110.

★★ **U Černého vola** HRADČANY One of the few remaining traditional pubs in the immediate area of Prague Castle. This is a gem. Big wooden tables, unfazed regulars who've seen and done it all, and excellent Kozel beer on tap. It's worth going out of your way for. Open daily 10am to 10pm. *Loretánské nám. 1.* ☎ *220-513-481.* Metro: Hradčanská. Map p 112.

★ **U Fleků** NOVÉ MĚSTO This 15th-century brewpub falls somewhere between "tourist trap" and "must see." I think the former, but nevertheless it remains popular with locals. It's no stranger to tour buses that stop here nightly at the front door. On the other hand, U Fleků might well be the most famous watering hole in the city. Its strong house lager, dark and sweet, is made from a recipe that's more than 500 years old. The Czech food is decent. Open daily 10am to 11pm. *Křemencová 11.* ☎ *224-934-019. www.ufleku.cz.* Metro: Karlovo náměstí. Map p 110.

U Medvídků.

★★ U Medvídků STARÉ MĚSTO

This popular pub and restaurant offers two delights for beer connoisseurs: high-quality original Budweiser from the southern Bohemian city of České Budějovice on tap; and a small microbrew that produces excellent small-batch lagers, including "X-33," reputed to be one of the world's strongest beers by alcohol content, at around 12%. *Be forewarned:* This place is immensely popular, so time your arrival to avoid mealtimes or book in advance. Open daily 10am to 11pm. *Na Perštýně 7.* ☎ *224-211-916. www.umedvidku.cz. Metro: Mustek. Map p 110.*

★★ U Pinkasů NOVÉ MĚSTO

A standard in nearly every guidebook on Prague, but still worth recommending for the excellent Pilsner Urquell beer, passable Czech food, and wonderfully old-fashioned pub feel. In cold weather, settle back at your table and just let the waiters bring round after round. In summer, tables in the back become an impromptu inner-city beer garden. Open daily 10am to 3am. *Jungmannovo nám. 16.* ☎ *221-111-151. www.upinkasu.cz. Metro: Mustek. Map p 110.*

★ U Vejvodů STARÉ MĚSTO

Back in the early '90s, this was a classic Czech pub: smoky, dirty, and filled with drunken old codgers, yet it always had great beer and tons of atmosphere. Now it's been remodeled into one of the slickest, biggest, and busiest taverns in the center of town, serving beer by the keg-load to hundreds and hundreds of customers—mostly tourists—each night. On the plus side, the beer (Pilsner Urquell) is still pretty good, and the place is so big you'll never be turned away for a lack of seats. Open daily 10am to 3am. *Jilská 4.* ☎ *224-219-999. www. restauraceuvejvodu.cz. Metro: Mustek. Map p 110.*

★ U Zlatého tygra STARÉ

MĚSTO   The "Golden Tiger" is one of the few true-blue Czech pubs in the center that hasn't sold its soul to the tourist trade. The regulars still line up for the 3pm opening as they always have. The Pilsner Urquell served here is reputed to be some of the best in the city. Former U.S. President Bill Clinton once raised a glass here with the late Václav Havel and fabled Czech writer Bohumil Hrabal. Open daily 3 to 11pm.

Husová 17. ☎ 222-221-111. Metro:
Staroměstská. Map p 110.

Map p 110.

Gay & Lesbian Bars & Clubs

★★ Friends STARÉ MĚSTO   A
centrally located bar and club that's
popular with both locals and tourists. Runs a weekly lesbian night on
Fridays. *Bartolomějská 11.* ☎ *224-
236-772. www.friendsprague.cz.
Metro: Mustek. Map p 110.*

★★ Saints Bar VINOHRADY
This welcoming, British-owned pub
hosts regular theme parties and
quiz nights in a relaxed, informal
atmosphere. Thursday night is
ladies' night. The website has a
good overview of other bars and
Prague's gay scene. *Open daily
until 4am. Polská 32.* ☎ *222-250-
326. www.praguesaints.cz. Metro:
Jiřího z Poděbrad. Map p 110.*

★ Termix VINOHRADY   This
small basement-level club is one of
the city's most popular gay discos
and can get impossibly crowded on
weekend evenings. Enter by ringing
the buzzer and the doorman will let
you in. Go early to ensure entry.
*Open Wednesday to Saturday 9pm
to 5am. Třebižského 4a.* ☎ *222-
710-462. www.club-termix.cz. Metro:
Muzeum plus tram 11. Map p 110.*

Music & Dance Clubs

★★★ Cross Club HOLEŠOVICE
This cavernous, industrial-style club,
bar, and cafe draws a scruffy but
hip crowd of college kids and
young professionals who come for
the edgy vibe. The location is in a
remote part of Holešovice but easy
enough to find by metro; exit the
station, find the street Plynární, and
walk about 100 yards. Look for the
metallic sculptures in the yard.
*Open daily from 6pm to 4am.
Plynární 23.* ☎ *736-535-053. www.
crossclub.cz. Cover 100 Kč. Metro:
Nádraží Holešovice. Map p 112.*

★ Duplex NOVÉ MĚSTO   The
main advantage of this crowded
rooftop dance club is location—
right in the middle of Václavské
náměstí. A bit more sophisticated
than Karlovy Lázně (see below),
with a slightly older, more estab-
lished (and occasionally sleazier) clientele. Mick Jagger thought so
much of the place that he picked
Duplex for his 60th birthday party
several years ago (though most of
the customers are well south of 60).
*Open Tuesday to Saturday 9pm to
4am. Václavské nám. 21.* ☎ *732-
221-111. www.duplex.cz. Cover 150
Kč. Metro: Mustek. Map p 110.*

Friends.

Duplex.

★ **Karlovy Lázně** STARÉ MĚSTO
Karlovy Lázně advertises itself as
Central Europe's biggest dance
club, and that may well be true.
Each of the several floors of dancing has a different sound and
theme: techno, metal, pop, oldies,
funk, depending on the night. Popular with tourists and students, who
start lining up at the door at 11pm
and stay until dawn. Open daily
from 9pm to 5am. *Smetanovo náb.
198.* ☎ *222-220-502. www.karlovy
lazne.cz. Cover 180 Kč. Metro:
Staroměstská. Map p 110.*

★ **Mecca** HOLEŠOVICE   This
cool, designer disco tends to draw
a successful, trendy crowd in their
20s and 30s. It has great DJs. Wear
your best club clothes and take a
map—you'll need it to find this
place, located in a still-scruffy part
of Holešovice. Open Friday and
Saturday 10pm to 5am. *U průhonu
3.* ☎ *734-155-300. www.mecca.cz.
Cover 150 Kč. Metro: Nádraží
Holešovice. Map p 110.*

★★★ **SaSaZu** HOLEŠOVICE
This remains arguably Prague's

hottest night club, anchoring
Holešovice's claim as the go-to district for fun after dark. A cavernous
dance club shares a name and
space with an excellent Asian restaurant, meaning it's possible to
slide right from dinner to the dance
floor. Open daily 11am to 3am.
Located in a warehouse on the
grounds of the open-air Pražská
Tržnice (Prague Market). *Bubenské
náb. 306.* ☎ *284-097-455. www.
sasazu.com. Cover 150 Kč–1,000 Kč.
Metro: Vltavská plus tram 1 or 25.
Map p 112.*

★ **Vodka Bar/Propaganda Club**
STARÉ MĚSTO   This club, in an
ancient Gothic cellar in Old Town,
is owned by an expat American and
employs English-speaking bartenders, making it very visitor-friendly.
Music can be hit or miss, but some
nights (especially weekends) bring
a great party vibe. Open daily 8pm
to 3am. *Michalská 12.* ☎ *242-480-
728. www.propagandapub.cz. Cover
100 Kč. Metro: Staroměstská. Map
p 110.* ●

8 The Best Arts & Entertainment

Arts & Entertainment Best Bets

Best **Opera House**
★★ Státní Opera, *Wilsonová 4* (p 128)

Best **Place to Hear Classical Music**
★★★ Rudolfinum, *Náměstí Jana Palacha* (p 128)

Best **Place to See Classical Music**
★★★ Obecní dům's Smetana Hall, *Náměstí Republiky 5* (p 128)

Best **Theater for English Speakers**
★★ Švandovo Divadlo na Smíchově, *Stefaníková 57* (p 131)

Best for **Don Giovanni**
★★ Stavovské Divadlo, *Ovocní trh 1* (p 131)

Best for **"Donnie" Giovanni**
★ Národní Divadlo Marionet (National Puppet Theater), *Žatecká 1* (p 130)

Best **Black Light Theater**
★★ Divadlo Image, *Pařížská 4* (p 129)

Best **Jazz Club**
★★ AghaRTA, *Železná 16* (p 126)

Best **Jazz Club with a River View**
★★★ JazzDock, *Janáčkovo nábřeží 2* (p 127)

Best **Place for Indie Rock**
★★★ Palác Akropolis, *Kubelíková 27* (p 130)

Best **Place for Alternative**
★★ Roxy, *Dlouhá 33* (p 130)

A performance of Candide at the Státní Opera.

Malá Strana Area A&E

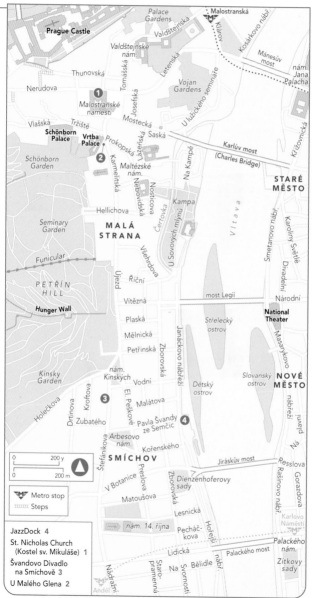

JazzDock 4

St. Nicholas Church
(Kostel sv. Mikuláše) 1

Švandovo Divadlo
na Smíchově 3

U Malého Glena 2

Photo p 121: Prague Symphony Orchestra performing at Obecní dům's Smetana Hall.

Staré Město Area A&E

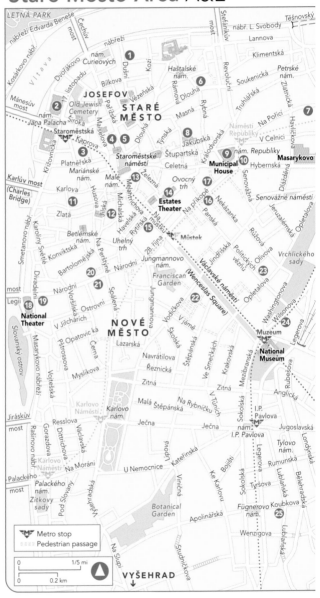

Metro stop
Pedestrian passage

0 — 1/5 mi
0 — 0.2 km

VYŠEHRAD

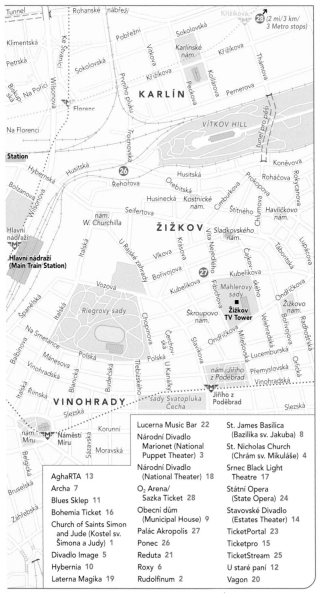

Lucerna Music Bar 22
Národní Divadlo Marionet (National Puppet Theater) 3
Národní Divadlo (National Theater) 18
O₂ Arena/ Sazka Ticket 28
Obecní dům (Municipal House) 9
Palác Akropolis 27
Ponec 26
Reduta 21
Roxy 6
Rudolfinum 2

St. James Basilica (Bazilika sv. Jakuba) 8
St. Nicholas Church (Chrám sv. Mikuláše) 4
Srnec Black Light Theatre 17
Státní Opera (State Opera) 24
Stavovské Divadlo (Estates Theater) 14
TicketPortal 23
Ticketpro 15
TicketStream 25
U staré paní 12
Vagon 20

AghaRTA 13
Archa 7
Blues Sklep 11
Bohemia Ticket 16
Church of Saints Simon and Jude (Kostel sv. Šimona a Judy) 1
Divadlo Image 5
Hybernia 10
Laterna Magika 19

Prague A&E A to Z

Church Concerts

★★ Church of Saints Simon and Jude (Kostel sv. Šimona a Judy) STARÉ MĚSTO For a real treat, try to catch one of the Prague Symphony Orchestra's occasional chamber concerts here. Check the symphony website for details. *Corner of Dušní and U Milosrdných.* ☎ 222-002-336. www.fok.cz. *Tickets 260 Kč–460 Kč. Metro: Staroměstská. Map p 124.*

★★ St. James Basilica (Bazilika sv. Jakuba) STARÉ MĚSTO The church's enormous 18th-century organ has been restored to its original sound, and this is an excellent place to catch organ recitals and concerts. The best times are during the Easter and Christmas holidays or in September, when the church hosts an annual festival of organ music. Check the website for schedules. *Malá Štupartská 6.* ☎ 604-208-490. www.auditeorganum.cz. *Tickets 300 Kč–500 Kč. Metro: Staroměstská. Map p 124.*

★ St. Nicholas Church (Chrám sv. Mikuláše) STARÉ MĚSTO A popular venue for afternoon and early-evening concerts done by private outfits looking to make a little

cash on the side. Quality is uneven, but the Baroque church makes for a lovely place to sit and listen. Note that this St. Nicholas Church is located on Old Town Square. Buy tickets at the door. *Staroměstské nám.* ☎ 224-190-994. *Tickets 400 Kč–600 Kč. Metro: Staroměstská. Map p 124.*

★★ St. Nicholas Church (Kostel sv. Mikuláše) MALÁ STRANA The interior of this church is one of the great treasures of Prague Baroque. The concerts here are of high quality and the organizers are determined to vary the program, which like everywhere else seems top-heavy on Mozart, Brahms, and Vivaldi. Note that this St. Nicholas Church is located in Malá Strana. Buy tickets at the door or through Ticketpro (see below). *Malostranské nám.* ☎ 257-534-215. *Tickets 300 Kč–400 Kč. Metro: Malostranská. Map p 123.*

Jazz

★★ AghaRTA STARÉ MĚSTO This atmospheric cellar from the Middle Ages is a wonderful place to catch a jazz concert. The hitch is that seating is limited. The only way

St. Nicholas Church.

AghaRTA.

to get a chair is to arrive by 7pm and camp out until showtime at 9pm. Buy tickets at the door. *Železná 16.* ☎ *222-211-275. www. agharta.cz. Tickets 250 Kč. Metro: Staroměstská. Map p 124.*

★ **Blues Sklep** STARÉ MĚSTO A relative and welcome newcomer to Prague's jazz scene, the Blues Sklep (Blues Cellar) focuses, not surprisingly, on blues, bringing in bands and singers from around town and Central Europe. Buy tickets at the door. *Liliová 10.* ☎ *608-848-074. www.bluessklep.cz. Tickets 150 Kč–200 Kč. Metro: Staroměstská. Map p 124.*

★★★ **JazzDock** SMÍCHOV This riverside jazz club in Smíchov brings in some of Central Europe's best jazz, blues, and soul singers, along with good food and beautiful views out over the river. The club is big enough to give at least some of the tables good sightlines to the stage (unlike many clubs in Prague); at the same time, it's small enough to be intimate. If you're looking for a romantic night of music and a view, this is your place. In summer, they run two shows nightly at 7 and 10pm. Buy tickets at the door. *Janáčkovo nábřeží 2.* ☎ *774-058-838. www.jazzdock.cz. Tickets 150 Kč–200 Kč. Metro: Anděl. Map p 123.*

★ **Reduta** NOVÉ MĚSTO Thirty years ago, this was Prague's preeminent venue for live music, and the interior hasn't changed a lot since then. If you'd like to see fusion jazz played in an authentic '70s-style room, this is for you. Buy tickets at the door or through Ticketpro or Bohemia Ticket (see below). *Národní třída 20.* ☎ *224-933-487. www. redutajazzclub.cz. Tickets 200 Kč – 300 Kč . Metro: Mustek. Map p 124.*

★★ **U Malého Glena** MALÁ STRANA The name ("At Little Glen's") refers to the owner, a shortish American guy named Glen, but it could also apply to the microscopic size of this cellar club. That's a shame, because on good nights you can't get anywhere near the music. The key is to arrive early. Sunday night brings a weekly jam session that, depending on who shows, can be the best show in town. *Karmelitská 23.* ☎ *257-531-717. www.malyglen.cz. Tickets 200 Kč–300 Kč. Metro: Malostranská plus tram 12, 20, 22. Map p 123.*

★★ **U staré paní** STARÉ MĚSTO One of the few jazz clubs in town where you can also eat dinner. This can be convenient when a big name is on the card and you have to get there early to get a table. Features mostly Czech players

U Malého Glena.

doing '70s- and '80s-style fusion and Latin mixes. Limited seating, so plan on standing if you arrive after 9pm. Buy tickets at the door. *Michalská 9.* ☎ *605-285-211. www. jazzstarapani.cz. Tickets 250 Kč. Metro: Staroměstská. Map p 124.*

Opera, Dance & Classical
★★★ Obecní dům (Municipal House) STARÉ MĚSTO Inside the Art Nouveau Municipal House, you'll find the country's most beautiful space for listening to classical music: the Bedřich Smetana Hall. This is the home of the Prague Symphony Orchestra (abbreviated as "fok") and the main venue for the annual Prague Spring Music Festival. The classical music season runs from September through the spring; in summer, the Obecní dům hosts some of the Prague Proms festival concerts and is also rented out by private musicians, who hold concerts of varying quality aimed at tourists. Buy tickets at the box office or through Bohemia Ticket (see below). *Náměstí Republiky 5.* ☎ *222-002-336 (box office). www. obecni-dum.cz. Tickets 300 Kč–1,100 Kč. Metro: Náměstí Republiky. Map p 124.*

★ Ponec ŽIŽKOV A beacon of civility in an otherwise dreary part of town, Ponec is Prague's center for contemporary dance and

movement theater. Home to the annual Tanec Praha dance festival. Buy tickets through Ticketpro or the theater box office (Mon–Fri 5–8pm as well as 1 hr. before performances). *Husítská 24a.* ☎ *222-721-531. www.divadloponec.cz. Tickets 290 Kč. Metro: Florenc. Map p 124.*

★★★ Rudolfinum STARÉ MĚSTO This beautiful neo-Renaissance concert hall hosts the Czech Philharmonic Orchestra and boasts arguably the best sound quality of any classical venue in the country. Attracts some big-name musicians. Most concerts take place in the main Dvořák hall. The smaller Suk hall toward the back is used for chamber concerts. The theater box office is open Monday to Friday from 10am to 6pm. *Náměstí Jana Palacha.* ☎ *227-059-227. www. ceskafilharmonie.cz. Tickets 200 Kč–1,000 Kč. Metro: Staroměstská. Map p 124.*

★★ Státní Opera (State Opera) NOVÉ MĚSTO The leading opera house in Prague, offering a highly polished repertoire of classics like *Carmen, Rigoletto, Madame Butterfly,* and *The Magic Flute.* Operas are sung in the original language, with Czech and occasionally English captions. Also hosts regular performances of ballet and modern dance. The location is less than ideal, across a busy highway and sandwiched between the main train station and the modern building that houses the annex to the National Museum. Buy tickets through Bohemia Ticket (see below) or at the theater box office. *Wilsonová 4.* ☎ *224-901-448. www.narodni-divadlo.cz. Tickets 400 Kč– 1,150 Kč . Metro: Muzeum. Map p 124.*

Puppet & Black Light Theater
★★ kids Divadlo Image STARÉ MĚSTO   Highly popular black light theater in Old Town. The popular production *Black Box* mixes traditional black light techniques with high-tech imagery, dance, and music. Entertaining. Suitable for children ages 12 and up (younger children will like the lights but may not be able to follow the plot). Buy tickets at the box office. *Pařížská 4.* ☎ *222-314-448. www.imagetheatre. cz. Tickets 480 Kč. Metro: Staroměstská. Map p 124.*

★★ Srnec Black Light Theater STARÉ MĚSTO   Well-respected black light theater from one of the innovators of the concept back in

the 1960s. In summer, when the company is not traveling, they offer daily performances of "The Best of Black Light Theater," essentially a montage of great scenes from the past 50 years. Check the website for the schedule and buy tickets at the box office. *Na Příkopě 31 (Broadway passage).* ☎ *774-574- 475. www.blacktheatresrnec.cz. Tickets 380 Kč–680 Kč. Metro: Mustek. Map p 124.*

★★ Laterna Magika NOVÉ MĚSTO   The original black light theater troupe that traces its roots back to the 1958 Brussels World Expo, where this peculiarly Czech form of drama first hit the international stage. In 2013, the theater was again staging its long-running and highly entertaining epic, *Wonderful Circus.* Performances take place in the *Nová Scéna* wing of the National Theater, and tickets are available online or at the National Theater box office. *Národní 4.* ☎ *224-901-448. www. narodni-divadlo.cz. Tickets 260 Kč– 690 Kč. Metro: Staroměstská plus tram 17, 18. Map p 124.*

Národní Divadlo Marionet.

★ kids **Národní Divadlo Mario-net (National Puppet Theater)** STARÉ MĚSTO This is the best of Prague's handful of puppet theaters. The company's mainstay for years has been Mozart's *Don Giovanni*. It's entertaining, but you might want to bone up on the opera's storyline beforehand so that you have a better idea of what's going on. Buy tickets at the box office or through Bohemia Ticket or Ticketpro outlets (see below). *Žatecká 1.* ☎ *224-819-322. www.mozart.cz. Tickets 590 Kč. Metro: Staroměstská. Map p 124.*

Rock & Live Music
★★ **Archa** NOVÉ MĚSTO This experimental stage hosts everything from visiting bands like The Cult and Sonic Youth to local groups, and alternative dance and theater troupes. Check the website to see what's on. It's invariably good. Box office is open weekdays from 10am to 6pm and 2 hours before performances. *Na Poříčí 26.* ☎ *221-716-333. www.archatheatre. cz. Tickets 200 Kč–600 Kč. Metro: Florenc. Map p 124.*

★★ **Lucerna Music Bar** NOVÉ MĚSTO A great underground bar and stage located below the Lucerna Pasáž shopping center just off Wenceslas Square. The weekday live acts tend toward medium-sized

Lucerna Music Bar.

Czech bands, with a few international musicians thrown in. Weekends are given over to a wildly popular retro '80s and '90s disco extravaganza. Buy tickets at the venue box office. *Vodičková 36.* ☎ *224-217-108. www.musicbar.cz. Tickets 100 Kč–500 Kč. Metro: Mustek. Map p 124.*

★ **O₂ Arena** LIBEŇ This is not a club, but an indoor arena that normally hosts the HC Slavia ice hockey team. Throughout the year, and especially in summer, it's also the city's main venue for visiting rock and pop giants like Kiss, Black Sabbath, Bruno Mars, and many more. Check the website for upcoming shows. Buy tickets online at www.sazkaticket.cz or at the arena box office. *Českomoravská 17, Prague 9 Libeň.* ☎ *266-771-000. www.o2arena.cz. Metro: Českomoravská. Map p 124.*

★★★ **Palác Akropolis** ŽIŽKOV This former theater was rescued from demolition in the '90s and has morphed into the most interesting performance venue in the city. The Akropolis regularly hosts great Czech rock and folk acts as well as indie alternative groups from around the world. On off nights, DJs spin for dancing and drinking in the smaller rooms off the main hall. Buy tickets through Ticketpro or at the venue box office. *Kubelíková 27.* ☎ *296-330-913. www.palacakropo lis.cz. Tickets 50 Kč–500 Kč. Metro: Jiřího z Poděbrad. Map p 124.*

★★ **Roxy** STARÉ MĚSTO Like the Akropolis, another former theater that's carved a niche as the city's leading venue for live performances of techno, electronic music, Asian dub, and other alternative sounds. The Old Town location puts a crimp on late-night noise, so concerts here tend to start and finish early. But, rest assured, the hot, sweaty after-party goes on all night long. Buy tickets at the box office or through Ticketpro (see listing below). *Dlouhá 33.* ☎ *224-826-296. www.roxy.cz. Tickets 200 Kč–600 Kč. Metro: Staroměstská. Map p 124.*

★ **Vagon** NOVÉ MĚSTO Informal rock venue with live acts most days of the week. The card is heavy on Czech and local revival bands. A recent month featured revival bands for no less than Led Zeppelin, Queen, and Elvis Presley. Some of these guys are pretty good. *Národní třída 25.* ☎ *733-737-301. www.vagon.cz. Tickets 100 Kč–200 Kč. Metro: Mustek. Map p 124.*

Theater

★ **Hybernia** NOVÉ MĚSTO In season (Sept–June), this glitzy theater focuses on big-budget musicals and spectacles. In summer, the program switches to more tourist-friendly fare like the "Best of Swan Lake" or the "Best of Carmen," or an occasional performance of the Prague Proms music festival. Check the website for an updated program. Buy tickets at the venue box office or through Ticketpro (www. ticketpro.cz). *Náměstí Republiky 4.* ☎ *221-419-420. www.hybernia.eu. Tickets 750 Kč–1,200 Kč. Metro: Náměstí Republiky. Map p 124.*

★★★ **Národní Divadlo (National Theater)** NOVÉ MĚSTO For more than a century, the leading stage in the Czech Republic has offered an alternating program of high-end theater, ballet, and opera. For non-Czech speakers, the ballet and opera performances will be of most interest (many of the operas are supertitled in English and German). The program has become more innovative in recent years, breaking away from bread-and-butter Czech classics in favor of more international offerings. Performances usually start at 7pm; the box office is open daily

Vagon.

from 10am to 6pm and 45 minutes before performances. Dress up. *Národní třída 2. www.narodni-divadlo.cz.* ☎ *224-901-448. Tickets 100 Kč–1,000 Kč. Metro: Staroměstská plus tram 17, 18. Map p 124.*

★★ **Stavovské Divadlo (Estates Theater)** STARÉ MĚSTO An offshoot of the National Theater, with a similar repertoire. The theater's claim to fame is that it hosted the premier of Mozart's *Don Giovanni* in 1787—with none other than Wolfgang Amadeus himself in the conductor's role. In summer, a private company offers nightly performances of opera for tourists. In season, a more demanding, experimental version of *Don Giovanni* is performed. Buy advance tickets at the National Theater box office (see above) or at the theater's historic box office 45 minutes before the performance. *Ovocní trh 1.* ☎ *224-901-448 (National Theater box office). www. narodni-divadlo.cz. Tickets 30 Kč–1,000 Kč. Metro: Mustek. Map p 124.*

★★ **Švandovo Divadlo na Smíchově** SMÍCHOV Experimental space offering an eclectic and often high-quality program of theater, dance, and music. The repertoire leans toward modern and alternative works, with a commitment to international artists. Many of the theater performances are subtitled in English. Buy tickets at the venue box office. *Stefaníková 57.* ☎ *257-318-666. www.svando-vodivadlo.cz. Tickets 180 Kč–400 Kč. Metro: Anděl plus tram 12, 20. Map p 123.*

Buying Tickets

Cultural events are refreshingly affordable and accessible, and except for a few high-profile performances at the National Theater or a big-time visiting rock act at O₂ arena, they rarely sell out. To check on schedules and secure tickets before arriving, surf the websites of the venues you might want to visit. The cheapest and easiest place to get tickets is usually at the theater or venue box office (normally open Mon–Fri 10am–6pm, and an hour or so before performances start). Many venues also allow you to purchase tickets directly through their website and pick up the tickets at the box office.

You can also buy tickets online through the major ticket agencies, all of which have English-language pages and are geared toward serving incoming visitors. The major agencies include: Bohemia Ticket (www.bohemiaticket.cz); Sazka Ticket (www.sazkaticket.cz); Ticketpro (www.ticketpro.cz); and TicketStream (www.

Foyer of the National Theater.

ticketstream.cz; see below). Once you've ordered the tickets, you can print them out on your home printer, have them sent to your hotel (for a fee), or pick them up at the agency's in-town office.

Bohemia Ticket NOVÉ MĚSTO Good source for performances at the Národní Divadlo, Státní Opera, and the Stavovské Divadlo. Offers hotel delivery for 200 Kč. *Na Příkopě 16.* ☎ *224-215-031. www.bohemia ticket.cz. Metro: Mustek. Map p 124.*

Sazka Ticket LIBEŇ Handles tickets for big-name rock and pop concerts as well as other major events held at O2 Arena (including home games for the HC Slavia hockey team). Buy tickets online or at the arena box office (located near entrance no. 10). *Českomoravská 17, Prague 9.* ☎ *266-771-000. www. sazkaticket.cz. Metro: Českomoravská. Map p 124.*

TicketPortal NOVÉ MĚSTO Decent ticket agency oriented mostly toward concerts and musical theater productions. The tricky website is only partly in English. *Politických vě zňů 15.* ☎ *224-091-439. www.ticketportal.cz. Metro: Mustek. Map p 124.*

Ticketpro NOVÉ MĚSTO Probably the best all-around agency, with an easy-to-use website and helpful staff. The main office near the Mustek metro station is a good place to check for special events and big concerts that might be on while you're here. *Václavské nám. 38.* ☎ *234-704-204. www.ticketpro.cz. Metro: Mustek. Map p 124.*

TicketStream NOVÉ MĚSTO This general ticketing agency is a good source for clubs, church concerts, and sporting events, as well as local music fests around the country. *Koubková 8.* ☎ *224-263-049. www.ticketstream.cz. Metro: I.P. Pavlova. Map p 124.* ●

Lodging Best Bets

Best **Views**
★★★ U Zlaté Studně $$$ *U Zlaté Studně 166/4 (p 147)*

Best **Hot Stones**
★★★ Le Palais $$$$ *U Zvonařky 1 (p 145)*

Best for **Fashionistas**
★★ Buddha-Bar Hotel $$$$ *Jakubská 8 (p 139)*

Best **Budget Hotel**
★★ Dahlia Inn $ *Lipová 20 (p 141)*

Best for **Minimalists**
★★ Anděl's Hotel Prague $$ *Stroupežnického 21 (p 138)*

Best for **Music Lovers**
★★ Aria $$$$ *Tržiště 9 (p 139)*

Best **if You Miss the '60s**
★★★ Sax $$ *Jánský Vršek 3 (p 146)*

Best **Socialist Realist Architecture**
★ Crowne Plaza $$ *Koulová 15 (p 141)*

Best **Luxury Chain Hotel**
★★★ Boscolo $$$ *Senovážné nám 8 (p 139)*

Best **Art Nouveau**
★★ Paříž $$$ *U Obecního Domu 1 (p 146)*

Best **Hideaway**
★★★ House at the Big Boot $$ *Vlašská 30 (p 143)*

Best **Breakfast Buffet**
★★ Hotel Josef $$$ *Rybná 20 (p 143)*

Best for **Incurable Romantics**
★★★ Alchymist Grand Hotel and Spa $$$$ *Tržiště 19 (p 138)*

Best **Business Hotel**
★★ Sheraton $$$ *Žítna 8 (p 147)*

Alchymist Grand Hotel and Spa.

Malá Strana Area Lodging

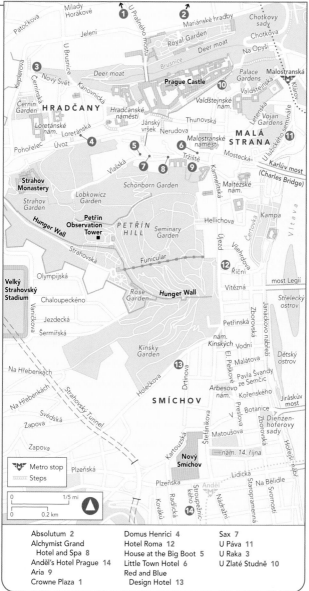

Absolutum 2	Domus Henrici 4	Sax 7
Alchymist Grand	Hotel Roma 12	U Páva 11
Hotel and Spa 8	House at the Big Boot 5	U Raka 3
Anděl's Hotel Prague 14	Little Town Hotel 6	U Zlaté Studně 10
Aria 9	Red and Blue	
Crowne Plaza 1	Design Hotel 13	

Photo p 133: The Royal Tower Suite at Paříž.

Staré Město Area Lodging

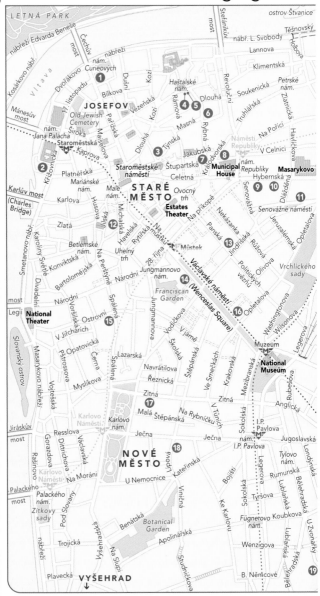

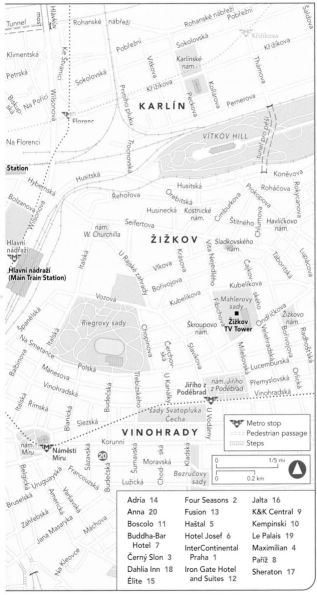

Adria 14
Anna 20
Boscolo 11
Buddha-Bar Hotel 7
Černý Slon 3
Dahlia Inn 18
Élite 15

Four Seasons 2
Fusion 13
Haštal 5
Hotel Josef 6
InterContinental Praha 1
Iron Gate Hotel and Suites 12

Jalta 16
K&K Central 9
Kempinski 10
Le Palais 19
Maximilian 4
Paříž 8
Sheraton 17

Metro stop
Pedestrian passage
Steps

Prague Lodging A to Z

★ **Absolutum** HOLEŠOVICE A sleek, modern hotel with designer rooms at relatively reasonable prices. The rack rates aren't great, but the reception desk will offer discounts on slow nights. The location, across the street from the Holešovice train and metro station, wouldn't win a beauty contest, but it's convenient for getting to the center or for checking out Holešovice nightspots like SaSaZu and Cross Club (the latter being across the street). The house restaurant is the best around, and a good place to get a bite if you're stuck waiting on a train at Holešovice nádraží. *Jablonského 4.* ☎ *222-541-406. www.absolutumhotel.cz. 34 units. Doubles 2,750 Kč. AE, DC, MC, V. Metro: Nádraží Holešovice. Map p 135.*

★ **Adria** NOVÉ MĚSTO An 18th-century burgher's house on Wenceslas Square houses this fully renovated hotel. It's a good value if you want to be close to the action. The rooms are small but tasteful in a contemporary chain-hotel style. The Adria cuts rates during summer and offers attractive discounts if you book online. *Václavské nám. 26.* ☎ *221-081-111. www.adria.cz. 88 units. Doubles 2,600 Kč–3,600 Kč. AE, DC, MC, V. Metro: Mustek. Map p 136.*

★★★ **Alchymist Grand Hotel and Spa** MALÁ STRANA Portions of this extravagantly restored Baroque town house date back to the 15th century. The owners spared no expense in creating arguably the most opulent, luxurious lodging in Prague, with canopy beds, hardwood floors, beautifully tiled bathrooms, and statues of cherubs peering from every pedestal. The website often offers weekend packages, with prices shaved by as much as a third off rack rates. *Tržiště 19.* ☎ *257-286-011. www.alchymisthotel.com. 47 units. Doubles 6,200 Kč, suites from 9,000 Kč. AE, DC, MC, V. Metro: Malostranská plus tram 12, 20, 22. Map p 135.*

★★ **Anděl's Hotel Prague** SMÍCHOV You'll find this arty design hotel in up-and-coming Smíchov, 10 minutes by metro from the center. The aesthetic here could be described as hard-core

Hotel Anna.

Buddha-Bar Hotel.

minimalist, with the spare decor relieved by colorful pillows and spreads. The hotel's 2-day "Golden Prague" package includes a complimentary dinner, tour of the city, and airport transfers at about 80% of the standard room rate. *Stroupežnického 21.* ☎ *296-889-688. www.andels hotel.com. 231 units. Doubles 2,600 Kč–4,500 Kč. AE, DC, MC, V. Metro: Anděl. Map p 135.*

★ **Anna** VINOHRADY This elegant, family-run hotel occupies a 19th-century neoclassical townhouse in residential Vinohrady. There's not much in the way of services, but you'll get a warm welcome at the reception desk and satisfaction from knowing you're getting good value. Check the website for special offers. There are two small suites on the top floor, one with a distant view out toward Prague Castle. *Budečská 17.* ☎ *222-513-111. www.hotelanna.cz. 24 units. Doubles 2,200 Kč. AE, DC, MC, V. Metro: Náměstí Miru. Map p 136.*

★★ **Aria** MALÁ STRANA Aria compares favorably to the nearby Alchymist Grand in terms of jaw-dropping luxury and room prices to match, but it's a little less showy. In keeping with the music theme, each of the 51 rooms and suites is named after a different composer

or musical performer. Each has a different decor, ranging from tasteful contemporary to 19th-century period piece. The rooftop terrace restaurant has excellent food and commands an incredible view. *Tržiště 9.* ☎ *225-334-111. www. ariahotel.net. 51 units. Doubles from 5,800 Kč, suites from 8,000 Kč. AE, DC, MC, V. Metro: Malostranská plus tram 12, 20, 22. Map p 135.*

★★★ **Boscolo** NOVĚ MĚSTO The Boscolo occupies a sumptuous 19th-century neoclassical town *palais* that's been added to the Marriott Hotel chain's 'Autograph' collection of unique properties. The emphasis here is on luxury and the target market is well-heeled corporate travelers, but the big beautiful rooms complete with marble tiling, and the breathtaking public areas also make this a great splurge or honeymoon option. The location is convenient to the train station, and the center is just 5 to 10 minutes on foot. *Senovážné nám. 8.* ☎ *224-593-111. www.marriott.com. 152 units. Doubles 3,600 Kč–5,400 Kč. AE, DC, MC, V. Metro: Náměstí Republiky. Map p 136.*

★★ **Buddha-Bar Hotel** STARÉ MĚSTO If you've got the spare crowns, you can hardly do better than this chic French-Asian inspired

Surviving Sticker Shock

Prague is a moderately priced destination, cheaper than London or Paris, but a bit more expensive than neighboring Central European cities like Kraków or Budapest. Thankfully (if that's the right word), the global economic crisis put an end to the trend of ever-rising prices, but rack rates can still be surprisingly high.

There are some steps you can take to minimize the pain. Always check the hotel's website beforehand. Hotel owners are adept at adjusting rates according to demand, and impromptu cuts of up to 30% posted on the Web are not uncommon to fill beds. Also, consider traveling out of season if possible. January, February, November, and most of December are considered "low" season, and prices fall as much as 50% from spring and fall rates. Midsummer (July and Aug) is "shoulder" season (neither high nor low), and a prime time to wheel and deal. The flip side of this is to avoid Prague over the New Year's and Easter holidays. Not only are there no deals to be had, but there are no beds either.

Several agencies offer short-term apartment rentals for as short as a few days or as long as a month. These are often very nice apartments, with good locations, at around half the price of comparable hotels (without the services, of course). **Apartments in Prague** (Vlašska[as] 8, Malá Strana; ☎ 775-588-511; http://apartments-in-prague.org) offers several units in Malá Strana and Old Town. Another popular agency, **Mary's Apartments** (Italská 31, Vinohrady; ☎ 222-254-007; www.marys.cz), has properties all around the city at nearly every price point. **Prague-Stay.com** (Na Perštýně 2, Prague 1 (☎ 222-328-281; http://prague-stay.com) is operated by the local upscale real estate agency **Svoboda & Williams.** Prices here are a bit higher than elsewhere, but the apartments are beautifully appointed and well located in the center of town.

Prague has tons of hostels and budget accommodations, including several combination hostel/hotels that do double duty, offering hostel-style dorm beds in one part of the property and surprisingly attractive private singles and doubles in another part. These "flashpacker" hostels can be great deals and are open to travellers of any age. Some of our favorites include the **Czech Inn** at Francouzská 76, Vršovice (☎ 267-267-600; www.czech-inn.com), and **Sir Toby's** (Dělnická 24, Holešovice; ☎ 246-032-610; www.sirtobys.com). Both offer beds in shared dorm rooms from around 250 Kč per person, and chic private doubles from around 1,200 Kč. Another highly recommended combination hostel/hotel is **Mosaic House** (Odboru 4, Nové Město; ☎ 221-595-350; www.mosaichouse.com). Mosaic House has an awesome central location, a lively sports bar and club on the ground floor, and beautiful private singles and doubles, some offering balconies and city views.

inn in the middle of the Old Town. The rooms are huge and furnished in a style that could be described as tastefully exotic, with warm reds and golds and bright tiles that recall the best of India or the Middle East. The in-house Buddha-Bar restaurant features great Asian-inspired cuisine, including a sushi bar, in a setting that manages to be both hip and ultra high-end at the same time. Check the website for discounts. *Jakubská 8.* ☎ *221-776-300. www.buddhabarhotelprague. com. 39 units. Doubles 7,500 Kč–9,000 Kč. AE, DC, MC, V. Metro: Náměstí Republiky. Map p ###.*

★★ Černý Slon STARÉ MĚSTO

This small hotel's ancient, atmospheric wine cellar sets it apart, as does its location—in a perfect part of the Old Town, a block away from Old Town Square. It's an excellent out-of-season choice, as rates drop by more than a quarter and the crowds that invariably stream past the hotel's doorstep thin to a mere trickle. The rooms are old-style charming, with creaky wooden floors and clean linens. *Týnská 1.* ☎ *222-321-521. www.hotelcerny slon.cz. 18 units. Doubles 2,500 Kč –3,200 Kč. AE, DC, MC, V. Metro: Staroměstská. Map p 136.*

★ Crowne Plaza DEJVICE

Fans of Socialist Realism architecture will want to give this place a close look: It's Prague's best example of early-1950s Stalinist "wedding cake" style and a real period piece. When the Holiday Inn group bought the property in the 1990s, they replaced the Communist-era red star on the top with their own corporate green one (now it's gold, reflecting the Crowne Plaza's colors). The interior has been thoroughly renovated, but many of the older Socialist murals and decorative elements thankfully remain. The location in suburban Dejvice,

on the western edge of the city, is convenient to the airport. *Koulová 15.* ☎ *296-537-111. www.ihg.com. 250 units. Doubles from 2,400 Kč. AE, DC, MC, V. Metro: Dejvická plus tram 8 to Podbaba. Map p 135.*

★★ Dahlia Inn NOVÉ MĚSTO

This popular budget option occupies a 19th-century townhouse, about 10 minutes' walk from central Václavské nám. The rooms are modest but tastefully appointed, with contemporary, minimalist design touches, clean, modern baths, and a small flat-screen TV on each desk. The outgoing, 20-something owner adds a dash of charm and energy to the place. *Lípová 20.* ☎ *222-517-518. www.dahliainn.com. 8 units. Doubles 1,600 Kč–2,000 Kč. AE, DC, MC, V. Metro: I.P. Pavlova. Map p 136.*

★★★ Domus Henrici

HRADČANY A sleek, upmarket bed-and-breakfast, a stone's throw from Prague Castle. There's been a house on this site since the 1300s, and Emperor Rudolf II was even a former owner. That feeling of exclusivity lingers in the well-proportioned rooms, tasteful contemporary furnishings, and gorgeous views out

Crowne Plaza Hotel.

Domus Henrici.

the back toward Petřín Hill and Strahov Monastery. Check the website for specials. Rates generally drop in midsummer. *Loretánská 11.* ☎ *220-511-369. www.domus-henrici.cz. 8 units. Doubles 2,500 Kč–4,000 Kč. AE, DC, MC, V. Metro: Malostranská plus tram 22. Map p 135.*

★★ **Élite** NOVÉ MĚSTO Another nicely renovated 14th-century townhouse, this one on a side street in one of the busiest parts of town. Night revelers will appreciate that the main stop on the city's nighttime tram service is right around the corner. The rooms are a pleasing mix of period and contemporary, with some authentic antiques tossed in for atmosphere. Ask to see the suite, with its 17th-century Renaissance frescoes. *Ostrovní 32.* ☎ *224-932-250. www.hotelelite.cz. 78 units. Doubles 2,000 Kč–3,200 Kč. AE, DC, MC, V. Metro: Karlovo náměstí. Map p 136.*

★★ **Four Seasons** STARÉ MĚSTO When the Four Seasons opened its doors in 2001, it set new standards for Prague hotels. Everything—from the heart-stopping views toward the Charles Bridge to the seamless service to the highly acclaimed in-house CottoCrudo restaurant—is what you'd expect

from the Four Seasons name. Oddly for these prices, breakfast is not included in the rate. Check the web for seasonal "4th night free" deals. *Veleslavínová 2a.* ☎ *221-427-000. www.fourseasons.com/prague. 161 units. Doubles from 9,000 Kč; suites up to 25,000 Kč. AE, DC, MC, V. Metro: Staroměstská. Map p 136.*

★★ **Fusion** NOVÉ MĚSTO New in 2012, the Fusion offers both hostel-style dorm rooms and private singles and doubles at prices that

The Four Seasons.

are a bit above youth hostel rates, but which represent amazing value given the quality of the rooms and central location. The private rooms offer distinct mid-century designer touches like Eames chairs and funky retro lamps. Some rooms are designed by theme, such as the Rock Room or the Vintage Room, the latter fitted out with high-end thrift shop finds. *Panská 9.* ☎ *226-222-888. www.fusionhotels.com. 88 units. Dorm beds from 400 Kč, doubles from 2,000 Kč. AE, DC, MC, V. Metro: Mustek. Map p 136.*

Haštal STARÉ MĚSTO The location, a beautiful and quiet part of the Old Town not far from the St. Agnes cloister, is the major draw at this smaller, locally owned hotel. The rooms are plain to the point of drab, but the prices, particularly off-season, are reasonable. Big discounts are available if you book online. *Haštalská 6.* ☎ *222-314-335. http://hotelhastalprague.com. 24 units. Doubles 2,100 Kč–3,200 Kč. AE, DC, MC, V. Metro: Staroměstská. Map p 136.*

★★ Hotel Josef STARÉ MĚSTO The Josef was one of the first contemporary boutique hotels to open in Prague, and fans of updated midcentury modern—in chrome and white—will find a second home here. The high style extends to the lobby and the all-white cocktail bar—so cool you'd expect to see Tom Ford himself perched on one of the stools. The gorgeous chrome-and-glass rooms receive dashes of color from bedspreads or pillowcases. The breakfast buffet is the best in town, filled with fresh fruits, fish, cheeses, and meats. This is one hotel breakfast you don't want to sleep through. *Rybná 20.* ☎ *221-700-111. www.hoteljosef. com. 110 units. Doubles 4,200 Kč–5,000 Kč. AE, DC, MC, V. Metro: Náměstí Republiky. Map p ###.*

Iron Gate Hotel and Suites.

★ Hotel Roma MALÁ STRANA A decent four-star option in Malá Strana. The standard rooms are small and the stripped-down modern aesthetic is more plain than trendsetting. Nevertheless, it's a nice fallback with a great location, not far from the funicular to Petřín Hill. Ask to see a few rooms before choosing, since some retain atmospheric period details like hardwood flooring. At the time of writing, the hotel website was discounting rooms for stays of at least 3 nights. *Újezd 24.* ☎ *222-500-120. www.hotelromaprague.com. 90 units. Doubles 3,000 Kč–4,400 Kč. AE, DC, MC, V. Metro: Malostranská plus tram 12, 20, 22. Map p 135.*

★★★ House at the Big Boot MALÁ STRANA This small, family-run inn occupies a 17th-century townhouse on a quiet square and feels like a well-kept secret. There's no sign on the door, or indeed any indication outside that it's a hotel. Inside, the rooms are eclectically furnished, with beds and dressers in styles ranging from 19th-century Biedermeier to 1930s Art Deco. The friendly owners are happy to show you around the property and advise on what to see and do during your stay. *Vlašská 30.* ☎ *257-532-088.*

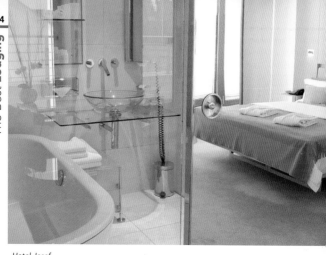

Hotel Josef.

www.dumuvelkeboty.cz. 10 units. *Doubles from 2,500 Kč. No credit cards. Metro: Malostranská plus tram 12, 20. Map p 135.*

InterContinental Praha STARÉ MĚSTO The hotel's eye-catching (or jarring, depending on your point of view) 1970s Brutalist architecture was actually intended to mesh with the surrounding Jewish quarter in a style dubbed "ghetto moderne." Inside, it's easier on the eyes, with sleek sofas and silky fabrics. The rooms are clean and quiet, but smallish for the money. Ask for an upper-floor room with a view out over the river or the Old Town. The fitness club downstairs, with an indoor pool, has great equipment. Popular with package tours. *Pař ížská 30.* ☎ *296-631-111. www.ihg. com. 364 units. Doubles 3,600 Kč –4,800 Kč. AE, DC, MC, V. Metro: Staromě stská. Map p 136.*

★★ Iron Gate Hotel and Suites STARÉ MĚSTO Another beautiful boutique hotel carved out of a series of Baroque burghers' houses, with many of the facade

reliefs still intact. The rooms are different, so look at a couple before deciding. Many have the original wood-beamed ceilings. The tasteful contemporary decor toes the line between high style and comfort. *Michalská 19.* ☎ *225-777-777. www. irongate.cz. 43 units. Doubles from 5,000 Kč. AE, DC, MC, V. Metro: Staromě stská. Map p 136.*

★ Jalta NOVÉ MĚSTO Even under Communism, the Jalta was one of the better hotels in Prague. The Socialist Realism facade from the 1950s was thoroughly renovated in 2007 and has UNESCO protection as a world heritage site. The superior deluxe rooms are the biggest and best, with smart contemporary furnishings and new bathrooms. The hotel's location, on the upper reaches of Wenceslas Square, is ideal for sightseeing. The rooms facing the square have balconies, allowing a broad view of the busy square and a chance to imagine how it might have looked in November 1989, when thousands came out onto the streets to bring down Communism. *Václavské nám. 45.* ☎ *222-822-888. www.hoteljalta. com. 94 units. Doubles 2,800 Kč– 4,000 Kč. AE, DC, MC, V. Metro: Muzeum. Map p 136.*

★★ **K+K Central** NOVÉ MĚSTO It wasn't that long ago that Hybernská Street was a forgotten corner of the city and slightly derelict. Now, it's one of the hottest properties for upscale hotels, including the Kempinski (reviewed below) and this ornate Art Nouveau palace that is nearly as nice and a better value. Fans of early 20th-century architecture will love the highly stylized exterior and public areas. The rooms are on the small side, but done up in a retro Functionalist style that recalls the 1920s. The dining and breakfast areas are opulent in the extreme, a series of archways carved into the wall and festooned with 1920s period lighting. Check the website for discounts. *Hybernská 10.* ☎ *225-022-000. www.kk hotels.com. 127 units. Doubles 3,000 Kč–5,000 Kč. AE, DC, MC, V. Metro: Náměstí Republiky. Map p 136.*

★★ **Kempinski** NOVÉ MĚSTO A beautiful five-star hotel that opened on the eve of the global economic recession in 2008 (but seems to be prospering lately). The setting is a refurbished 17th-century town house. The rooms feature a stylish contemporary interior with retro hints. Its Le Grill restaurant is easily one of the best in the city. *Hybernská 12.* ☎ *226-226-132. www.kempinski.com/en/prague. 74 units. Doubles 5,000 Kč–7,500 Kč. AE, DC, MC, V. Metro: Náměstí Republiky. Map p 136.*

★★★ **Le Palais** VINOHRADY A special luxury boutique hotel in a 19th-century Belle Époque town house. With all the little reading rooms, hidden nooks, and places to cozy up to the fire with a glass of brandy, you may not want to leave the hotel. The fitness room is one of the nicest in the city, complete with aromatherapy, hot stones, and all the rest. The quiet location in leafy Vinohrady is a big plus. *U Zvonařky 1.* ☎ *234-634-111. www.vi-hotels. com. 60 units. Doubles 4,000 Kč, suites 10,000 Kč. AE, DC, MC, V. Metro: Náměstí Miru. Map p 136.*

★ **Little Town Hotel** MALÁ STRANA This remodeled 13th-century palace on the upper end of Malostranské nám. offers several

Le Palais.

multibed rooms (some with kitchens) that are ideal for groups or long stays. Some rooms give views of Prague Castle in the distance, so ask to see what's available when you check in. The actual room furnishings are modest at best, but the price is right for this part of town. *Malostranské nám. 11.* ☎ *242-406-964. www.littletownhotel.cz. 10 units. Doubles 1,500 Kč–3,000 Kč. AE, DC, MC, V. Metro: Malostranská plus tram 12, 20, 22. Map p 135.*

★★ Maximilian STARÉ MĚSTO

The Maximilian goes for the same light, modern, minimalist aesthetic as Hotel Josef (see above), but it's not quite as chic. It does have a superb location, however, in an overlooked and beautiful part of the Old Town. Ask for a room with a view toward the nearby St. Agnes cloister. The rooms are spare, in keeping with the overall look, but comfortable. The Planet Zen wellness studio is an added draw. *Haštalská 14.* ☎ *225-303-118. www.maximilianhotel.com. 71 units. Doubles 3,200 Kč–5,000 Kč. AE, DC, MC, V. Metro: Staroměstská. Map p 136.*

★★ Paříž STARÉ MĚSTO

This beautiful Art Nouveau hotel recalls much of the glory of turn-of-the-20th-century Prague and that fabled interwar period under the First Republic. The "Paris" is a local landmark, and was immortalized in Czech author Bohumil Hrabal's hilarious book *I Served the King of England.* The public areas, restaurant, and cafe are pure Art Nouveau museum pieces. The rooms are plainer but comfortable. *U Obecního Domu 1.* ☎ *222-195-195. www.hotel-paris.cz. 86 units. Doubles 3,500 Kč–5,200 Kč. AE, DC, MC, V. Metro: Náměstí Republiky. Map p 136.*

★★ Red and Blue Design Hotel MALÁ STRANA

This fully remodeled townhouse on the southern end of Malá Strana offers 52 clean and well-appointed modern rooms (26 done out in red, 26 in blue). The rooms are divided into "design" and "superior design," with the chief difference being size (and the more expensive rooms have a tub). The location is a 10- to 15-minute walk from the center, but easy to reach by public transport. *Holečkova 13.* ☎ *220-990-100. www.redandbluehotels.com. 52 units. Doubles 2,100 Kč–3,000 Kč. AE, DC, MC, V. Metro: Malostranská plus tram 12, 20. Map p 135.*

★★★ Sax MALÁ STRANA

Why settle for standard-issue hotel decor when you can have this beautiful throwback 1960s vintage hotel for the same price? They also throw in a picture-perfect Malá Strana setting. Colorful period

Paříž.

☎ 225-999-999. www.starwood hotels.com. 160 units. Doubles 3,500 Kč–5,000 Kč. AE, DC, MC, V. Metro: Karlovo náměstí plus tram 4, 6, 10, 16, 22. Map p 136.

★★ U Páva MALÁ STRANA

"At the Peacock" is situated on Kampa Island, with views both toward the river and up to the castle. Each room is slightly different, but many have the original wooden ceilings and antique furnishings. Check the website for photos and ask to see a few different rooms on arrival. The location is perfect for a stroll across the Charles Bridge. U Lužického Semináře 32. ☎ 257-533-360. www.hotel-upava.cz. 27 units. Doubles 2,700 Kč, castle-view suites 5,000 Kč. AE, DC, MC, V. Metro: Malostranská plus tram 12, 20, 22. Map p 135.

★★ U Raka HRADČANY

A special place, where you can relax in the garden courtyard of this secluded luxury log cabin and imagine you're at a country cottage. Stroll Nový Svět, the timeless lane on the far side of Prague Castle that leads up to U Raka, and feel like you have the entire city to yourself. Royal treatment is provided at the Japanese spa. And by all means, book far in advance; the five rooms fill up fast. Černínská 10. ☎ 220-511-100. www.romantikhotel-uraka.cz. 5 units. Doubles 3,200 Kč—4,000 Kč. AE, DC, MC, V. Metro: Malostranská plus tram 22. Map p 135.

★★★ U Zlaté Studně MALÁ STRANA

An all-around perfect boutique hotel, with drop-dead views of Malá Strana, gorgeous rooms with parquet floors and period furnishings, and a renowned chef turning out gourmet meals for a bite on the terrace. The Renaissance

U Páva.

furniture (think kidney-bean coffee tables and lava lamps), stylish wallpaper, and lots of charm mix with some gorgeous views out over the terra-cotta Malá Strana rooftops. Excellent value. Jánský Vršek 3. ☎ 257-531-268. www.sax.cz. 22 units. Doubles 2,500 Kč–3,200 Kč. AE, DC, MC, V. Metro: Malostranská plus tram 12, 20, 22. Map p 135.

★★ Sheraton NOVÉ MĚSTO

A stunning addition to a five-star Prague lineup that already included the likes of the Four Seasons, Buddha-Bar, Kempinski, and several others. This is arguably the city's best business hotel and everything you would expect from the luxury Sheraton name, though the location is slightly away from the main tourist area and a 15 minute walk to the Old Town Square. Check the website for discounts. Žitna 8.

U Raka.

house once belonged to Emperor Rudolf II and for a time housed the famed—or was it infamous?—Danish astronomer Tycho de Brahe. The hike up here can be quite steep, so splurge on a taxi if you're carrying luggage. *U Zlaté Studně 4.* ☎ *257-011-213. www.goldenwell.cz. 19 units. Doubles 5,000 Kč–6,500 Kč. AE, DC, MC, V. Metro: Malostranská plus tram 12, 20, 22 (and then walk uphill). Map p 135.* ●

Fairy-Tale Karlštejn

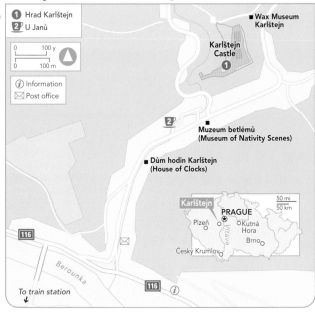

1 Hrad Karlštejn
2 U Janů

0   100 y
0   100 m

ⓘ Information
✉ Post office

■ Wax Museum Karlštejn

Karlštejn Castle 1

■ Muzeum betlémů (Museum of Nativity Scenes)

■ Dům hodin Karlštejn (House of Clocks)

Karlštejn

PRAGUE
Plzeň ○   ○ Kutná Hora
   Brno ○
Český Krumlov ○

Vltava

50 mi
50 km

116

Berounka

To train station ↓

116   ⓘ

Karlštejn is far and away the most popular Prague day trip—for both city residents and visitors. It's an easy 40-minute ride out on the train, and the quaint village, with its gingerbread-style houses guarded over by an enchanted-kingdom castle, is a welcome antidote to the big city. The surrounding countryside is lovely and unspoiled. Plan on a leisurely day of strolling along the town's main road, popping in at the numerous gift shops and pubs as you make your way slowly up to the castle.

1 ★★★ **Hrad Karlštejn.** They don't come much more majestic than Karlštejn Castle, a high-Gothic beauty that dates from the middle of the 14th century (although much of the exterior was restored and embellished in the 19th century). The castle was built on orders of Charles IV to protect what were then the coronation jewels of the Holy Roman Empire. The jewels

Previous page: Český Krumlov.

were later moved to Prague Castle during the turbulent 17th century (where they sit today under lock and key), leaving Karlštejn Castle pretty much empty. Even if you're not that into castles, it's still fun to make the climb up here for the fabulous views. There are two main tours on offer. Tour 1 is quicker and cheaper, and includes a nice overview of highlights like the Imperial Palace

Karlštejn: Practical Matters

There are no buses to Karlštejn from Prague, so trains are the only public transportation option. Trains leave approximately once an hour during the day from Prague's main station (Hlavní nadráží). If you don't see Karlštejn on the timetable, look for trains heading in the direction of Beroun. The trip costs about 60 Kč each way and takes about 40 minutes. The walk into the village from the train station takes about 20 minutes. If you'd like to drive, head west along the D5 motorway out of the city in the direction of Plzeň and then follow the signs to Karlštejn. Depending on traffic, you can make the drive in about 40 minutes.

and Royal Bedroom. But it omits the real treasure: the jewel-studded Chapel of the Holy Rood, with its 2,000 precious and semiprecious inlaid stones. The chapel visit comes only with Tour 2, but the catch is you have to book that one in advance. If you have the time and interest, it's worth the effort. Note that Tour 2 is only offered from May to October. ⏲ *2 hr. with tour, 1 hr. without. Karlštejn.* ☎ *224-497-492 (call to reserve Tour 2). www.hrad karlstejn.cz. 270 Kč (Tour 1, includes guide), 300 Kč (Tour 2, includes guide). May–Sept Tues–Sun 9am–5pm; Oct–Dec Tues–Sun 9am–3pm; Mar–Apr 9am–3pm. Closed Jan–Feb.*

Karlštejn Castle.

2 **U Janů.** Let's face it: None of the restaurants in Karlštejn is going to win a Michelin star, but this little tavern at the top of the village, not far from the castle, at least has the advantage of a terrace in summer and a cozy fireplace inside during the colder months. The menu includes Czech standards like fried cheese, roast pork and dumplings, and even a decent trout. The prices are excellent. *Karlštejn 90.* ☎ *311-681-210. $.*

Charming Český Krumlov

1 Náměstí Svornosti
2 Regional Museum
3 Hotel Růže
4 St. Vitus Church
5 Na louži
6 Egon Schiele Art Centrum
7 Marionette Museum
8 Castle

Information
Pedestrian passage
Steps

After Prague, it's hard to imagine being totally wowed by yet another riverside town in the Czech Republic. Well, prepare to be wowed. Český Krumlov's location, south of České Budějovice, feels impossibly remote. But back in the heyday of the landed aristocracy—in the 14th and 15th centuries—this was the seat of the powerful Rožmberk (Rosenberg) family, whose influence once spread far and wide in these parts. The family insignia—a five-petal rose—adorns castles and houses throughout southern Bohemia. The town's startling castle is second only to Prague Castle in terms of sheer impact. Český Krumlov is relatively compact and can easily be walked in a day. As you take the tour outlined below, feel free to meander at will, crossing the various bridges and poking down little alleyways and behind gates. There are surprises at every turn.

1 Náměstí Svornosti. Český Krumlov's main square is surprisingly quiet, but a good place to get your bearings. The Town Hall at no. 1—easily identified by the Renaissance arcades—houses the highly proficient tourist information office (www.ckrumlov.info), a great source for learning about special events or exhibits that might be going on. The buildings on this square are some of the oldest in town, with cellars dating from the 13th century. ⏱ *15 min. Náměstí Svornosti.*

Český Krumlov's town square.

❷ Regional Museum (Okresní Muzeum). From Náměstí Svornosti, follow picturesque Horní street, with some great panoramas over the city. This small museum and picture gallery offers an informative overview of the history of the town; it's worth the 30 minutes or so it takes to familiarize yourself with the basics. The very realistic miniature town model will help you get your bearings. ⏱ *30 min. Horní 152.* ☎ *380-711-674. 50 Kč. Tues–Sun 9am–5pm.*

❸ Hotel Růže. Just across the street from the museum, this former Jesuit residence (and later army barracks) from the 16th century is now a privately owned luxury hotel. It's worth a peek inside to see how the Renaissance and Baroque touches have been restored. ⏱ *10 min. Horní 154.* ☎ *380-772-100.*

❹ ★ St. Vitus Church (Kostel sv. Víta). Walk back toward the center of town and turn off on Kostelní. This enormous church was intended as an ecclesiastical counterweight to the secular authority of the castle. The church's steeple can be seen for miles around—and the view from on high is impressive. Construction of the church began in the late 14th century and was completed about 50 years later. It underwent the typical transformation into a more ornate Baroque church in the 17th century with the rise of Austrian influence. In the 19th century, many of these Baroque elements, including an onion dome on top, were stripped away to restore its original Gothic appearance. ⏱ *15 min. Kostelní. No phone. Daily 9am–5pm.*

Allow some time to wander Český Krumlov's cobblestone streets.

5️⃣ Na louži. Continue walking along Kostelní, which then becomes Kájovská Street (don't worry if you get lost—all roads eventually lead back to the center). Na louži is a classic Czech pub that's been spruced up to accommodate visitors. They serve delicious home-cooked meals and some of the best fruit dumplings (ovocné knedlíky) in the Czech Republic. It can get crowded, so try to visit slightly before or after traditional meal hours. They also offer comfortable, clean, and reasonably priced rooms upstairs, if you want to plan an overnight. *Kájovská 66.* ☎ *380-711-280. www.nalouzi.cz. $.*

6️⃣ ★★★ Egon Schiele Art Centrum. Walk left out the door from Na louži to find Široká Street. Český Krumlov has always had a love-hate relationship with the controversial Austrian portraitist Egon Schiele. Schiele's mother was born here, and the painter had a fondness for the place. But when he moved here in the early years of the 20th century to paint his now-prized portraits of scantily clad girls, he was run out of town as a pornographer. Today, the Egon Schiele Art Centrum is one of the most innovative and outward-looking art museums in the Czech Republic. In addition to displaying a small but important collection of Schiele's own portraits and graphics, it hosts often-fascinating visiting exhibitions. ⏱ *1 hr. Široká 71.* ☎ *380-704-011. www.schieleart centrum.cz. 120 Kč. Daily 10am–6pm.*

7️⃣ ★ 🄺🄸🄳🅂 Marionette Museum. Continue walking along Široká, then follow painfully picturesque Dlouhá (leaving time to pop in at shops along the way). Turn right at the main street, Radniční, to find this excellent collection of historical puppets, most dating from the 19th century, as well as sets from puppet theater. This museum is a local offshoot of the National Puppet Theater in Prague (p 130). ⏱ *30 min. Radniční 29.* ☎ *380-713-422. http://expozice. krumlovskainspirace.cz. 80 Kč. Daily 10am–6pm.*

8️⃣ ★★★ Castle (Hrad). This, the town's main sight, was the residence of the powerful Rožmberk family until the line died out at the beginning of the 17th century. It later fell into the hands of the

Krumlov Castle.

Český Krumlov: Practical Matters

From Prague, you can take either the bus or the train to Český Krumlov, but bear in mind it's at least a 3-hour trip each way, so planning an overnight stay makes sense. Buses are quicker and cheaper, and drop you off at Český Krumlov's convenient bus station, just a 5- to 10-minute walk from the main sites. Buses usually depart from Prague's Na Knížecí bus station in the outlying district of Smíchov (☎ 841-101-101; metro: Anděl). Try to arrive well before departure time to get a seat; the buses tend to fill to capacity, especially on weekends. Trains leave from Prague's Hlavní nadráží and require a change in České Budějovice. Figure on about 4 hours in total. Český Krumlov's train station is a good 25-minute walk into town. If you're driving, follow the D1 motorway out of Prague, heading south toward Brno. Follow the signs first to České Budějovice and then once there to Český Krumlov. Depending on traffic, the trip takes about 3 hours.

Eggenberg family and then the Schwarzenberg family, the largest noble landholders in the Czech Republic. The castle was built up in stages; the oldest part is the 13th-century observation tower, which was given its current Renaissance appearance in the 16th century. The gardens are open year-round, but the interiors are accessible only from April to October, and by guided tour only. The tour possibilities are confusing, but most visitors will be content with **Tour 1** (focusing on the Renaissance and Baroque interiors) and perhaps a scramble up the 162 steps to the top of the observation tower. **Tour 2** focuses on the Schwarzenberg family. It's also possible to visit the lapidary and the castle museum. **Tour 3** presents the castle's fascinating Baroque Theater, which is still in operation. The tours take around an hour each. Be sure to leave yourself at least another hour to wander around and take in the upper gardens. ⏱ 2 hr. Zámek 59. ☎ 380-704-721 (for tour info and reservations). www.zamek-cesky krumlov.eu. Tour 1, 250 Kč (includes

English-language guide); Tour 2, 240 Kč (includes guide); Tour 3, 300 Kč; lapidary 35 Kč. Apr–Oct Tues–Sun 9am–5pm (last tours 1 hour before closing).

A fountain on the castle grounds.

Bone-Chilling Kutná Hora

1. Bone Church
2. Stone House
3. Plague Column
4. Italian Court
5. Church of St. James
6. Czech Silver Museum
7. Pivnice Dačický
8. St. Barbara's Cathedral

Back in the early years of the Bohemian kingdom, in the 13th and 14th centuries, Kutná Hora was Prague's main rival for power and influence. The town grew rich on the back of the silver mines, and became a major financial center and even a secondary royal residence. Decline began to set in around the 16th century and what you see today is a smallish Czech town overshadowed by its splendiferous medieval past. That makes it all the more fun for a trip back into time. Kutná Hora is easily reachable from Prague by bus or rail in about an hour and a half. The bus will drop you at Kutná Hora's in-town bus station, while the train will leave you about 2km (1.2 miles) outside of town in the village of Sedlec, but within easy walking distance of the Bone Church (see below).

1 ★★★ kids Bone Church
(Kostnice). Mesmerizing or just plain creepy? You be the judge. The interior of this small church, part of a larger monastery complex dating from the 12th century, is made up entirely of human bones. Altars, chalices, chandeliers . . . it simply must be seen to be

believed. For centuries, the area was used as a mass burial ground for victims of the plague or war. In the 19th century, a Czech wood-carver named František Rint came up with this unique solution for using the bones. It's estimated some 40,000 people are "interred" here. ⏱ *45 min. Zámecká 127*

The fascinating, creepy Bone Church.

(Sedlec). ☎ 326-551-049. 60 Kč. Apr–Sept 8am–6pm; Oct–Mar 9am–noon, 1–4pm.

❷ ★ Stone House (Kamenný dům). The triangular gable on the front of the house is widely considered one of the high points of late Czech Gothic architecture. Parts of the house were designed by the same man who built the immense town hall in the Polish city of Wrocław (formerly Breslau). Now it holds a small offshoot of the Czech Silver Museum that focuses on life in the 18th century; it's worth the admission price for a look around inside. ⏱ 20 min. Václavské nám. ☎ 327-512-821. 50 Kč. May–Sept 10am–6pm; Apr 10am–5pm; Oct–Nov 10am–4pm. Closed Dec–Mar.

❸ Plague Column (Morový sloup). The "Black Death" swept through Kutná Hora in 1713, killing some 6,000 residents. This Baroque column dates from the period immediately after and was meant to ward off the plague. Look for the miners' motifs around the column—a sure sign that you're in Kutná Hora. Šultysová.

❹ ★ Italian Court (Vlašský dvůr). During the Middle Ages, this was the seat of considerable wealth and influence—even the

Kutná Hora: Practical Matters

Kutná Hora lies about 80km (50 miles) to the east of Prague, with regular connections during the day by train or bus. The hitch is that the train station is in Sedlec—relatively far from town, but close to the Bone Church—while the bus station is much closer to the center of town and the other main sights. The tour above assumes that you take the train into Kutná Hora, walk to the Bone Church from there, and then proceed into town (on foot, or by taxi or bus). The return trip to Prague is by bus. Of course, you could easily do it in reverse, taking the bus to Kutná Hora and then returning to Prague via the train. Whatever route you choose, figure on about 90 minutes of travel each way and a cost of around 70 Kč (by bus) or 100 Kč (by train) per trip. If you're driving, head east out of Prague along Vinohradská třída, continuing straight, picking up local highway no. 2 until you see signs to Kutná Hora. Figure on about an hour's drive. Once in Kutná Hora, you'll see signs directing you to public parking lots. The local **Kutná Hora Information Center** (Palackého nám. 377; ☎ 327-512-378; www.kutnahora.cz; Apr–Sept daily 9am-6pm; Oct–Mar Mon–Fri 9am–5pm, Sat–Sun 10am–4pm) has a wealth of information about the town, and can help advise on transport and sleeping options.

king maintained a part-time residence. It was here where the main workshops were housed for reworking the silver and minting coins. The "Italian" in the name refers to the Italian lawyers who worked out the early code for mining and minting. The court reached the height of its power in the 15th century with the circulation of the highly coveted Prague Groschen. Operations were halted toward the end of the 16th century and the building fell into ruin. It was "rediscovered" in the 19th century and given a thorough neo-Gothic makeover, essentially what you see today. ⏱ *30 min. Havlíčkovo nám.* ☎ *327-512-873. 100 Kč. Apr–Sept 9am–6pm; Oct–Mar 10am–4pm.*

⑤ Church of St. James (Kostel sv. Jakuba). This stately, somber Gothic church, with its high steeple, is visible for miles around. The church was originally intended to have two steeples, but the ground below proved too unstable. The interior was reworked as Baroque in keeping with the fashion of the 17th century. Unfortunately, it's seldom open to the public, but you may be able to catch a Sunday service for a peek inside. *Havlíčkovo nám. No phone. Sometimes open Sun for mass.*

St. Barbara's Cathedral.

⑥ ★★★ kids Czech Silver Museum (České Muzeum Stříbra/Hrádek). This 15th-century town residence houses the main branch of the Czech Silver Museum and its impressive collection of coins from the Middle Ages. The Renaissance-style painted ceilings are also valuable. But the real highlight of a visit here is the chance to descend into an abandoned silver mine. You even get to don miners' smocks and headgear. Great for kids, but not recommended for claustrophobics. ⏱ *1 hr. Barborská 28.* ☎ *327-512-159. 140 Kč. Apr–Oct 9am–5pm.*

⑦ Pivnice Dačický. This popular beer hall, done out to resemble a medieval knights' chamber, is the perfect retreat for a town that never really left the Middle Ages. Good grilled meats, as well as Czech and Moravian staples like roast pork and goulash, at reasonable prices. There's even Kutná Hora's own Dačický beer on tap. *Raková 8.* ☎ *327-512-248. www.dacicky.com. $$.*

⑧ ★★★ St. Barbara's Cathedral (Chrám sv. Barbory). This is widely considered the second-most-impressive Gothic cathedral in the country after St. Vitus at Prague Castle. The original builders were from the family of Peter Parler, the main architect of the Charles Bridge. Over the years, the masters who worked on the church read like a who's who of Czech Gothic and late-Gothic architecture. St. Barbara is considered the patron saint of miners, and miner motifs are seen throughout the church. Leave yourself the better part of an hour to see the frescoes and chapels. The church lay dormant for a century before being completed in 1905. ⏱ *1 hr. Barborská. No phone. 60 Kč. May–Sept Tues–Sun 9am–6pm; Oct–Apr Tues–Sun 9am–noon, 2–4pm.* ●

Before You Go

Government Tourist Offices

The official agency for tourism promotion is the **Czech Tourist Authority** (www.czechtourism.com). It has offices around the world, including in the **U.S.** (1109 Madison Ave., New York, NY 10028; ☎ 212/288-0830) and **U.K.** (13 Harley St., London W1G 9QG; ☎ 0207-631-0427).

The Best Times to Go

Prague is gorgeous in **spring**, when the trees blossom and the city shrugs off a long winter. **Fall** can be equally pleasant, with long, warm days and usually reliably sunny weather. Avoid travel over **Christmas, New Year's,** and **Easter,** when the city fills to brimming with tour groups from Germany and Italy. Midsummer is considered "in-between" season, with slightly lower hotel prices, but it can be stiflingly hot and many hotels lack air-conditioning. You might consider coming in low season, February or November, when the crowds thin and you finally feel you have this beautiful city to yourself.

Festivals & Special Events

SPRING The **Prague Spring Music Festival** (www.festival.cz), held in late spring, is a world-famous, 3-week series of symphony, opera, and chamber performances. **Prague Khamoro** (www.khamoro. cz), usually held at the end of May, is a celebration of Roma (gypsy) culture. **Febiofest** (www.febiofest. cz), in March, is one of the largest noncompetitive film and video festivals in Central Europe. Many of the films are shown in English or with English subtitles. The **One**

Previous page: Prague's trams let you cover a lot of ground for a little money.

World film festival (www.jedensvet. cz), also in March, brings together the best human rights and documentary films of the past year. Many of the screenings are in English. Spring normally ends with the **Prague Fringe Festival** (www. praguefringe.com), a week of English-language drama, comedy, and performance art, held in late May and early June.

SUMMER **Prague Proms** (www. pragueproms.cz) is a month-long international music festival that attracts all genres, from classical to jazz, over a series of evenings from mid-June to mid-July. **Tanec Praha** (Dance Prague; www.tanecpraha.cz) is a dance festival in June that focuses on contemporary dance and movement theater. The **United Islands** (www.unitedislands.cz) festival, usually a long weekend in June, is a carnival of jazz, rock, folk, and house music spread out over several islands in the Vltava River.

FALL In September, Prague's theaters, concert halls, and opera houses return to life after the summer break. October's 2-week-long **Prague International Jazz Festival** (www.jazzfestivalpraha.cz) attracts some of the world's best jazz musicians. Performances are usually held in the Lucerna Music Hall and the city's oldest jazz venue, Reduta.

WINTER The Christmas season begins on **St. Nicholas Eve** (Dec. 5), when children traditionally dress as St. Nicholas, the devil, or an angel. The annual **Prague Christmas Market** in Old Town Square gets going about then. Stalls hawk all manner of food, mulled wine, ornaments, and cheap gifts in a festive atmosphere that toes a fine line between traditional and tacky. **New Year's Eve** is literally a blowout—and the

MONTHLY AVERAGE TEMPERATURE						
	JAN	FEB	MAR	APR	MAY	JUNE
Daily Temp (°F)	30	33	40	48	57	63
Daily Temp (°C)	0.9	0.8	4.6	9.2	14.2	17.5
	JULY	AUG	SEPT	OCT	NOV	DEC
Daily Temp (°F)	66	65	58	49	39	33
Daily Temp (°C)	19.1	18.5	14.7	9.7	4.4	0.9

entire town comes out to light fire-crackers on Old Town Square, Wenceslas Square, and Charles Bridge. Watch your head, as every year hundreds of people are injured by errant bottle rockets.

The Weather
Late **spring** (May and June) and **fall** generally bring the best weather for touring, with warm days and cool nights. **Summers** can be hit or miss, with some years bringing lots of rain and others weeklong stretches of hot sunshine. **Winters** can be cold and unusually long, sometimes lasting into April. Rain is a possibility at any time of year, so be sure to pack an umbrella.

Useful Websites
- **www.praguewelcome.cz:** The city's main tourist information portal. Good source for general information and cultural calendars. Includes an excellent interactive guide to help visitors plan their activities depending on how long they will stay.

- **www.prague-information.eu:** Another highly useful tourist information portal (this one privately operated), with lots of suggestions on sights and activities, as well as tons of practical information.

- **www.mapy.cz:** Online maps and journey planner; covers Prague and the entire Czech Republic. Simply type in an address and a map shows you exactly where it is.

- **www.dpp.cz:** The ins and outs of Prague's public transportation system, including system maps and info on tickets and travel passes.

- **www.idos.cz:** Online timetable for trains and buses, including international destinations. Just type in the city (using the Czech spellings, for example, "Praha" for Prague) and you'll get a complete listing of train and bus connections.

- **www.praguemonitor.com:** Excellent English online magazine about all things Prague and Czech. Good sections on politics and economics, and a lifestyle section that includes cultural listings and restaurant reviews.

Cellphones (Mobile Phones)
Czech cellphones operate on a GSM band of 900/1800MHz. This is the same standard in use throughout Europe but different from the one used in the U.S. **U.S. mobiles** will work here, provided that they are tri-band phones (not all phones are tri-band) and that you've contacted your service provider to allow for international roaming. Keep calls to a minimum, however, since roaming charges can be steep. **U.K. mobiles** should work without any problem, provided that you've contacted your service provider to activate international

roaming (the same precautions about steep prices apply to U.K. mobiles). One way of avoiding international roaming charges is to **purchase a pay-as-you-go SIM card** for your cellphone and a pre-paid calling card. This provides you with a local number and allows you to make calls and send text messages at local rates. All of the major local telephone operators offer this service.

The situation for **smartphones** like iPhones and Android models is more complicated. Local networks support 3G (and 4G is on the way), but unless you have an international data plan with your provider,

data roaming fees can add up quickly. The best advice is to turn off "data roaming" and use your phone as a Wi-Fi device at the many hotels and cafes that offer free Wi-Fi.

Car Rentals

There's little need to rent a car in Prague, but if you're determined to do so, it's usually cheapest to book a car online before you leave home. All of the major rental agencies offer cars in Prague (with pick-up either in town or at the airport). Try **Hertz** (www.hertz.com), **Avis** (www.avis.com), or **Budget** (www.budget.com).

Getting There

By Plane
Václav Havel Airport Prague
(code PRG; ☎ 220-111-888, www.prg.aero) is the main international air gateway to the Czech Republic. The airport lies in the suburb of Ruzyně, about 12 miles (18km) northwest of the center. The airport has two main passenger terminals: 1 and 2. **Terminal 1** handles destinations outside the E.U., including overseas flights to and from the U.S. as well as flights from the U.K. (which is outside the E.U.'s Schengen common border zone). **Terminal 2** handles what are considered to be internal flights within the E.U., including flights to and from France, Germany, Italy, and Switzerland.

Prague is well served by major European and international carriers, including several budget airlines. The Czech national carrier, **CSA** (www.czechairlines.com), no longer flies directly to North America, but it is a useful airline for accessing

major European cities. **Delta Airlines** (www.delta.com) offers direct service between Prague and New York JFK, though these flights normally operate only from May to October.

From Ruzyně to town: Taxis are the quickest but most expensive option. Two companies are licensed to operate at the airport: **AAA** (☎ 222-333-222; www.aaa-taxi.cz) and **1.1.1. RadioCab Taxi** (☎ 220-113-892; www.111radiocab.cz). Both operate stands outside the two main terminals. Fares average 650 Kč to the center. The trip normally takes about 25 minutes (but up to 45 min. during rush hour).

If you're staying near the immediate center of town, a cheaper alternative is to share a minibus operated by **CEDAZ** (☎ 220-116-758; www.cedaz.cz). Minibuses run regularly between the airport and the center for a flat fee of 150 Kč per person.

The most affordable option is public transportation. **City bus no. 119** stops at both terminals and runs regularly from the airport to the Dejvická metro station (on Line A), from which the center is just three metro stops away. **Bus no. 100** runs south from the airport to the area of Zličín, and connects to metro Line B. Travel on both requires a 32 Kč ticket purchased from yellow ticketing machines at the bus stop (*Note:* The machines only accept change). Buy two tickets if you're carrying large luggage.

A special **Airport Express** (designated "AE" on buses) runs to and from Prague's main train station and costs 50 Kč per person each way. This is convenient if you are connecting directly to an international train.

By Car
Prague is easily accessible by major highway from around Europe. The main four-lane highways leading into and out of the city include the D1 motorway running south and east to Brno (2 hr.), Bratislava (3 hr.), and with connections to Kraków (8 hr.) and Budapest (5 hr.); the D5 motorway running southwest to Plzeň (Pilsen; 1 hr.) and Nuremberg (3 hr.), with connections to Italy and points in southern and western Europe; and the D8 running north to Dresden (2 hr.) and Berlin (5 hr.). Vienna is about 5 hours by car, with most of the trip along crowded two-lane highway.

By Train
Prague lies on major European rail lines, with good connections to Dresden (2 hr.) and Berlin (5 hr.) to the north, and Brno (2–3 hr), Vienna (4–5 hr.), Bratislava (3 hr.), and Budapest (7 hr.) to the south and east. High-speed rail service has been introduced on the Prague-Vienna run, shortening the travel time on some trains to as little as hours. More high-speed rail links are on the drawing board.

Most international trains arrive at the main station, **Hlavní nádraží** (Wilsonova 80, Prague 1; ☎ 224-614-071; www.cd.cz; Metro: Hlavní nádraží, Line C). A few trains to and from Berlin, Vienna, and Budapest, however, stop at the northern suburban station, **Nádraží Holešovice** (Vrbenského ul., Prague 7; ☎ 224-615-865; www.cd.cz; Metro: Nádraží Holešovice, Line C). Train information is available at ☎ 840-112-113 and http://jizdnirady.idnes.cz.

Hlavní nádraží is a bustling station, with all the services you might need, including currency exchange offices, ATMs, a left luggage counter, lockers, shops and restaurants. From the train platforms, you'll walk down a flight of stairs and through a tunnel before arriving in the ground-level main hall. Also useful is **ČD Centrum** (☎ 840-112-113; www.cd.cz), run by Czech Railways. This office sells domestic and international train tickets, seat reservations and sleepers, and it also provides information. It is open daily 7am to 7pm. Visa and MasterCard are accepted.

The Czech Republic is a member of the **Eurail** network and you won't have any problems validating and using your **Global Euralipass** and other rail passes (www.railpass.com). In addition to the Global pass, you can buy tailored regional passes that include the Czech Republic and Germany or Austria. There's also a **Czech Republic Pass** (4 days of second-class travel for $166), but domestic rail tickets are so cheap you're probably better off simply buying tickets as you go. **RailEurope** (www.raileurope.com) offers a similar menu of countries and passes. Check the website for details, but generally these passes only make financial sense if you're ver a lot of ground

sses are available in
travel to the Czech
including the popular **InterRail** and InterRail Youthpass (www.internationalrail.com). It's also possible to purchase an InterRail–Czech Republic pass offering 3 days of unlimited second-class travel in the Czech Republic within 1 month for £72. To purchase an InterRail pass, you must be a permanent resident of one of the participating countries (residents of the U.S. and Canada are prohibited).

By Bus
The main European international bus line, **Eurolines** (www.elines.cz),

maintains regular service to Prague from around Europe. Most international buses arrive and depart from Prague's **Florenc bus station** (Křižíkova 4, Prague 8; ☎ 900-144-444; Metro: Florenc, Line B, C). Florenc is also the main gateway for long-haul domestic coach service to cities like Brno and Karlovy Vary. For travel within the Czech Republic by bus, contact **Student Agency** (☎ 800-100-300; www.studentagency.cz).

Like many bus stations around the world, Florenc can be a fairly depressing place, though it's gotten a face-lift and now has a nice waiting room, a Burger King restaurant, and several stores catering to travelers' needs.

Getting **Around**

On Foot
Prepare to do plenty of walking. Most of the center of the city is closed to vehicles, including taxis, meaning you'll have to walk pretty much everywhere. Distances are relatively close, but be sure to wear comfortable shoes, since many of the streets are paved (if that's the right word . . .) with cobblestones.

By Public Transportation
Prague's public transportation system (www.dpp.cz) of metros, trams, and buses is excellent. A 32- Kč ticket, which you can buy at tobacco kiosks or from yellow ticket machines, gives you 90 minutes of unlimited travel on any metro, tram, or bus. For shorter journeys, a 24-Kč ticket gives you 30 minutes of travel on metros, trams, and buses. You can also buy a 1-day pass for 110 Kč or a 3-day pass for 310 Kč.

On metros, validate tickets in punching machines located at the

top of the escalators. On trams and buses, these machines are located in the vehicle. Hold on to your ticket until the end of the journey. Spot-checks are infrequent, but fines are steep.

By Taxi
Taxi rates are reasonable, but watch for dishonest drivers. In an honest cab, the meter will start at around 40 Kč and rise 28 Kč per kilometer after that. Fares for destinations near the center should not be higher than 200 Kč. Refrain from hailing cabs on the street; instead order cabs by phone. **AAA** (☎ 222-333-222; www.aaa-taxi.cz) employs honest drivers, and operators speak English. Rates are also cheaper if ordered by phone.

By Car
Driving is not recommended because traffic is heavy and many areas of the central city are closed

to motor vehicles. Parking can be difficult. You'll need a special sticker to park in the center (available only to residents) or pay very high short-term rates. Note too that street parking is now restricted in several districts outside of the center, leaving you with few reasonably priced options.

Prague's Architectural Mix

Look up. That's maybe the best advice I can give you. Prague's majestic mix of Medieval, Renaissance, and Art Nouveau architecture shares one fairly universal element—the most elegant and well-appointed facades and fixtures aren't at eye level or even street level, but are on top floors and roofs. Hundreds of buildings are decorated with intricately carved cornices or ornamental balconies and friezes depicting mythical, religious, or heroic figures.

The grime of Prague pollution has been gradually stripped away, and each restored building reveals previously obscured details. What's interesting, though, is how visitors react to the grime. When people visit Paris or Venice and see dirty, crumbling buildings, they consider them quaint. When they see the same old, dirty, crumbling buildings in Prague, however, they point to the failure of Communism—not entirely fair. If you look at photos of Prague taken in 1900, you'll also see dirty, crumbling buildings.

The city's earliest extant forms are Romanesque, dating from 1100 to 1250. The long Gothic period followed from 1250 to 1530. You'll find many Gothic buildings in Staré Město. Plus Prague Castle's most visible superstructure, St. Vitus Cathedral, is a Gothic masterpiece—that is, its older east-facing half (the cathedral's western sections exemplify Renaissance and neo-Gothic styles). From 1500 to the early 1600s, the Italian Renaissance style prevailed.

Many of the best-known structures are Baroque and Rococo, sharply tailored in the high Austrian style inspired by the Habsburgs of the 17th and 18th centuries.

Some of the most flamboyant buildings are Art Nouveau, popular from 1900 to around 1920. The movement that swept across Europe developed with the Industrial Revolution. Innovative building materials—primarily steel and glass—opened endless possibilities for artistic embellishments. Architects abandoned traditional stone structures built in a pseudo-historic style. Art Nouveau is characterized by rich, curvaceous ornamentation.

Several intriguing cubist designs from that era have also been hailed for their ingenuity. As an architectural style, cubism thrived in Bohemia, and you can find many examples in the neighborhood below Vyšehrad Park.

The late 20th century played havoc with Prague's architecture. Communists were partial to functionalism with virtually no character. Their buildings shed all decorative details. You shouldn't leave Prague before taking the metro out to Prosek to see the thousands of Communist-era flats, called "rabbit huts" even by their occupants. Created partly out of socialist dogma and partly out of economic necessity, these prefabricated apartment buildings (paneláks) were named after the concrete slabs used to build them. Cheap and unimaginatively designed, the apartment buildings are surrounded by a featureless world. Exteriors were made of plain, unadorned cement, and halls were lined with linoleum. The same room, balcony, and window design was stamped over and over.

But *panelák* living wasn't always viewed as a scourge. Unlike the larger, older apartments, *paneláks* had new plumbing and heating and in the 1960s, '70s, and '80s they were considered the modern way to live.

The post-Communist period has seen a boom in new building, but has been much less fruitful from an architectural perspective. One

notable exception is the so-called Dancing Building on the embankment at the Rašínovo nábřeží, which is both loved and loathed in equal measure. Its design strays from the 19th-century Empire classical houses lining the river, but in a most peculiar way. Controversial U.S. architect Frank Gehry, who designed the American Center in Paris, and New Wave designer Vlado Milunič have created a building that ironically pays tribute to the most classic of film dancing pairs: Fred Astaire and Ginger Rogers. Built as the Prague office of a Dutch insurance company, the building depicts the two intertwined in a spin above the Vltava.

Recommended Films & Books

Films

Czech filmmaking has a long tradition. The Prague studios in the Barrandov Hills churned out glossy pre-Communist romantic comedies and period pieces rivaling the output of Paris, Berlin, and even Hollywood at the time.

While Czech literature and music have carved their places in classical culture, the country's films and their directors have collected the widest praise in the mid– to late 20th century. Cunning, melancholy views of Bohemian life under Communism were captured by some of the finest filmmakers in the era known as the "Czech New Wave" of the 1960s.

Directors Jiří Menzel and Miloš Forman were in the vanguard. An easy-to-find example of this period's work (with English subtitles) is Menzel's Oscar-winning *Closely Watched Trains*, a snapshot of the

odd routine at a rural Czech train station.

Forman made his splash with a quirky look at a night in the life of a town trying to have fun despite itself. *The Fireman's Ball* shows Forman's true mastery as he captures the essence of being stone-bored in a gray world, yet he still makes it strangely intriguing. Of course, this was made before Forman emigrated to the big budgets of Hollywood and first shocked Americans with *Hair*. He then directed the Oscar-winning *One Flew Over the Cuckoo's Nest*. For *Amadeus*, Forman sought authenticity, so he received special permission from the Communists to return to Prague; while filming, he brought back to life the original Estates Theater (Stavovské divadlo), where Mozart first performed.

Czech-based directors after the New Wave mostly disappeared

from view, but one stunningly brave film was made in 1970, as the repressive post-invasion period known as "normalization" began its long, cold freeze of talent. In *The Ear (Ucho),* director Karel Kachyňa presents the anguished story of a man trapped in an apartment wired for sound, subject to the Communist leaders' obsession and paranoia. That *The Ear* was made in the political environment of the time was astounding. That it was quickly banned wasn't. Fortunately, local TV has dusted off copies from the archives, and it has begun playing to art-house audiences again.

But maybe a new Czech wave has begun. The father-and-son team of Zdeněk and Jan Svěrák won the Best Foreign Film Oscar in 1997 for *Kolja,* the bittersweet tale of an abandoned Russian boy grudgingly adopted by an aging Czech bachelor on the cusp of the 1989 revolution. After a previous Oscar nomination for the 1992 *Elementary School (Obecná škola),* the 30-something director Jan and his actor father are making an industry out of golden reflections about Czech life.

In the 1990s and the early 2000s, Prague became a popular location for major motion pictures. Producer/actor Tom Cruise and director Brian De Palma chose it for the stunning night shots around Charles Bridge in the early scenes of the first *Mission: Impossible* movie. During shooting, a verbal brawl broke out with Czech officials, who jacked up the rent for use of the riverside palace that acts as the American Embassy in the film (the palace is actually claimed by the von Liechtenstein family). *Immortal Beloved,* a story of Beethoven, made use of Prague's timeless streets (shooting around the graffiti).

Dozens of other films have been shot here or have used Prague locations. A partial list includes the 2006 James Bond installment *Casino Royale* as well as parts of the popular *Narnia* and *Bourne Identity* series. As costs have risen locally, however, fewer and fewer movies are being made here as producers look for even cheaper locations in countries like Romania and Hungary. Officials have recently proposed a series of tax breaks for the film industry in hopes of luring a few productions back.

The film about Prague probably most familiar to American audiences is *The Unbearable Lightness of Being,* based on the book by émigré author Milan Kundera. Set in the days surrounding the Soviet invasion, the story draws on the psychology of three Czechs who can't escape their personal obsessions while the political world outside collapses around them. Many Czechs find the film disturbing, some because it hits home, others because they say it portrays a Western stereotype.

Books

Any discussion of Czech literature with visiting foreigners usually begins with Milan Kundera. Reviled among many Czechs who didn't emigrate, Kundera creates a visceral, personal sense of the world he chose to leave in the 1970s for the freedom of Paris. In *The Unbearable Lightness of Being,* the anguish over escaping the Soviet-occupied Prague he loves tears the libidinous protagonist Dr. Tomáš in the same way the love for his wife and the lust for his lover do. More Czech "life under Communism" angst can be found in *The Book of Laughter and Forgetting* and *Laughable Loves.* Kundera's biting satire of Stalinist purges in the

1950s, *The Joke*, is regarded by Czech critics as his best work.

The late Arnošt Lustig, a survivor of the Nazi-era Terezín concentration camp and author of many works, including *Street of Lost Brothers*, shared the 1991 *Publishers Weekly* award for best literary work with John Updike and Norman Mailer. In 1995, he later went on to become the editor of the Czech edition of *Playboy*.

The best work of renowned writer Ivan Klíma, also a survivor of Terezín, is translated as *Judge on Trial*, a study of justice and the death penalty.

Jaroslav Hašek wrote the Czech harbinger to *Forrest Gump* in *The Good Soldier Švejk*, a post–World War I satire about a simpleton soldier who wreaks havoc in the Austro-Hungarian army during the war.

Bohumil Hrabal, noted for writing about the Czech Everyman and maybe the country's all-time favorite author, died in early 1997 when he fell (so they said officially) out of a fifth-story window while trying to feed pigeons. His death was eerily similar to the fate of a character in one of his stories. He had two internationally acclaimed hits: *Closely Watched Trains* (also translated as *Closely Observed Trains*, on which the Menzel film was based) and *I Served the King of England*, which was also later made into a film. When then-President Bill Clinton visited Prague in 1994, he asked to have a beer with Hrabal in the author's favorite Old Town haunt, the pub U Zlatého tygra (at the Golden Tiger). Clinton may have gotten more than he bargained for, as the gruff but lovable Hrabal, who turned 80 that year, lectured the president on his views of the world.

No reading list would be complete without reference to Franz Kafka, Prague's most famous novelist, who wrote his originals in his native German. *The Collected Novels of Franz Kafka*, which includes *The Castle* and *The Trial*, binds his most claustrophobic works into a single volume.

If it's contemporary philosophy you want, there is, of course, the late philosopher and former president, Václav Havel. His heralded dissident essay, "The Power of the Powerless," explained how the lethargic masses were allowing their complacency with Communism to sap their souls. His "Letters to Olga," written to his first wife while in prison in the 1980s, takes you into his cell and his view of a moral world. Available are two solid English-translated compilations of his dissident writings: *Living in Truth* and *Open Letters*. *Disturbing the Peace* is an autobiographical meditation on childhood, the events of 1968, and Havel's involvement with Charter 77. His first recollections about entering politics are in "Summer Meditations," a long essay written during a vacation.

Havel died in 2011 at the age of 75, following a long bout with cancer.

Finally, for an epic intellectual tour of the long, colorful, and often tragic history of the city, try the 1997 release of *Prague in Black and Gold* by native son and Yale literature professor Peter Demetz. In 2008, Demetz followed that book up with a more personal recollection of Prague during World War II, *Prague in Danger*, including touching memories of his mother, who died at the Terezín concentration camp.

Fast **Facts**

APARTMENT RENTALS **Apartments in Prague** at Vlašská 8, Prague 1 (☎ 775-588-511; http://apartments-in-prague.org), has beautiful properties for 2-6 occupants in Malá Strana and elsewhere starting at around 2,000 Kč a night (higher over the Easter, Christmas, and New Year's holidays). Local real estate agency Svoboda & Williams operates **Prague-Stay.com** at Na Perštýně 2, Prague 1 (☎ 222-311-084; http://prague-stay.com). They offer a similar selection of luxury short-term rentals starting at about 2,000 Kč a night. Check both companies' websites for apartment photos.

ATMS/CASHPOINTS The easiest and best way to get cash abroad is through an ATM—the Cirrus and PLUS networks span the globe. Bank fees average about 1% to 2% of the transaction. ATMs are common in commercial areas. Czech ATMs require a four-digit PIN code.

BABYSITTING **BabyAgency**(☎ 739-310-848; www.baby-agency.eu) offers babysitting services as well as activity programs for young children.

BANKING HOURS Most banks are open Monday to Friday from 8:30am to 5pm.

BIKE RENTALS Try **City Bike Prague** (Královdvorská 5, Prague 1; ☎ 776-180-284; www.citybike-prague.com). **Biko Adventures** (Lidická 5, Prague 5; ☎ 736-441-710; www.bikoadventures.com) offers guided adventure routes to destinations around the city.

BUSINESS HOURS Stores are typically open Monday to Friday from 9am to 6pm and on Saturday from 9am to 1pm; those in the center often keep longer hours and may be open on Sundays and holidays as well. Museums are often closed on Mondays.

CLIMATE Prague has a continental climate with four distinct seasons, including often cold and snowy winters and occasionally hot summers, though temperatures rarely exceed about 32°C (90 °F).

CONSULATES & EMBASSIES **United States Embassy,** Tržiště 15 (☎ 257-022-000); **Canadian Embassy,** Muchová 6 (☎ 272-101-800); **United Kingdom Embassy,** Thunovská 14 (☎ 257-402-111); **Irish Embassy,** Tržiště 13 (☎ 257-530-061); **Australian Consulate,** Klimentská 10 (☎ 221-729-260).

CREDIT CARDS Credit (or debit) cards are a safe way to carry money. They also provide a convenient record of all your expenses, and they generally offer good exchange rates. You can also withdraw cash advances from your credit cards at banks or ATMs, provided you know your PIN. (Call the number on the back of your card if you don't know yours.) Keep in mind that when you use your credit card abroad, most banks assess a 2% fee above the 1% fee charged by Visa, MasterCard, or American Express.

CUSTOMS Baggage checks at airports are rare. You're permitted to bring in reasonable amounts of tobacco products and alcohol for personal use.

DENTISTS & DOCTORS See "Emergencies," below.

DRUGSTORES After regular hours, ask at your hotel for the location of the nearest 24-hour pharmacy. You'll also find the address posted on the doors or windows of other drugstores in the neighborhood. One drugstore that often keeps late hours is **Lékárna U Svaté Ludmily**, in Vinohrady (Prague 2), Belgická 37 (☎ 222-513-396).

ELECTRICITY The Czech Republic operates on the standard European 220V with a two-pronged plug with round pins. U.S. appliances will need a transformer and a plug adapter. Laptops have a built-in transformer and usually require only a plug adapter.

EMBASSIES See "Consulates & Embassies," above.

EMERGENCIES Dial the following telephone numbers in an emergency: 112 (general emergency, equivalent to U.S. 911); 155 (ambulance); 158 (state police); 150 (fire); 1230, 1240 (emergency road service). For emergency medical treatment, go to the **Nemocnice Na Homolce** (Hospital Na Homolce), Roentgenova 2, Prague 5 (☎ 257-271-111). If you need non-urgent medical attention, practitioners in most fields can be found at the **Canadian Medical Center,** Veleslavínská 1, Prague 6 (☎ 235-360-133; www.cmcpraha.cz). For routine dental service, call **American Dental Associates,** Hvězdova 33, Prague 4 (☎ 733-737-337; www.americandental.cz), Monday through Friday from 8am to 8pm.

EVENT LISTINGS The best source of weekly information in English is *The Prague Post* (www.praguepost.com), available at newsstands for 99 Kč a copy. The Prague edition of the *In Your Pocket* guides—updated quarterly—is available at bookstores and is a good source of restaurant, hotel, and club listings, as well as an entertaining, opinionated overview of what's out there.

GAY & LESBIAN TRAVELERS The Czech Republic is a relatively tolerant society, and gay and lesbian travelers should have no particular problems. The website **prague.gayguide.net** is a useful resource for events, clubs, and gay-friendly hotels and restaurants.

HOLIDAYS Public holidays include New Year's Day (Jan 1); Easter Monday (Mar or Apr); Labor Day (May 1); Liberation Day (May 8); Sts. Cyril & Methodius Day (July 5); Death of Jan Hus (July 6); St. Wenceslas Day (Sept 28); Founding of the Czechoslovak Republic (Oct 28); Student Demonstration of 1989 (Nov 17); Christmas (Dec 24, 25); and St. Stephen's Day (Dec 26).

INSURANCE U.S., Canadian, and Australian citizens should obtain medical insurance with international coverage prior to arrival in the Czech Republic, as any doctor or hospital visits must be paid out of pocket. Hospitals may demand cash pre-payment before rendering services, but be sure to save all of the paperwork for later reimbursements. The Czech Republic and the E.U. have a reciprocal health insurance agreement that covers U.K. citizens provided they have a European Health Insurance Card (EHIC).

North Americans with homeowner's or renter's insurance are probably covered for lost luggage. If not, inquire with **Travel Assistance International** (☎ 800/821-2828) or **Travelex** (☎ 800/228-9792). These insurers can also provide trip-cancellation, medical, and emergency-evacuation coverage abroad. The website www.moneysupermarket.com compares prices across a wide range of providers for single- and multitrip policies. For U.K. citizens, insurance is always advisable.

INTERNET CAFES Central Prague is filled with Internet cafes. Rates run about 2 Kč a minute. To surf the net or check e-mail, try **Bohemia Bagel** at Masná 2 (Old Town; ☎ 224-812-560; www.bohemiabagel.cz).

LIQUOR LAWS You can buy alcohol (beer, wine, and spirits) at supermarkets, convenience stores, cafes, and bars. The legal age for buying and consuming alcohol is 18, though ID checks are practically unheard of. The blood-alcohol limit for driving a car is zero, and motorists face a stiff fine.

LOST PROPERTY If your luggage is lost, immediately file a lost-luggage claim at the airport, detailing the luggage contents. For most airlines, you must report delayed, damaged, or lost baggage within 4 hours of arrival.

MAIL & POSTAGE Most post offices in Prague are open Monday through Friday from 8am to 7pm. The **main post office** (Hlavní pošta), at Jindřišská 14, Prague 1 (☎ 221-131-111), is open 24 hours a day. Stamps can sometimes be purchased from your hotel reception desk.

MONEY The Czech currency is the crown (*koruna* in Czech, noted as Kč in shops and CZK in banks). One crown, in theory, is divided into 100 *haler* but the tiny haler coins no longer circulate. Coins come in denominations of 1, 2, 5, 10, 20, and 50 crowns. Bills come in denominations of 100, 200, 500, 1,000, 2,000 and 5,000 crowns. The euro is not in circulation in the Czech Republic, though euros are sometimes accepted at large hotels and at some shops. Dollars are usually not accepted as payment. At press time, one U.S. dollar was worth about 20 Kč; one euro was worth about 25 Kč; and one pound was worth about 30 Kč.

ORIENTATION TOURS See "Tours," below.

PARKING Parking in Prague is a nightmare. To park in the center requires a special permit available only to residents. Parking garages and paid parking lots can be very expensive. In public parking areas, there are no parking meters; instead buy temporary parking permits at machines and display the piece of paper on your dashboard. Parking rates in the center run about 20 Kč to 40 Kč an hour. Parking on streets outside the center is usually free, but good luck finding a spot.

PASSES The **Prague City Card** (www.praguecitycard.com) offers free entry to around 40 attractions, including Prague Castle and the various museums run by the National Gallery (but not the Jewish Museum). Cards are available from 2 to 4 days, starting at 880 Kč for adults and 580 Kč for students. You can buy the pass at select hotels and travel agencies, and at Prague Welcome offices (see "Tourist Offices" below). Most museums and museum attractions will offer sizable discounts for kids and teens aged 5 to15 and seniors over 65. Children 5 and under are often free.

PASSPORTS If your passport is lost or stolen, contact your country's embassy or consulate immediately. (See "Consulates & Embassies," above.) Before you travel, you should copy the critical pages and keep them in a separate place.

PHARMACIES Pharmacies (*apteka* in Czech) are recognizable by the big green cross on the door. Pharmacies sell both prescription and over-the-counter medicines. Most are well stocked, though pharmacists may not always be willing to fill an out-of-country prescription (so be sure to carry extra medication if needed). Most pharmacies are open from 8am to 6pm, though a few maintain 24-hour service. Your hotel should be able to locate an all-night pharmacy in a pinch.

SAFETY Violent crime against tourists is rare, but pickpockets and scams are common. Watch your purses and wallets while on crowded trams and metro cars. Tram no. 22 is especially notorious for pickpockets. Report any theft to police for insurance purposes, and immediately cancel all credit cards. For more information, consult the U.S. State Department's website at www.travel.state.gov; in the U.K., consult the Foreign Office's web-site, www.fco.gov.uk; and in Australia, consult the government travel advisory service at www.smartraveller.gov.au.

SENIOR TRAVELERS Mention that you're a senior when you make your travel reservations. As in most cities, people over the age of 65 (occasionally 60) qualify for reduced admission to theaters, museums, and other attractions, as well as discounted fares on public transport.

SMOKING Restaurants are now required to post smoking policies at the door and to offer segregated nonsmoking seating. Ask the manager to seat you in a nonsmoking area if you are bothered by cigarette smoke. Pubs, particularly the older, more traditional pubs, can be very smoky, and little provision is made for the nonsmoker.

SPECTATOR SPORTS The Czech Republic is an ice hockey superpower. Prague has two professional teams that traditionally battle it out for hockey supremacy during the season, which goes from September through April. **HC Sparta Praha** plays its home matches at **Tipsport Arena,** Za Elektrárnou 419, Prague 7 (☎ 266-727-443; www.hcsparta.cz). Tickets are available at the stadium box office, Monday to Friday 1 to 5:30pm, or at www.ticketportal.cz. The stadium is part of the Výstaviště exhibition grounds: metro C to Holešovice and then tram no. 5, 12 or 17 one stop to Výstaviště.

The second Prague hockey team, **HC Slavia,** plays its home games at **O₂ Arena,** Ocelářská 460, Prague 9 (☎ 266-121-122; www.hc-slavia.cz), the country's biggest and most modern indoor sports facility. Buy tickets at the O₂ Arena box office starting from 10am on the day of the event or at www.sazkaticket.cz. To find the arena, take metro Line B to the stop Českomoravská and it's a short walk from there.

Soccer is also popular, with the season running from July to May (with a break during the coldest months of Dec and Jan). The city's main team is **AC Sparta Praha.** Games typically draw rowdy crowds to **Generali Arena,** Milady Horákové 98, Prague 7 (☎ 296-111-400; www.sparta.cz). Buy tickets at the stadium box office, open Monday to Friday 9am to noon, 1 to 5pm, or on game days 3 hours before kick-off. Take metro Line A to Hradčanská and then tram no. 1, 8, 12, 25, or 26 to the Sparta stop.

STAYING HEALTHY Prague poses no particular health hazards. Tap water is safe to drink, but if in doubt, drink bottled water, which is cheap and abundant.

TAXES Value-added tax, or VAT (DPH in Czech), is 21% on many goods, but non–E.U. visitors can get a partial refund if you spend 2,000 Kč or more within 1 day at shops that participate in the VAT refund program. The shops will give you a form, which you must then get stamped at the Customs desk at the airport on departure (allow yourself extra time at the airport to do this, as lines can be long). Mark the paperwork to request a credit card refund; otherwise, you'll be stuck with a check in euros. For an overview of how the system works and a list of participating stores in Prague, consult the **Global Blue** (www.globalblue.com) website.

TAXIS Watch out for dishonest drivers. Avoid hailing cabs on the street or in popular tourist areas like Wenceslas Square. The best bet is to have someone phone for a taxi or to call one yourself. Two reliable taxi companies include **AAA** (☎ 222-333-222; www.aaa-taxi.cz) and **City Taxi** (☎ 257-257-257; www.citytaxi.cz).

TELEPHONES Working public phones are few and far between thanks to the rapid growth of mobile phones. To use a pay phone, you must buy a prepaid card from tobacco and magazine kiosks (cards are available for 200 Kč). Insert the card, listen for a dial tone, and dial. You can use pay phones with pre-paid cards to dial abroad.

The country code for the Czech Republic is 420. To dial the Czech Republic from abroad, dial the international access code (011 in the U.S.) plus 420 and then the unique nine-digit local number (there are no area or city codes in the Czech Republic). Once you are here, to dial any number anywhere in the Czech Republic, simply dial the nine-digit number.

To make a direct international call from the Czech Republic, dial 00 plus the country code of the country you are calling and then the area code and number. The country code for the U.S. and Canada is 1; Great Britain, 44; Ireland, 353; Australia, 61; and New Zealand, 64.

TIPPING The Czech Republic is not a tipping culture, but waiters still expect small gratuities at restaurants. As a rule of thumb, on small bills round up to the next 10 Kč interval (if the bill comes to 74 Kč, for example, give the server 80 Kč and tell him or her to keep the change). On larger bills or in fancier places, tip up to 10% (but not higher) for good service. Tip taxi drivers a few crowns. For example, if the fare is 152 Kč, give the driver 160 Kč and tell him or her to keep the change.

TOILETS Every large metro station has a passably clean public toilet that you can use for 5 Kč. Otherwise, search out restaurants or cafes and use the facilities in return for the price of a coffee or soft drink.

TOURIST OFFICES The city's official tourist office is called **Prague**

Welcome (☎ 221-714-7... praguewelcome.cz). It h... lent English-language... several helpful branch off... located around town: Staroměstske nám. 1 (inside the Old Town Hall); Rytířská 31; the Malá Strana bridge tower (open Apr–Oct only); and Prague's Václav Havel Airport. In addition to dispensing maps and advice, the staff can help book tours, excursions, concert tickets, and hotel rooms.

TOURIST TRAPS Prague has its share of scams. Don't be tempted to change money on the street; you'll inevitably get ripped off. Be very wary of anyone who might approach you claiming to be a police officer and asking for identification. Also, be sure to watch wallets and valuables on crowded tram and metro cars. Pickpockets abound.

TOURS Several companies offer bus and walking tours (often combined) of Prague. **Martin Tour** at Št ěpánská 61 (☎ 224-212-473; www. martintour.cz) and **Premiant** at Na Příkopě 12 (☎ 606-600-123; www. premiant.cz) have a similar range of tours at similar prices. **Wittmann Tours,** Novotného lávka 5 (☎ 222-252-472; www.wittmann-tours.com), offers daily walks around Prague's compact Jewish Quarter. A thousand years of history are discussed during the 3-hour stroll.

TRAVELERS WITH DISABILI-TIES Wheelchair-bound travelers or those with restricted mobility will have endless problems with Prague's stairs, cobblestones, and curbs. Though some newer buildings, and many four- and five-star hotels, are wheelchair-accessible, the city is years behind in making its streets and public buildings available to all.

VAT See "Taxes," above.

WEATHER See "Climate," above.

Useful Phrases & Menu Terms

Although Czech is a very difficult language to master, you should at least make an attempt to learn a few phrases. Czechs will appreciate the effort and will be more willing to help you out.

Czech Alphabet

There are 32 vowels and consonants in the Czech alphabet, and most of the consonants are pronounced about as they are in English. Accent marks over vowels lengthen the sound of the vowel, as does the *kroužek*, or little circle "°," which appears only over "u."

A, a father	N, n no
B, b boy	Ň, ň Tanya
C, c gets	O, o awful
Č, č choice	P, p pen
D, d day	R, r slightly trilled r
Ď, d' Dior	Ř, ř slightly trilled r + zh as in Persian
E, e never	S, s seat
F, f food	Š, š crush
G, g goal	T, t too
H, h unhand	Ť, t' not yet
Ch, ch Loch Lomond	U, u room
I, i need	V, v very
J, j yes	W, w vague
K, k key	Y, y funny
L, l lord	Z, z zebra
M, m mama	Ž, ž azure, pleasure

Everyday Expressions

ENGLISH	CZECH	PRONUNCIATION
Hello	**Dobrý den**	*doh-*bree den
Good morning	**Dobré rano**	*doh-*breh *rah-*noh
Good evening	**Dobrý večer**	*doh-*bree *veh-*chair
How are you?	**Jak se máte?**	*yahk* seh *mah-*teh
Very well	**Velmi dobře**	*vel-*mee *doh-*brsheh
Thank you	**Děkuji vám**	dyek-*ooee* vahm
You're welcome	**Prosím**	*proh-*seem
Please	**Prosím**	*proh-*seem
Yes	**Ano**	*ah-*no
No	**Ne**	neh
Excuse me	**Promiňte**	*proh-*min-teh
How much does it cost?	**Kolik to stojí?**	*koh-*leek taw *stoh-*ee
I don't understand.	**Nerozumím.**	*neh-*roh-zoo-meem
Just a moment.	**Moment, prosím.**	*moh-*ment, *proh-*seem
Good-bye	**Na shledanou**	*nah* skleh-dah-noh-oo

Traveling

ENGLISH	CZECH	PRONUNCIATION
Where is the . . . ?	Kde je . . . ?	gde yeh . . .
bus station	autobusové nádraží	au-toh-boos-oh-veh nah-drah-zhee
train station	nádraží	nah-drah-zhee
airport	letiště	leh-tyish-tyeh
baggage check	úschovna zavazadel	oo-skohv-nah zah-vahz-ah-del
Where can I find a taxi?	Kde najdu taxi?	gde nai-doo tahks-eh
Where can I find a gas station?	Kde najdu benzínovou pumpu?	gde nai-doo ben-zeen-oh-voh poomp-oo
How much is gas?	Kolik stojí benzín?	koh-leek stoh-yee ben-zeen
Please fill the tank.	Naplňte mi nádrž, prosím.	nah-puln-teh mee nah-durzh, proh-seem
How much is the fare?	Kolik je jízdné?	koh-leek yeh yeesd-neh
I am going to . . .	Pojedu do . . .	poh-yeh-doo doh . . .
One-way ticket	Jízdenka	yeez-den-kah
Round-trip ticket	Zpáteční jízdenka	zpah-tech-nee jeez-den-kah
Car-rental office	Půjčovna aut	poo-eech-awv-nah ah-oot

Accommodations

ENGLISH	CZECH	PRONUNCIATION
I'm looking for . . .	Hledám . . .	hleh-dahm . . .
a hotel	hotel	hoh-tel
a youth hostel	studentskou ubytovnu	stoo-dent-skoh oo-beet-ohv-noo
I am staying . . .	Zůstanu . . .	zoo-stah-noo . . .
a few days	několik dnů	nyeh-koh-leek dnoo
2 weeks	dva týdny	dvah tid-neh
a month	jeden měsíc	yeh-den myeh-seets
I have a reservation.	Mám zamluvený nocleh.	mahm zah-mloo-veh-ni nohts-leh
My name is . . .	Jmenuji se . . .	meh-noo-yee seh . . .
Do you have a room . . . ?	Máte pokoj . . . ?	mah-teh poh-koy . . .
for tonight	na dnešek	nah dneh-sheck
for 3 nights	na tři dny	nah trshee dnee
for a week	na týden	nah tee-den
I would like . . .	Chci . . .	khtsee . . .
a single	jednolůžkový pokoj	jed-noh-loosh-koh-vee poh-koy
a double	dvojlůžkový pokoj	dvoy-loosh-koh-vee poh-koy

ENGLISH	CZECH	PRONUNCIATION
I want a room . . .	**Chci pokoj . . .**	khtsee *poh-koy* . . .
with a bathroom	**s koupelnou**	*skoh-pehl-noh*
without a bathroom	**bez koupelny**	*behz koh-pehl-nee*
with a shower	**se sprchou**	*seh spur-choh*
without a shower	**bez sprchy**	*bez sprech-eh*
with a view	**s pohledem**	*spoh-hlehd-ehm*
How much is the room?	**Kolik stojí pokoj?**	*koh-leek stoh-yee paw-koy*
with breakfast?	**se snídaní?**	*seh snee-dan-nyee*

Getting Around

ENGLISH	CZECH	PRONUNCIATION
I'm looking for . . .	**Hledám . . .**	*hleh-dahm* . . .
a bank	**banku**	*bahnk-oo*
the church	**kostel**	*kohs-tell*
the city center	**centrum**	*tsent-room*
the museum	**muzeum**	*moo-zeh-oom*
a pharmacy	**lékárnu**	*lek-ahr-noo*
the park	**park**	*pahrk*
the theater	**divadlo**	*dee-vahd-loh*
the tourist office	**cestovní kancelář**	*tses-tohv-nee kahn-tseh-larsh*
the embassy	**velvyslanectví**	*vehl-vee-slahn-ets-tvee*
I would like to buy . . .	**Chci koupit . . .**	khtsee *koh-peet* . . .
a stamp	**známku**	*znahm-koo*
a postcard	**pohlednici**	*poh-hlehd-nit-seh*
a map	**mapu**	*mahp-oo*

Signs

No Trespassing	**Cizím vstup zakázán**
No Smoking	**Kouření zakázáno**
No Parking	**Neparkovat**
Arrivals	**Příjezd/Přílet**
Departures	**Odjezd/Odlet**
Entrance	**Vchod**
Exit	**Východ**
Toilets	**Toalety**
Information	**Informace**
Danger	**Pozor, nebezpečí**

Numbers

1	**jeden** (*yeh*-den)		9	**devět** (*deh*-vyet)
2	**dva** (*dvah*)		10	**deset** (*deh*-set)
3	**tři** (*trzhee*)		11	**jedenáct** (*yeh*-deh-nahtst)
4	**čtyři** (*chtee*-rshee)		12	**dvanáct** (*dvah*-nahtst)
5	**pět** (*pyet*)		13	**třináct** (*trshee*-nahtst)
6	**šest** (*shest*)		14	**čtrnáct** (*chtur*-nahtst)
7	**sedm** (*seh*-duhm)		15	**patnáct** (*paht*-nahtst)
8	**osm** (*aw*-suhm)		16	**šestnáct** (*shest*-nahtst)

177

Useful Phrases & Menu Terms

17 **sedmnáct** (*seh*-doom-nahtst)	60 **šedesát** (*she*-deh-saht)
18 **osmnáct** (*aw*-soom-nahtst)	70 **sedmdesát** (*seh*-duhm-deh-saht)
19 **devatenáct** (*deh*-vah-teh-nahtst)	80 **osmdesát** (*aw*-suhm-deh-saht)
20 **dvacet** (*dvah*-tset)	90 **devadesát** (*deh*-vah-deh-saht)
30 **třicet** (*trshee*-tset)	100 **sto** (staw)
40 **čtyřicet** (*chti*-rshee-tset)	500 **pět set** (*pyet* set)
50 **padesát** (*pah*-deh-saht)	1,000 **tisíc** (tyee-seets)

Dining

ENGLISH	CZECH	PRONUNCIATION
Restaurant	**Restaurace**	*rehs*-tow-rah-tseh
Breakfast	**Snídaně**	*snee*-dah-nyeh
Lunch	**Oběd**	*oh*-byed
Dinner	**Večeře**	*veh*-chair-sheh
A table for two, please. (Lit.: There are two of us.)	**Jsme dva.**	*ees*-meh dvah
Waiter	**Číšník**	*cheess*-neek
Waitress	**Servírka**	ser-*veer*-ka
I would like . . .	**Chci . . .**	*khtsee* . . .
a menu	**jídelní lístek**	*yee*-del-nee *lees*-teck
a fork	**vidličku**	*veed*-leech-koo
a knife	**nůž**	noosh
a spoon	**lžičku**	lu-*shich*-koo
a napkin	**ubrousek**	*oo*-broh-seck
a glass (of water)	**skleničku (vody)**	*sklehn*-ich-koo (vod-*dee*)
the check, please	**účet, prosím**	*oo*-cheht, *proh*-seem
Is the tip included?	**Je v tom zahrnuto spropitné?**	yeh *ftohm*-zah *hur*-noo-toh *sproh*-peet-neh

Menu Terms

GENERAL

ENGLISH	CZECH	PRONUNCIATION
Soup	**Polévka**	*poh*-lehv-kah
Eggs	**Vejce**	*vayts*-eh
Meat	**Maso**	*mahs*-oh
Fish	**Ryba**	*ree*-bah
Vegetables	**Zelenina**	*zehl*-eh-nee-nah
Fruit	**Ovoce**	*oh*-voh-tseh
Desserts	**Moučníky**	*mohch*-nee-kee
Beverages	**Nápoje**	*nah*-poy-yeh
Salt	**Sůl**	sool
Pepper	**Pepř**	*peh*-psh
Mayonnaise	**Majonéza**	*mai*-o-neza
Mustard	**Hořčice**	*hohrsh*-chee-tseh
Vinegar	**Ocet**	*oh*-tseht
Oil	**Olej**	*oh*-lay

ENGLISH	CZECH	PRONUNCIATION
Sugar	**Cukr**	*tsoo-ker*
Bread	**Chléb**	*khlehb*
Butter	**Máslo**	*mahs-loh*
Wine	**Víno**	*vee-noh*
Beer	**Pívo**	*pee-voh*
Fried	**Smažený**	*smah-sheh-nee*
Roasted	**Pečený**	*pech-eh-nee*
Boiled	**Vařený**	*vah-rsheh-nee*
Grilled	**Grilovaný**	*gree-loh-vah-nee*

SOUP

Potato	**Bramborová**	Tomato	**Rajská**
Lentil	**Čočková**	Chicken	**Slepičí**
Goulash	**Gulášová**	Vegetable	**Zeleninová**

MEAT

Steak	**Biftek**	Sausage	**Klobása**
Goulash	**Guláš**	Rabbit	**Králík**
Beef	**Hovězí**	Mutton	**Skopové**
Liver	**Játra**	Veal	**Telecí**
Lamb	**Jehněčí**	Veal Cutlet	**Telecí kotleta**
Duck	**Kachna**	Pork	**Vepřové**

FISH

Carp	**Kapr**	Pike	**Štika**
Caviar	**Kaviár**	Cod	**Treska**
Fish Filet	**Rybí filé**	Eel	**Úhoř**
Herring	**Sleď**	Oysters	**Ústřice**

SALAD

Bean Salad	**Fazolový salát**	Cucumber Salad	**Okurkový salát**
Mixed Green Salad	**Hlávkový salát**	Beet Salad	**Salát z červené řepy**

VEGETABLES

Potatoes	**Brambory**	Cauliflower	**Květák**
Celery	**Celer**	Carrots	**Mrkev**
Asparagus	**Chřest**	Peppers	**Paprika**
Onions	**Cibule**	Tomatoes	**Rajská jablíčka**
Mushrooms	**Houby**	Cabbage	**Zelí**

DESSERT

Cake	**Koláč**	Apple Strudel	**Jablkový závin**
Cookies	**Cukroví**	Pancakes	**Palačinky**
Chocolate Ice Cream **Čokoládová zmrzlina**		Vanilla Ice Cream **Vanilková zmrzlina**	

FRUIT

Lemon	**Citrón**	Apple	**Jablko**
Pear	**Hruška**	Plum	**Švestka**

BEVERAGES

Tea	**Čaj**	Red wine	**Červené víno**
Coffee	**Káva**	White wine	**Bílé víno**
Milk	**Mléko**	Beer	**Pívo**
Wine	**Víno**	Water	**Voda**

Index

22 Gold Lane, 29

A

Abbreviations, meaning, vi
Absolutum, 138
Accommodations, 134–138
Adria, 138
Adult entertainment, 116–117
AghaRTA, 122, 126–127
Akropolis, 6
Alchymist Grand Hotel and Spa, 134, 138
Alma Antiques, 74
Anděl's Hotel Prague, 134, 138–139
Anna, 139
Antikvariát Pařížská, 70, 74
Antikvariát Ztichlá klika, 74
Antiquarian books and maps, 74
Antiques, 74–75
Apartment rentals, 140, 169
Apartments in Prague, 140, 169
Archa, 130
Archbishop's Palace, 62
Architecture, 70, 165–166
Aria, 134, 139
Aromi, 94, 98
Art Deco Galerie, 74
Art Decoratif, 81–82
Art galleries, 75
Artel, 70, 76
Arts, see Entertainment
Astronomical Clock, 11–12
ATMs, 169
Atrium Flora, 77–78
Au Gourmand, 80

B

BabyAgency, 169
babysitting, 169
Bakeshop Praha, 80
Bakeshop, 98
Banking hours, 169
Baráčnická Rychta, 60
Bars, 115
Bellevue, 94, 98
Bethlehem Chapel, 67–68
Bike rentals, 169
Black light theater, 122, 129–130
Blues Sklep, 127
Boat rentals, 49–50
Boheme, 79
BohemiaTicket, 132
Bone Church, 156–157
Books, 167–168

Boscola, 134, 139
Botanicus, 70, 81
Breakfast buffet, lodging, 134
Bric a Brac, 74–75
Buddha-Bar Hotel, 134, 139, 141
Bugsy's, 115
Burger joint, 94
Bus travel, 164
Business
  hours, 169
  lodging, 134

C

Cabarets, 116–117
Café Arco, 28
Café Imperial, 106
Café Louvre, 106–107
Café Savoy, 107
Café Slavia, 107
Cafes, 105–108
Car rentals, 162
Car travel, 163–165
Castle District, 62–63
  Archbishop's Palace, 62
  Černin Palace, 63
  Hradčanské náměstí, 62
  Loreta, 63
  Nový Svět, 63
  Schwarzenberg Palace, 63
  Sternberg Palace, 62
  Strahov Monastery, 63
  U Černého vola, 63
Castle (Hrad), 154–155
Celebrity sightings, 94, 114
Cellphones, 161–162
Ceremonial Hall, Jewish Quarter, 55
Černin Palace, 63
Černý Slon, 141
Český Krumlov, 152–155
Čestr, 94, 98
Charles Bridge, 2, 4, 13–14, 50
Child-friendly shopping, 75–76
China, 76–77
Church concerts, 126
Church of Our Lady Before Týn, 10–11
Church of Our Lady Below the Chain, 60
Church of Our Lady Victorious—Infant Jesus of Prague, 60
Church of Saints Simon and Jude, 126
Church of St. Giles, 66–67
Church of St. James, 158
Cili Bar, 114–115

Classical music, 122, 128–129
Climate, 169
Coal Market, 68
Coccinelle, 79
Cocktail bar, 114
Collectibles, 74-75
Communist Prague, 38–43
  Hotel International (Crowne Plaza Hotel), 42–43
  Kinský Palace, 41–42
  Letná, 42
  Lokál, 42
  Máj department store, 39–40
  Melantrich Balcony, 40–41
  Museum of Communism, 41
  Národní třída 16, 39
  Vitkov National Memorial, 43
  Wenceslas Square, 40
  Žižkov TV Tower, 43
Consulates, 169
Credit cards, 169
Cross Club, 14, 119
Crowne Plaza Hotel, 134, 141; see also Hotel International
Crystal, 76–77
Cukrkávalimonáda, 14, 99
Culinaria, 68, 70, 80
Customs, 169
Czech Inn, 140
Czech pubs, 117–119
Czech Silver Museum, 158

D

Dahlia Inn, 134, 141
Dalibor Tower, Prague Castle, 34
Dance, 128–129
Dance clubs, 119–120
Darling Cabaret, 116–117
Department stores, 77–78
Dining, 93–108
  Aromi, 94, 98
  Bakeshop, 98
  Bellevue, 94, 98
  best list, 94
  burger joint, 94
  Café Imperial, 106
  Café Louvre, 106–107
  Café Savoy, 107
  Café Slavia, 107
  cafes, 105–108
  celebrity sightings, 94
  Čestr, 94, 98
  Cukrkávalimonáda, 99
  Ferdinanda, 99

Dining, (cont.)
Grand Café Orient, 107–108
Hergetova Cihelna, 94, 99
Ichnusa Botega,99
Kampa Park, 94, 99–100
kid-friendly, 94
Kofein, 94, 100
La Degustation, 94, 100
La Finestra in Cucina, 100
Lal Qila, 100–101
Las Adelitas, 94, 101
Lehká Hlava, 94, 101
Lokál, 94, 101
Maitrea, 101–102
Malá Strana, 95
Mistral, 102
Obecní dům, 108
Osteria da Clara, 102
Pepe Nero, 102
Peperoncino, 94, 103
Pho Vietnam Tuan & Lan, 94, 103
Pizza Nuovo, 103
Rugantino, 94, 103–104
SaSaZu, 104
Staré Město, 96–97
Sushi Bar, 94, 104
The Tavern, 94, 104
Taverna Olympos, 104–105
U bílé krávy, 105
V Kolkovne, 94, 105–106
V Zátiší, 106
value, 94
vegetarian, 94
Villa Richter, 105
Divadlo Image, 122, 129
Domus Henrici, 141–142
Dorotheum, 75
Drugstores, 169
Dům Porcelánu, 76–77
Duplex, 119–120

E

Egon Schiele Art Centrum, 154
Electricity, 170
Élite, 142
Embassies, 169
Emergencies, 170
English publications, 70, 79
Entertainment, 121–132
best list, 122
black light theater, 129–130
church concerts, 126
classical, 128–129
dance, 128–129

jazz, 126–128
Malá Strana, 123
music, live, 130–131
opera, 128–129
puppets, 129–130
rock music, 130–131
Staré Město, 124–125
theater, 131–132
tickets, 132
Estates Theater, 10
Events, 170
Exlibris, 70, 74

F

Farmer's Market, 80
Fashion, 79–80
Ferdinanda, 99
Festivals, 160–161
Films, 166–167
Fish & Chips, 57
Food, shopping, 80
Foot travel, 164
Four Seasons, 142
Fraktal, 115
Franz Kafka Museum, 29
Friends, 114, 119
Funicular Railway, 85
Fusion, 142–143

G

Galerie Art Praha, 75
Gardens Below Prague, 18, 91
Gay & lesbian travelers, 170
Gay bars and clubs, 114, 119
Gifts, shopping, 81
Globe Bookstore and Coffeehouse, 70, 79
Golden Lane, Prague Castle, 34
Granát, 82
Grand Café Orient, 107–108
Gravestone, Kafka, 29

H

H&M, 81
Hanavský Pavilon, 89
Hapu, 114–115
Haštal, 143
Havelský trh, 68
Hemingway, 114–115
Hergetova Cihelna, 94, 99
Hermès, 81
Holidays, 170
Home furnishings, 81–82
Hotel Evropa, 24
Hotel International, 42–43
Hotel Josef, 134, 143
Hotel Roma, 143
Hotel Růže, 153
House at the Big Boot, 134, 143–144

House of the Black Madonna, 9–10
House of the Lords of Kunstát, 67
Hrad Karlštejn, 150–151
Hradcanské naměstí, 62
Hunger Wall, 86
Hybernia, 131

I

Ichnusa Botega,99
Icons, meaning, vi
Indie rock, 122
Insurance, 170
InterContinental Praha, 144
Internet, 170
Iron Gate Hotel and Suites, 144
Italian Court, 157–158

J

Jalta, 144–145
Jáma, 116
Janský Vršek, 59
Jazz, 122, 126–128
JazzDock, 122, 127
Jewelry, 82
Jewish Community Center, 55–56
Jewish Quarter, 52–57
Ceremonial Hall, 55
Fish & Chips, 57
history, 54
Jewish Community Center, 55–56
Klausen Synagogue, 55
Maisel Synagogue, 56
Maiselova Street, 53
Old Jewish Cemetery, 54–55
Old New Synagogue, 55
Pinkas Synagogue, 53–54
Shelanu Café & Deli, 55
Spanish Synagogue, 56–57
St. Agnes Convent, 57
ticket information, museums, 56
Jiří Švestka
John Lennon Peace Wall, 60–61

K

K5 Relax Club, 117
K+K Central, 145
Kafka, Franz, 26–29
22 Gold Lane, 29
birthplace, 27
Café Arco, 28
Franz Kafka Museum, 29
gravestone, 29

Kafka Snob Food, 27
Old Town Square, 27–28
Workers' Accident Insurance Company, 28
Kafka Snob Food, 27
Kampa Park, 61, 94, 99–100
Kampa, 92
Karlová, 12
Karlovy Lázně, 120
Karlštejn, 150–151
Kempinski, 145
Kid-friendly dining, 94
Kid-friendly tour, 44–47
National Technical Museum, 46–47
Oldtimer Tram, 45–46
Petřín Hill, 45
Podoli indoor pool, 46
Prague Zoo, 47
Rugantino's, 46
swimming, 46
Toy Museum, 45
Výstaviště, 47
Yellow Beach, 46
Kinský Palace, 41–42
Klára Nademlýnská, 79
Klausen Synagogue, 55
Kofein, 94, 100
Kogo, 68
Kotva, 70, 78
Kubista, 70, 82
Kutná Hora, 156–158

L

La Degustation, 94, 100
La Finestra in Cucina, 100
Lal Qila, 100–101
Las Adelitas, 94, 101
Laterna Magika, 129
Le Palais, 134, 145
Lehká Hlava, 94, 101
Les Moules, 94
Lesbian bars and clubs, 119
Lesser Town, 2, 5, 58–61
Baráčnická Rychta, 60
Church of Our Lady Below the Chain, 60
Church of Our Lady Victorious—Infant Jesus of Prague, 60
Janský Vršek, 59
John Lennon Peace Wall, 60–61
Kampa Park, 61
Museum Kampa, 61
Na Kampě, 61
Nerudova, 59
Nostitz Palace, 60
Schoenborn Palace, 59–60

Lesser Town Square, 14
Letenský Zámecek, 89
Letná, 42, 88–89
Letná Beer Garden, 2, 4
Letná Plain, 89
L'Institut Guerlain, 82
Liquor laws, 170–171
Little Town Hotel, 145–146
Lobkowicz Palace, Prague Castle, 35
Lodging, 133–148
Absolutum, 138
Adria, 138
Alchymist Grand Hotel and Spa, 134, 138
Anděl's Hotel Prague, 134, 138–139
Anna, 139
apartment rentals, 140
Apartments in Prague, 140
Aria, 134, 139
best list, 134
Boscola, 134, 139
breakfast buffet, 134
Buddha-Bar Hotel, 134, 139, 141
business, 134
Černý Slon, 141
Crowne Plaza, 134, 141
Czech Inn, 140
Dahlia Inn, 134, 141
Domus Henrici, 141–142
Élite, 142
Four Seasons, 142
Fusion, 142–143
Hastal, 143
Hotel Josef, 134, 143
Hotel Roma, 143
Hotel Růže, 153
House at the Big Boot, 134, 143–144
InterContinental Praha, 144
Iron Gate Hotel and Suites, 144
Jalta, 144–145
K+K Central, 145
Kempinski, 145
Le Palais, 134, 145
Little Town Hotel, 145–146
Malá Strana, 135
Mary's Apartments, 140
Maximilian, 146
Mosaic House, 140
Paríž, 134, 146
Prague-Stay.com, 140
Red and Blue Design Hotel, 146
romantic, 134

Sax, 134, 146–147
Sheraton, 134, 147
Sir Toby's, 140
Staré Město, 136–137
Svoboda & Williams, 140
U Páva, 147
U Raka, 147
U Zlaté Studne, 134, 147–148
Lokál, 3, 6, 42, 94, 101
Lokowicz Palace Café, Prague Castle, 36
Loreta, 63
Louis Vuitton, 81
Lucerna Music Bar, 130
Lucerna Pasáž, 3, 6, 23, 70, 78
Luggage, lost, 171

M

Mail, 171
Maisel Synagogue, 56
Maiselova Street, 53
Maitrea, 101–102
Máj department store, 39–40
Malá Strana, 50, 71
dining, 95
entertainment, 123
lodging, 135
nightlife, 110–111
shopping, 90–92
Mánes Bridge, 18
Manufaktura, 81
Marionette Museum, 154
Marionety, 70, 75
Martinis, 114
Mary's Apartments, 140
Material, 77
Maximilian, 146
Maze of Mirrors, 87
Mecca, 120
Melantrich Balcony, 40–41
Melantrichová, 66
Menu terms, 177–178
Metro, 49, 88
Michalská, 66
Microbrews, 114
Mistral, 102
Mobile phones, 161–162
Modernista, 82
Money, 171
Mosaic House, 140
Moser, 70, 77
Mucha Museum, 68
Municipal House, 3, 6, 9, 65
Museum Kampa, 61
Museum of Communism, 41
Music clubs, 119–120
Music, live, 130–131

N

Na Kampě, 61
Na louži, 154
Na Můstku, 68
Na příkopě, 24
Náměstí Svornosti, 152
Náprstek Museum of Asian, African, and American Cultures, 67
Národní Divadlo, 131
Národní Divadlo Marionet, 122, 130
Národní třída 16, 22, 39
National Museum, 23
National Technical Museum, 46–47
National Theater, 21–22
Nebozizek, 50
Neighborhoods, 51–68
    Castle District, 62–63
    Jewish Quarter, 52–57
    Lesser Town, 58–61
    Old Town, 64–68
Nerudova, 15, 59
Nightlife, 109–120
    adult entertainment, 116–117
    bars, 115
    best list, 114
    cabarets, 116–117
    Czech pubs, 117–119
    dance clubs, 119–120
    gay bars and clubs, 119
    lesbian bars and clubs, 119
    Malá Strana, 110–111
    music clubs, 119–120
    Staré Město, 112–113
Nostitz Palace, 60
Nový Svět, 63, 78

O

O2 Arena, 130
Obecní dům, 108, 128; see also Municipal House
Old Jewish Cemetery, 54–55
Old New Synagogue, 55
Old Royal Palace, Prague Castle, 33
Old Town, 64–68
    Bethlehem Chapel, 67–68
    Church of St. Giles, 66–67
    Coal Market, 68
    Culinaria, 68
    Havelský trh, 68
    House of the Lords of Kunštát, 67
    Kogo, 68
    Melantrichova, 66

Michalská, 66
Mucha Museum, 68
Municipal House, 65
Na Mustků, 68
Náprstek Museum of Asian, African, and American Cultures, 67
Old Town Square, 66
St. Gallus Church, 68
St. James Basilica, 65
Tynská Literární kavárna, 65
Týnská, 65
Ungelt, 65–66
Old Town Square, 2, 5, 10, 27–28, 66, 71
Oldtimer Tram, 45–46
One-day tour, 8–15
    Astronomical Clock, 11–12
    Charles Bridge, 13–14
    Church of Our Lady Before Týn, 10–11
    Cukrkávalimonáda, 14
    Estates Theater, 10
    House of the Black Madonna, 9–10
    Karlová, 12
    Lesser Town Square, 14
    Municipal House, 9
    Nerudova, 15
    Old Town Bridge Tower, 13
    Old Town Hall, 11
    Old Town Square, 10
    Powder Tower, 9
    Prague Castle, 15
    St. Nicholas Church, 15
    U zlatého tygra, 13
    Villa Richter, 15
Opera, 122, 128–129
Osteria da Clara, 102
Outdoor attractions, 83–92
    Funicular Railway, 85
    gardens below Prague Castle, 91
    Hanavský Pavilon, 89
    Hunger Wall, 86
    Kampa, 92
    Letenský Zámeček, 89
    Letná Plain, 89
    Letná, 88–89
    Malá Strana, hidden gardens, 90–92
    Maze of Mirrors, 87
    Metronome, 88
    Petřín Gardens, 87
    Petřín Hill, 84–87
    Petřín Observatory, 86
    Rose Garden, 85–86
    Štefánik Observatory, 85
    Vojan Gardens, 92

Vrtba Garden, 92
Wallenstein Gardens, 91–92

P–Q

Palác Akropolis, 3, 6, 122, 130
Palladium, 78
Pařiž, 134, 146
Parking, 171
Passes, 171
Passports, 171
Pepe Nero, 102
Peperoncino, 94, 103
Personal care salons, 82
Petřín Gardens, 87
Petřín Hill, 2, 4, 45, 84–87
Petřín Observatory, 86
Pharmacies, 171
Pho Vietnam Tuan & Lan, 94, 103
Phrases, 174–177
Picture Gallery, Prague Castle, 31–32
Pinkas Synagogue, 53–54
Pivnice Dačický, 158
Pivovarský Dům, 117
Pivovarský Klub, 114, 117
Pizza Nuovo, 103
Plague Column, 157
Plane travel, 162–163
Podoli indoor pool, 46
Ponec, 128
Porcelain, 76–77
Postage, 171
Powder Tower, 9
Prada, 81
Prague Castle, 2, 5, 15, 17, 30–37
    Dalibor Tower, 34
    Golden Lane, 34
    history, 35
    Lobkowicz Palace, 35
    Lokowicz Palace Café, 36
    Old Royal Palace, 33
    Picture Gallery, 31–32
    St. George's Basilica, 33–34
    St. Vitus Cathedral, 32–33
    ticket information, 37
    Toy Museum, 34
Prague Jewish Museum, 19
Prague Museum of Decorative Arts, 18–19
Prague Zoo, 47
Prague-Stay.com, 140
Prasná brána, see Powder Tower
Pricing guide, vii
Public transportation, 164
Puppets, 75–76, 129–130

R

Red and Blue Design Hotel, 146
Red Room, 116
Reduta, 127
Regional Museum, 153
Report's, 79
Riegrovy Sady, 50
Robertson, 80
Rock music, 130–131
Rocking Horse Toy Shop, 70, 75–76
Romantic lodging, 134
Romantic tour, 48–50
    boat rentals, 49–50
    Charles Bridge, 50
    Malá Strana, 50
    metro, 49
    Nebozízek, 50
    Riegrovy Sady, 50
    tram, 50
    Vltava, 49
    Vysehrad Castle, 49
Rose Garden, 85–86
Roxy, 122, 130–131
Rudolfinum, 18, 122, 128
Rudolfinum Café, 19
Rugantino's, 46, 94, 103–104

S

Sabai, 82
Safety, 171–172
St. Agnes Convent, 57
St. Barbara's Cathedral, 158
St. Gallus Church, 68
St. George's Basilica, 33–34
St. James Basilica, 65, 126
St. Nicholas Church, 15, 126
St. Vitus Cathedral, 32–33, 153
Saints Bar, 119
SaSaZu, 104, 114, 120
Sax, 134, 146–147
Sazka Ticket, 132
Schoenborn Palace, 59–60
Schwarzenberg Palace, 63
Senior travelers, 173
Shakespeare & Sons, 70, 79
Shelanu Café & Deli, 55
Sheraton, 134, 147
Shopping, 69–82
    antiquarian books and maps, 74
    antiques, 74–75
    art galleries, 75
    best list, 70
    centers, 77–78
    child-friendly, 75–76
    china, 76–77
    collectibles, 74–75
    crystal, 76–77
    department stores, 77–78

English publications, 79
fashion, 79–80
food, 80
gifts, 81
home furnishings, 81–82
jewelry, 82
Malá Strana area, 71
Old Town Square, 71
personal care salons, 82
porcelain, 76–77
puppets, 75–76
souvenirs, 81
Staré Mesto area, 72–73
toys, 75–76
Shopping centers, 77–78
Sir Toby's, 140
Slavia Café, 22
Slovanský dům, 78
Smetana Hall, 122
Smetanovo Embankment, 21
Smoking, 172
Souvenirs, shopping 81
Spanish Synagogue, 56–57
Sparky's, 76
Sports, 172
Square of the Republic, 24
Srnec Black Light Theater, 129
Staré Město
    dining, 96–97
    entertainment, 124–125
    lodging, 136–137
    nightlife, 112–113
    shopping, 72–73
Starozitnosti Ungelt, 75
Státní Opera, 122, 128–129
Statue of St. Wenceslas, 23
Stavovské Divadlo, 122, 131
Štefánik Observatory, 85
Sternberg Palace, 62
Stone House, 157
Strahov Monastery, 63
Studio Sperk, 70, 82
Sushi Bar, 94, 104
Švandovo Divadlo na Smíchově, 122, 131–132
Svoboda & Williams, 140
Swarovski, 77
swimming, 46

T

Tatiana, 79
The Tavern, 94, 104
Taverna Olympos, 104–105
Taxes, 172
Taxis, 164, 172
Telephones, 173
Termix, 119
Tesco, 78
Theater, 122, 131–132
Three-day tour, 20–24

Hotel Evropa, 24
Lucerna Pasáz, 23
Na príkope, 24
Národní trída 16, 22
National Museum, 23
National Theater, 21–22
Slavia Café, 22
Smetanovo Embankment, 21
Square of the Republic, 24
Statue of St. Wenceslas, 23
Vysehrad, 23–24
Wenceslas Square, 22–23
TicketPortal, 132
Ticketpro, 132
Tickets, entertainment, 132
TicketStream, 132
Time to travel, 160
Timoure et Groupe, 70, 79–80
Tipping, 173
Toilets, 173
Tourist offices, 160, 173
Tourist traps, 173
Tours, 173
Toy Museum, Prague Castle, 34, 45
Toys, shopping, 75–76
Train travel, 163–164
Tram, 2, 5, 50
Travelers with disabilities, 173
Tretter's New York Bar, 114, 116
Truhlár Marionetry, 76
Two-day tour, 16–19
    Gardens Below Prague, 18
    Les Moules, 19
    Mánes Bridge, 18
    Prague Castle, 17
    Prague Jewish Museum, 19
    Prague Museum of Decorative Arts, 18–19
    Rudolfinum, 18
    Rudolfinum Café, 19
Týnská, 65
Týnská Literární kavárna, 65

U

U bilé krávy, 105
U Černého vola, 63, 114, 117
U Fleků, 117
U Janů, 151
U Malého Glena, 127
U Medvídků, 118
U Páva, 147
U Pinkasů, 118
U Raka, 147
U staré paní, 127–128

Photo Credits

U Sudu, 114, 116
U Vejvodů, 118
U Zlaté Studne, 134, 147–148
U Zlatého Iva, 76
U Zlatého tygra, 2, 4–5, 13, 118–119
Ungelt, 65–66, 75

V

V Kolkovne, 94, 105–106
V Zátiší, 106
Vagon, 131
Vegetarian dining, 94

Villa Richter, 15, 105
Vitkov National Memorial, 43
Vltava, 49
Vodka Bar/Propaganda Club, 114, 120
Vojan Gardens, 92
Vrtba Garden, 92
Vyšehrad Castle, 23–24, 49
Výstaviště, 47

W–X

Wallenstein Gardens, 91–92
Weather, 161

Websites, 161
Wenceslas Square, 22–23, 40
Workers' Accident Insurance Company, 28

Y

Yellow Beach, 46

Z

Zara's, 81
Žižkov TV Tower, 43
Zlutá Pumpa, 116

Photo **Credits**